Samuel Carter Hall

The book of British ballads

Samuel Carter Hall

The book of British ballads

ISBN/EAN: 9783744771689

Printed in Europe, USA, Canada, Australia, Japan

Cover: Foto ©Thomas Meinert / pixelio.de

More available books at **www.hansebooks.com**

THE BOOK

OF

BRITISH BALLADS

EDITED BY

S. C. HALL

*WITH ILLUSTRATIONS
AFTER DESIGNS BY CRESWICK, GILBERT, AND OTHERS*

NEW YORK AND LONDON
G. P. PUTNAM'S SONS
The Knickerbocker Press
1888

INTRODUCTION.

Mr. S. C. Hall, the editor of this collection of British Ballads, gave a two-page introduction to each selection. These introductions have been abridged for the present edition. The source, both immediate and remote, of the poems, approximate date of their composition, historical foundation, if any were to be found, and the names of the authors, when known, have been given. Comparisons with more or less kindred ballads, and all historical or legendary matter merely suggested by, but not vital to, the subject of the poem, have been omitted.

The first person in England who called attention to ballad literature and who published an important modern collection was Thomas Percy, Bishop of Dromore (1728—1811). An old MS. of ballads came into his possession, which he published in addition to some others found in the libraries of Cambridge, Oxford, and the British Museum. This volume, "Reliques of Ancient Romance Poetry," has been the main fountain-head for all subsequent collections. Besides this, Mr. Hall is mainly indebted to Sir Walter Scott's "Minstrelsy of the Scottish Border," and Wm. Motherwell's "Minstrelsy, Ancient and Modern." Scott published in his book many songs which had been handed down by word of mouth. Many valuable and interesting ballads, never before printed, were obtained from a Mrs. Brown of Falkland. Her aunt, Mrs. Farquhar, had spent the best part of her life in Braemar, near the source of the Dee, among flocks and herds. She possessed a most retentive memory, and remembered all the songs and tales she had heard in that sequestered part of the country. Mrs. Brown, the child of Mr. Gordon, never forgot these tales thus related to her in childhood, and her nephew, Professor Scott, of Aberdeen, took down many ballads from her recitation. Later the editor of "Border Minstrelsy" took down many more.

In all poems of this class much is left to be inferred. The tale nearly always begins *in medias res*. To explain this it must be remembered that they were composed essentially for recitation, and the minstrels were in the habit of making long introductions and interpolations between the verses, which described in detail all that the poet had not fully explained. The different versions are not always due to variance in relation, but sometimes to the fact that one event was narrated by several bards. Certain phrases or couplets occur again and again in ballads composed at long intervals of time. The old bards had no scruples about plagiarizing, and if they remembered some lines descriptive of an event similar to the subject in hand, they adopted them without change.

CONTENTS.

	PAGE.
INTRODUCTION	iii
CHEVY-CHASE	1
THE CHILDREN IN THE WOOD	11
FAIR ROSAMOND	17
THE DEMON LOVER	25
THE NUT-BROWN MAID	29
KEMPION	41
THE CHILD OF ELLE	45
THE TWA BROTHERS	53
THE BEGGAR'S DAUGHTER	57
ROBIN GOODFELLOW	75
SIR PATRICK SPENS	79
GIL MORRICE	83
SIR ALDINGAR	91
SIR LANCELOT DU LAKE	99
KING ARTHUR'S DEATH	105
THE HEIRE OF LINNE	113
LORD SOULIS	121

Contents

Lord Thomas and Fair Annet	131
Fause Foodrage	137
Genevieve	143
Fair Margaret and Sweet William	147
The Birth of St. George	151
The Mermaid	159
Lord Ullin's Daughter	169
Sir Agilthorn	173
Johnie of Breadislee	181
The Dowie Dens of Yarrow	185
The Bonnie Bairns	189
Glenfinlas	193
The Gay Goss-Hawk	203
Colin and Lucy	209
Katharine Janfarie	213
Rudiger	217
The Eve of St. John	225
Barthram's Dirge	233
Sir Cauline	235
Ruth	249
Robin Hood and Guy of Gisborne	257
Robin Hood's Death and Burial	265
Sir James the Rose	269
The Clerk's Twa Sons	277
Sir Andrew Barton	283
Frennet Hall	297
King Estmere	298
The Cruel Sister	308
Fair Helen	312

Contents

THE LUCK OF EDEN HALL	316
LADY ANNE BOTHWELL'S LAMENT	324
AULD ROBIN GRAY	328
ELFINLAND WUD	334
THE TWA CORBIES	340
HENGIST AND MAY	342
APPENDIX	349
GLOSSARY	367

CHEVY-CHACE.*

God prosper long our noble king,
  Our lives and safetyes all;
A woeful hunting once there did
  In Chevy-Chace befall.

To drive the deere with hound and horne,
  Erle Percy took his way;
The child may rue that is unborne,
  The hunting of that day.

* See Appendix.

Chevy=Chace

The stout Erle of Northumberland
  A vow to God did make,
His pleasure in the Scottish woods
  Three summer days to take;

The cheefest harts in Chevy-Chace
  To kill and beare away.
These tydings to Erle Douglas came,
  In Scottland where he lay:

Who sent Erle Percy present word,
  He wold prevent his sport.
The English Erle, not fearing that,
  Did to the woods resort,

With fifteen hundred bow-men bold:
  All chosen men of might,
Who knew full well in time of neede
  To ayme their shafts arright.

The gallant greyhounds swiftly ran,
  To chase the fallow deere:
On Munday they began to hunt,
  When day-light did appeare;

And long before high noone they had
  An hundred fat buckes slaine;
Then having dined, the drovyers went
  To rouze the deere againe.

The bow-men mustered on the hills,
  Well able to endure;
And all their reare, with speciall care,
  That day was guarded sure.

The hounds ran swiftly through the wo
  The nimble deere to take,
That with their cryes the hills and dal
  An eccho shrill did make.

Chevy=Chace

Lord Percy to the quarry went,
   To view the slaughter'd deere;
Quoth he, "Erle Douglas promised
   This day to meet me heere:

"But if I thought he wold not come,
   Noe longer wold I stay."
With that, a brave younge gentleman
   Thus to the Erle did say:

"Loe, yonder doth Erle Douglas come,
   His men in armour bright;
Full twenty hundred Scottish speres
   All marching in our sight;

"All men of pleasant Tivydale,
   Fast by the river Tweede":   [said,
"Then cease your sports," Erle Percy
   "And take your bowes with speede:

"And now with me, my countrymen,
   Your courage forth advance;
For never was there champion yett,
   In Scottland or in France,

"That ever did on horsebacke come,
   But if my hap it were,
I durst encounter man for man,
   With him to break a spere."

Erle Douglas on his milke-white steede,
   Most like a baron bold,
Rode foremost of his company,
   Whose armour shone like gold.

"Show me," sayd hee, "whose men you
   That hunt soe boldly heere,   [bee,
That, without my consent, do chase
   And kill my fallow-deere.'

Chevy=Chace

The first man that did answer make,
  Was noble Percy hee;
Who sayd, "Wee list not to declare,
  Nor show whose men wee bee:

"Yet will wee spend our deerest blood,
  Thy cheefest harts to slay."
Then Douglas swore a solemne oathe,
  And thus in rage did say:

"Ere thus I will out-braved bee,
  One of us two shall dye:
I know thee well, an erle thou art;
  Lord Percy, soe am I.

"But trust me, Percy, pittye it were,
  And great offence to kill
Any of these our guiltlesse men,
  For they have done no ill.

"Let thou and I the battell trye,
  And set our men aside."
"Accurst bee he," Erle Percy sayd,
  "By whome this is denyed."

Then stept a gallant squier forth,
  Witherington was his name,
Who said, "I wold not have it told
  To Henry our king for shame,

"That ere my captaine fought on foote,
  And I stood looking on.
You two bee erles," quo' Witherington,
  "And I a squier alone:

"Ile doe the best that doe I may,
  While I have power to stand:
While I have power to weeld my sword,
  Ile fight with heart and hand."

Chevy=Chace

Our English archers bent their bowes,
   Their hearts were good and trew ;
Att the first flight of arrowes sent,
   Full four-score Scots they slew.

Yet bides Erle Douglas on the bent,
   As chieftain stout and good ;
As valiant captain, all unmov'd
   The shock he firmly stood.

His host he parted had in three,
   As leader ware and try'd ;
And soon his spearmen on their foes
   Bare down on every side.

Throughout the English archery
   They dealt full many a wound :
But still our valiant Englishmen
   All firmly kept their ground :

And throwing strait their bowes away,
   They grasp'd their swords so bright :
And now sharp blows, a heavy shower,
   On shields and helmets light.*

They closed full fast on everye side,
   Noe slacknes there was found ;
And many a gallant gentleman
   Lay gasping on the ground.

---

* The four preceding stanzas, taken chiefly from the old ballad, were introduced by Dr. Percy, in lieu of the following stanza :—

   " To drive the deere with hounde and horne,
     Douglas bade on the bent ;
   Two captaines moved with mickle might,
     Their speres to shivers went."

These lines are, as Dr. Percy states, "confused and obscure,"—and seriously interrupt the progress of the story. The black-letter copies, in the British Museum and the Pepysian Library, instead of "two captaines," have "a captain ; " and "the spere," in lieu of "their speres."

Chevy=Chace

O Christ! it was a griefe to see,
  How each one chose his spere,
And how the blood out of their brests
  Did gush like water cleere.

At last these two stout erles did meet,
  Like captaines of great might:
Like lyons wode, they layd on lode,
  And made a cruell fight:

They fought untill they both did sweat,
  With swords of tempered steele;
Until the blood, like drops of rain,
  They trickling downe did feele.

"Yeeld thee, Lord Percy," Douglas sayd;
  "In faith I will thee bringe,
Where thou shalt high advanced bee
  By James our Scottish king:

"Thy ransome I will freely give,
  And this report of thee,
Thou art the most couragious knight,
  That ever I did see."

"Noe, Douglas," quoth Erle Percy then,
  " Thy proffer I doe scorne ;
I will not yeelde to any Scott,
  That ever yett was borne."

With that, there came an arrow keene
  Out of an English bow,
Which struck Erle Douglas to the heart,
  A deepe and deadlye blow:

Who never spake more words than these,
  " Fight on, my merry men all ;
For why, my life is at an end ;
  Lord Percy sees my fall."

Chevy=Chace 7

Then leaving life, Erle Percy tooke
  The dead man by the hand ;
And said : " Erle Douglas, for thy life
  Wold I had lost my land.

" O Christ ! my verry heart doth bleed
  With sorrow for thy sake ;
For sure a more redoubted knight
  Mischance did never take."

A knight amongst the Scotts there was,
  Which saw Erle Douglas dye,
Who streight in wrath did vow revenge
  Upon the Erle Percy :

Sir Hugh Mountgomery was he call'd,
  Who, with a spere full bright,
Well-mounted on a gallant steed,
  Ran fiercely through the fight ;

And past the English archers all,
  Without a dread or feare ;
And through Erle Percy's body then
  He thrust his hatefull spere ;

With such vehement force and might
  He did his body gore,
The staff ran through the other side
  A large cloth-yard, and more.

So thus did both these nobles dye,
  Whose courage none could staine :
An English archer then perceiv'd
  The noble erle was slaine ;

He had a bow bent in his hand,
  Made of a trusty tree ;
An arrow of a cloth-yard long
  To the hard head haled he ;

Chevy=Chace

Against Sir Hugh Mountgomery
  So right the shaft he sett;
The grey goose wing that was thereon
  In his heart's bloode was wett.

This fight did last from breake of day,
  Till setting of the sunne;
For when they rung the evening-bell,
  The battel scarce was done.

With stout Erle Percy, there was slaine
  Sir John of Egerton,
Sir Robert Ratcliff, and Sir John,
  Sir James, that bold barròn.

And with Sir George and stout Sir James,
  Both knights of good account,
Good Sir Ralph Raby there was slaine,
  Whose prowesse did surmount.

For Witherington my heart is woe,
  That ever he slaine shold be:
For when his legs were hewn in two
  He knelt and fought on his knee.*

And with Erle Douglas, there was slaine
  Sir Hugh Mountgomery,
Sir Charles Murray, that from the feeld
  One foote wold never flee.

Sir Charles Murray of Ratcliff, too,
  His sister's sonne was hee;
Sir David Lamb, so well esteem'd,
  But saved he cold not bee.

* This stanza is introduced from the old ballad—in accordance with the suggestio of Dr. Percy; for although the death of Witherington, as described in the ancier copy, is exquisitely touching, in the modern version it "never fails to excit ridicule."

Chevy-Chace

And the Lord Maxwell in like case
  Did with Erle Douglas dye :
Of twenty hundred Scottish speres,
  Scarce fifty-five did flye.

Of fifteen hundred Englishmen,
  Went home but fifty-three ;
The rest in Chevy-Chace were slaine,
  Under the greene woode tree.

Next day did many widdowes come,
  Their husbands to bewayle ;
They washt their wounds in brinish teares,
  But all wold not prevayle.

Their bodyes, bathed in purple blood,
  They bore with them away :
They kist them dead a thousand times,
  Ere they were cladd in clay.

The newes was brought to Eddenborrow,
  Where Scottland's king did raigne,
That brave Erle Douglas suddenlye
  Was with an arrow slaine :

"O heavy newes," King James did say,
  "Scottland can witnesse bee,
I have not any captaine more
  Of such account as hee."

Like tydings to King Henry came,
  Within as short a space,
That Percy of Northumberland
  Was slaine in Chevy-Chace :

"Now God be with him," said our king,
  "Sith 't will noe better bee ;
I trust I have, within my realme,
  Five hundred as good as hee :

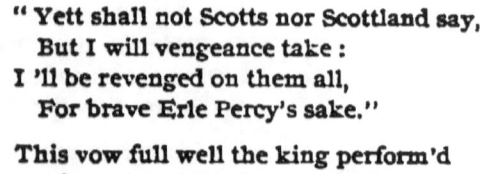

"Yett shall not Scotts nor Scottland say,
　But I will vengeance take:
I 'll be revenged on them all,
　For brave Erle Percy's sake."

This vow full well the king perform'd
　After, at Humbledowne:
In one day, fifty knights were slayne,
　With lords of high renowne:

And of the rest, of small account,
　Did many hundreds dye.
Thus endeth the hunting of Chevy-Chace,
　Made by the Erle Percy.

God save the king, and bless this land
　With plentye, joy, and peace;
And grant, henceforth, that foule debate
　'Twixt noblemen may cease.

The Children in the Wood

THE CHILDREN IN THE WOOD

Now ponder well, you parents deare,
  These wordes which I shall write;
A doleful story you shall heare,
  In time brought forth to light.
A gentleman of good account
  In Norfolke dwelt of late,
Whose wealth and riches did surmount
  Most men of his estate.

The Children in the Wood

Sore sicke he was, and like to dye,
  No helpe his life could save;
His wife by him as sicke did lye,
  And both possest one grave.
No love between these two was lost,
  Each was to other kinde,
In love they lived, in love they dyed,
  And left two babes behinde:

The one a fine and pretty boy,
  Not passing three yeares olde;
The other a girl more young than he,
  And made in beautyes molde.
The father left his little son,
  As plainlye doth appeare,
When he to perfect age should come,
  Three hundred poundes a yeare.

And to his little daughter Jane,
  Two hundred poundes in gold,
To be paid downe on marriage-day,
  Which might not be controll'd:
But if the children chance to dye,
  Ere they to age should come,
Their uncle should possesse their wealth;
  For so the wille did run.

"Now, brother," said the dying man,
  "Look to my children deare;
Be good unto my boy and girl,
  No friendes else have they here:
To God and you I do commend
  My children night and day;
A little while be sure we have
  Within this world to staye.

"You must be father and mother both,
  And uncle all in one;
God knowes what will become of them,
  When I am dead and gone."

The Children in the Wood

With that bespake their mother deare,
 "O brother kinde," quoth shee,
"You are the man must bring my babes
 To wealth or miserie:

"If you do keep them carefully,
 Then God will you reward;
If otherwise you seem to deal,
 God will your deedes regard."
With lippes as cold as any stone,
 They kist the children small:
"God bless you both, my children deare!"
 With that the teares did fall.

These speeches then their brother spoke
 To this sicke couple there:
"The keeping of your children deare
 Sweet sister, do not feare:
God never prosper me nor mine,
 Nor aught else that I have,
If I do wrong your children deare,
 When you are layd in grave."

Their parents being dead and gone,
 The children home he takes,
And brings them both unto his house,
 Where much of them he makes.
He had not kept these pretty babes
 A twelvemonth and a daye,
But, for their wealth, he did devise
 To make them both awaye.

He bargain'd with two ruffians rude,
 Which were of furious mood,
That they should take the children young,
 And slay them in a wood.
He told his wife, and all he had,
 He would the children send
To be brought up in faire London,
 With one that was his friend.

The Children in the Wood

Away then went the pretty babes,
  Rejoycing at that tide,
Rejoycing with a merry minde,
  They should on cock-horse ride.
They prate and prattle pleasantly,
  As they rode on the waye,
To those that should their butchers be,
  And work their lives' decaye :

So that the pretty speeche they had,
  Made murtherers heart relent :
And they that tooke the deed to do,
  Full sore they did repent.
Yet one of them, more hard of heart,
  Did vowe to do his charge,
Because the wretch that hired him
  Had paid him very large.

The other would not agree thereto,
  So here they fell at strife ;
With one another they did fight,
  About the childrens life :
And he that was of mildest mood,
  Did slaye the other there,
Within an unfrequented wood ;
  Where babes did quake for feare !

He took the children by the hand,
  When teares stood in their eye,
And bade them come and go with him,
  And look they did not crye :
And two long miles he ledd them thus,
  While they for bread complaine :
"Stay here," quoth he, "I'll bring ye bread,
  When I do come againe."

These pretty babes, with hand in hand,
  Went wandering up and downe ;
But never more they sawe the man
  Approaching from the towne ;

The Children in the Wood

Their prettye lippes with blackberries,
    Were all besmear'd and dyed,
And when they sawe the darksome night,
    They sat them downe and cryed.

Thus wandered these two pretty babes,
    Till deathe did end their grief,
And in one anothers armes they dyed,
    As babes wanting relief:
No burial these pretty babes
    Of any man receives,
Till robin-red-breast painfully
    Did cover them with leaves.

And now the heavy wrathe of God
    Upon their uncle fell;
Yea, fearfull fiends did haunt his house,
    His conscience felt an hell:
His barnes were fired, his goods consum'd,
    His landes were barren made,
His cattle dyed within the field,
    And nothing with him stayd.

And in the voyage of Portugal
    Two of his sonnes did dye;
And to conclude, himself was brought
    Unto much miserye:
He pawn'd and mortgaged all his land
    Ere seven years came about.
And now at length this wicked act
    Did by this meanes come out:

The fellowe, that did take in hand
    These children for to kill,
Was for a robbery judg'd to dye,
    As was God's blessed will:
Who did confess the very truth,
    The which is here exprest;
Their uncle dyed while he for debt
    Did long in prison rest.

FAIR ROSAMOND.*

When as King Henry rulde this land,
    The second of that name,
Besides the queene, he dearly lovde
    A faire and comely dame.

Most peerlesse was her beautye founde,
    Her favour, and her face;
A sweeter creature in this world
    Did never prince embrace.

Her crisped lockes like threads of golde
    Appeard to each mans sight;
Her sparkling eyes, like Orient pearles,
    Did cast a heavenlye light.

* See Appendix.

The blood within her chrystal cheekes
  Did such a colour drive,
As though the lillye and the rose
  For mastership did strive.

Yea Rosamond, fair Rosamond,
  Her name was called so,
To whom our queene, dame Elinor,
  Was known a deadlye foe.

The king, therefore, for her defence,
  Against the furious queene,
At Woodstocke builded such a bower,
  The like was never seene.

Most curiously that bower was built
  Of stone and timber strong,
An hundred and fifty doors
  Did to this bower belong:

And they so cunninglye contriv'd,
  With turnings round about,
That none but with a clue of thread
  Could enter in or out.

And for his love and ladyes sake,
  That was so faire and brighte,
The keeping of this bower he gave
  Unto a valiant knighte.

But fortune, that doth often frowne
  Where she before did smile,
The kinges delighte, the ladyes joy,
  Full soon shee did beguile;

For why, the kinges ungracious sonne,
  Whom he did high advance,
Against his father raised warres
  Within the realme of France.

Fair Rosamond

But yet before our comelye king
    The English land forsooke,
Of Rosamond, his ladye faire,
    His farewelle thus he tooke:

"My Rosamond, my only Rose,
    That pleasest best mine eye:
The fairest flower in all the worlde
    To feed my fantasye:

"The flower of mine affected heart,
    Whose sweetness doth excelle;
My royal Rose, a thousand times,
    I bid thee nowe farewelle!

"For I must leave my fairest flower,
    My sweetest Rose, a space,
And cross the seas to famous France,
    Proud rebelles to abase.

"But yet, my Rose, be sure thou shalt
    My coming shortly see,
And in my heart, when hence I am,
    Ile beare my Rose with mee."

When Rosamond, that ladye brighte,
    Did heare the kinge saye soe,
The sorrowe of her grieved heart
    Her outward looks did show;

And from her cleare and crystall eyes
    The teares gusht out apace,
Which like the silver-pearled dewe
    Ranne downe her comely face.

Her lippes erst like the corall redde,
    Did waxe both wan and pale,
And for the sorrowe she conceivde
    Her vitall spirits faile:

And falling down all in a swoone
  Before King Henryes face,
Full oft he in his princelye armes
  Her body did embrace;

And twentye times, with watery eyes,
  He kist her tender cheeke,
Until he had revivde againe
  Her senses milde and meeke.

"Why grieves my Rose, my sweetest Rose?"
  The king did often say.
"Because," quoth shee, "to bloodye warres
  My lord must pass awaye.

"But sith your grace in forrayne coastes,
  Amonge your foes unkinde
Must goe to hazarde life and limbe,
  Why should I staye behinde?

"Nay, rather let me, like a page,
  Your sworde and target beare,
That on my breast the blowes may lighte,
  Which would offend you there.

"Or lett mee, in your royal tent,
  Prepare your bed at nighte,
And with sweete baths refresh your grace,
  At your returne from fighte.

"So I your presence may enjoye
  No toil I will refuse;
But wanting you, my life is death:
  Nay, death Ile rather choose."

"Content thy self, my dearest love;
  Thy rest at home shall bee
In Englandes sweet and pleasant isle;
  For travell fits not thee.

"Faire ladies brooke not bloodye warres;
    Sweet peace their pleasures breede,
The nourisher of hearts content,
    Which fancy first did feede.

"My Rose shall rest in Woodstocke bower,
    With musickes sweete delight;
Whilst I, amonge the piercing pikes,
    Against my foes do fighte.

"My Rose in robes of pearle and golde,
    With diamonds richly dight;
Shall dance the galliards of my love,
    Whilst I my foes do fighte.

"And you, Sir Thomas, whom I trust
    To be my love's defence;
Be careful of my gallant Rose
    When I am parted hence."

And therewithall he fetcht a sigh,
    As though his heart would breake:
And Rosamond, for inward griefe,
    Not one plaine worde could speake.

And at their parting well they mighte
    In heart be grieved sore:
After that daye faire Rosamond
    The king did see no more.

For when his grace had passed the seas,
    And into France was gone;
With envious heart, Queene Elinor,
    To Woodstocke came anone.

And forth she calls the trustye knighte
    Which kept this curious bower;
Who with his clue of twined thread,
    Came from the famous flower.

And when that they had wounded him,
   The queene his thread did gette,
And went where Lady Rosamond
   Was like an angell sette.

And when the queene with stedfast eye
   Beheld her heavenlye face,
She was amazed in her minde
   At her exceeding grace.*

* In the old ballad,—" Rosamond's Overthrow," to which we have referred in our introductory remarks,—the interview between the enraged queen and her hapless rival is thus described:—

*   *   *   *   *

The angry Queen with malice fraught,
   Could not herself contain,
Till she Fair Rosamond had brought
   To her sad, fatal bane.
The sweet and charming precious Rose,
   King Henry's chief delight!
The Queen she to her bower goes,
   And wrought her hateful spight.

But when she to the bower came,
   Where Lady Clifford lay,
Enraged Ellinor by name,
   She could not find the way,
Until the silken clew of thread,
   Became a fatal guide
Unto the Queen, who laid her dead
   Ere she was satisfied.

Alas! it was no small surprise
   To Rosamond the fair;
When death appeared before her eyes,
   No faithful friend was there,
Who could stand up in her defence,
   To put the potion by;
So, by the hands of violence,
   Compelled she was to die.

*   *   *   *   *

"I will not pardon you," she said,
   "So take this fatal cup;
And you may well be satisfied
   I 'll see you drink it up."
Then with her fair and milk-white hand
   The fatal cup she took;
Which being drank, she could not stand,
   And soon the world forsook.

*   *   *   *   *

"Cast off from thee thy robes," she said,
  "That riche and costlye bee;
And drinke thou up this deadlye draught,
  Which I have brought to thee."*

But presentlye upon her knees
  Sweet Rosamond did falle;
And pardon of the queene she crav'd
  For her offences all.

"Take pittie on my youthfull yeares,"
  Fair Rosamond did crye;
"And lett mee not with poison stronge
  Enforced bee to dye.

"I will renounce my sinfull life,
  And in some cloyster bide;
Or else be banisht, if you please,
  To range the world soe wide;

"And for the fault that I have done,
  Though I was forc'd theretoe,
Preserve my life, and punish mee
  As you thinke good to doe."

And with these words, her lillie handes
  She wrunge full often there;
And downe along her comelye face
  Did trickle many a teare.

* In "The Lamentation of Queen Elinor," during her "twenty-six years'" Imprisonment, she is made to confess the crime:
  "The which I did with all despite,
    Because she was the King's delight."
And in "Queen Elinor's Confession," she informs the king:
  "The next vile thing that ever I did,
    To you I will discover;
  I poysoned faire Rosamond,
    All in faire Woodstocke Bower."

But nothing could this furious queene
  Therewith appeased bee;
The cup of deadlye poyson stronge,
  As she knelt on her knee,

Shee gave the comelye dame to drinke;
  Who tooke it in her hand,
And from her bended knee arose,
  And on her feet did stand;

And casting up her eyes to heaven,
  Shee did for mercye calle;
And drinking up the poison stronge,
  Her life she lost withalle.

And when that death through everye limbe
  Had showde his greatest spite,
Her chiefest foes did there confesse
  Shee was a glorious wight.

Her body then they did entombe,
  When life was fled away,
At Godstowe, neere to Oxford towne,
  As may be scene this day.

THE DEMON LOVER.*

"O where have you been my long, long love,
   This long seven years and mair?"
"O I'm come to seek my former vows,
   Ye granted me before."

"O hold your tongue of your former vows,
   For they will breed sad strife;
O hold your tongue of your former vows,
   For I am become a wife."

* See Appendix.

The Demon Lover

He turned him right and round about,
   And the tear blinded his e'e ;
"I wad never hae trodden on Irish ground,
   If it had not been for thee.

"I might have had a king's daughter,
   Far far beyond the sea ;
I might have had a king's daughter,
   Had it not been for love o' thee."

"If ye might have had a king's daughter,
   Yersell ye had to blame ;
Ye might have taken the king's daughter,
   For ye kend that I was nane."

"O faulse are the vows o' womankind,
   But fair is their faulse bodie ;
I never would hae trodden on Irish ground,
   Had it not been for love o' thee."

"If I was to leave my husband dear,
   And my two babes also,
O what have you to take me too,
   If with you I should go?"

"I have seven ships upon the sea,
   The eighth brought me to land ;
With four-and-twenty bold mariners,
   And music on every hand."

She has taken up her two little babes,
   Kissed them baith cheek and chin :
"O fare ye weel, my ain two babes,
   For I 'll never see you again."

She set her foot upon the ship,
   No mariners could she behold ;
But the sails were o' the taffetie,
   And the masts o' the beaten gold.

The Demon Lover

She had not sailed a league, a league
    A league but barely three,
When dismal grew his countenance,
    And drumlie grew his e'e.

The masts that were like the beaten gold,
    Bent not on the heaving seas;
And the sails that were o' the taffetie,
    Filled not in the eastland breeze.

They had not sailed a league, a league,
    A league but barely three,
Until she espied his cloven foot,
    And she wept right bitterlie.*

"O hold your tongue of your weeping," says
    "Of your weeping now let me be;   [he,
I will show you how the lilies grow
    On the banks of Italy."

"O what hills are yon, yon pleasant hills,
    That the sun shines sweetly on?"
"O yon are the hills of heaven," he said,
    "Where you will never win."

"O whaten a mountain is yon," she said,
    "All so dreary wi' frost and snow?"
"O yon is the mountain of hell," he cried,
    "Where you and I will go."

---

* In Mr. Buchan's ballad, remorse is made to visit the heroine, not by the sight of the "cloven foot," but by a feeling more natural and more worthy:—
> She minded on her dear husband,
>   Her little son tee.

And at the same time,—
> The thoughts o' grief came in her mind,
>   And she langed for to be hame;

While the miserable woman thus prays:—
> "I may be buried in Scottish ground,
>   Where I was bred and born."

And aye when she turned her round about
    Aye taller he seemed to be ;
Until that the tops o' the gallant ship
    Nae taller were than he.
                                 [loud,
The clouds grew dark, and the wind grew
    And the levin filled her e'e ;   [sprites,
And waesome wailed the snow-white
    Upon the gurlie sea.

He struck the topmast wi' his hand,
    The foremast wi' his knee ;
And he brake that gallant ship in twain,
    And sank her in the sea.

Be it right or wrong, these men among
  On women do complayne
Affermyng this, how that it is
  A labour spent in vayne,
To love them wele ; for never a dele
  They love a man agayne :
For lete a man do what he can,
  Theyr favour to attayne,
Yet, yf a newe do them pursue,
  Theyr first true lover than
Laboureth for nought: and from her thought
  He is a banyshed man.

* See Appendix.

I say not nay, but that all day
  It is bothe writ and sayde
That womans faith is, as who sayth,
  All utterly decayde ;
But, neverthelesse, ryght good wytnèsse
  In this case might be layd,
That they love trewe, and contynew :
  Recorde the Nut-brown Mayd :
Which, from her love (when her to prove,
  He cam to make his mone),
Wolde not depart ; for in her herte
  She loved but hym alone.

Than, betweine us, lete us discusse
  What was all the manere
Betwene them two : we wyll also
  Tell all the payne, and fere,
That she was in. Now I begyn,
  So that ye me answère ;
Wherfore, ye, that present be,
  I pray you, gyve an eare
I am the knyght ; I come by nyght,
  As secret as I can :
Sayinge, "Alas ! thus standeth the case,
  I am a banyshed man."

" And I your wyll for to fulfyll
  In this wyll not refuse ;
Trustyinge to shewe, in wordès few,
  That men have an ille use
(To theyr own shame) women to blame,
  And causelesse them accuse ;
Therfore to you I answere nowe,
  All women to excuse,—
My owne hart dere, with you what chere ?
  I pray you, tell anone ;
For, in my mynde, of all mankynde
  I love but you alone."

"It stondeth so; a dede is do
  Whereof moche harme shall growe:
My destiny is for to dy
  A shamefull deth, I trowe;
Or ellés to flee: the one must bee.
  None other way I knowe,
But to withdrawe as an outlawe,
  And take me to my bowe.
Wherfore, adue, my owne hart true!
  None other rede I can;
For I must to the grene wode go,
  Alone, a banyshed man."

"O Lord, what is thys worldys blysse
  That changeth as the mone!
My somers day in lusty may
  Is derked before the none.
I here you say, farewell: nay, nay,
  We dèpart not so sone.
Why say yé so? wheder will ye go?
  Alas! what have ye done?
All my welfàre to sorrowe and care
  Sholde chaunge, yf ye were gone;
For, iu my mynde, of all mankynde
  I love but you alone."

"I can beleve, it shall you greve,
  And somewhat you dystrayne;
But, aftyrwarde, your paynes harde
  Within a day or twayne
Shall sone aslake; and ye shall take
  Comfort to you agayne.   [thought,
Why sholde ye nought? for, to make
  Your labour were iu vayne.
And thus I do; and pray you to,
  As hartely, as I can;
For I must to the grene wode go,
  Alone, a banyshed man."

"Now, syth that ye have shewed to me
  The secret of your mynde,
I shall be playne to you agayne,
  Lyke as ye shall me fynde.
Sith it is so, that ye wyll go,
  I wolle not leve behynde;
Shall never be sayd, the Nut-brown Mayd
  Was to her love unkynde:
Make you redy, for so am I,
  Allthough it were anone;
For, in my mynde, of all mankynde
  I love but you alone."

"Yet I you rede to take good hede
  What men wyll thynke, and say:
Of yonge and olde it shall be tolde,
  That ye be gone away,
Your wanton wyll for to fulfill,
  In grene wode you to play;
And that ye myght from your delyght
  No lenger make delay.
Rather than ye sholde thus for me
  Be called an yll woman,
Yet wolde I to the grene wode go
  Alone, a banyshed man."

"Though it be songe of old and yonge,
  That I sholde be to blame,
Theyrs be the charge, that speke so large
  In hurtynge of my name:
For I wyll prove, that faythfulle love
  It is devoyd of shame;
In your dystresse, and hevynesse,
  To part with you the same:
And sure all tho, that do not so,
  True lovers are they none;
For, in my mynde, of all mankynde,
  I love but you alone."

"I councelye you, remember howe,
  It is no maydens lawe,
Nothynge to dout, but to renne out,
  To wode with an outlâwe:
For ye must there in your hand bere
  A bowe, redy to drawe;
And, as a thefe, thus must you lyve,
  Ever in drede and awe;
Wherby to you grete harme myght growe:
  Yet had I lever than,
That I had to the grene wode go,
  Alone, a banyshed man."

"I thinke not nay, but as ye say,
  It is no maydens lore:
But love may make me for your sake,
  As ye have sayd before
To come on fote, to hunt, and shote
  To gete us mete in store;
For so that I your company
  May have, I aske no more:
From which to part, it maketh my hart
  As colde as ony stone:
For, in my mynde, of all mankynde
  I love but you alone."

"For an outlawe this is the lawe,
  That men hym take and bynde;
Without pytee, hanged to be,
  And waver with the wynde.
If I had nede, (as God forbede!)
  What rescous coude ye fynde?
Forsoth, I trowe, ye and your bowe
  For fere wolde drawe behynde:
And no mervayle; for lytell avayle
  Were in your counceyle than:
Wherfore I to the wode will go,
  Alone, a banyshed man."

"Right wele knowe ye, that women be
  Ful feble for to fyght;
No womanhede is it indede
  To be bolde as a knyght:
Yet, in such fere yf that ye were
  With enemyes day and nyght,
I wolde withstande, with bowe in hande,
  To greve them as I myght,
And you to save; as women have
  From deth saved many one:
For, in my mynde, of all mankynde
  I love but you alone."

"Yet take good hede; for ever I drede
  That ye coude not sustayne
The thornie wayes, the depe valeies,
  The snowe, the frost, the rayne,
The colde, the hete: for dry or wete,
  We must lodge on the playne;
And, us above, none other rofe
  But a brake bush, or twayne;
Which sone sholde greve you, I beleve;
  And ye wolde gladly than
That I had to the grene wode go,
  Alone, a banyshed man."

"Syth I have here bene partynere
  With you of joy and blysse,
I must also parte of your wo
  Endure, as reson is:
Yet am I sure of one plesùre;
  And, shortely, it is this:
That, where ye be, me semeth, perdè,
  I coude not fare amysse.
Without more speche, I you beseche
  That we were sone agone;
For, in my mynde, of all mankynde
  I love but you alone."

The Nut-Brown Mayd

"If ye go thyder, ye must consyder,
  Whan ye have lust to dyne,
There shall no mete be for to gete,
  Nor drinke, bere, ale, ne wyne.
No shetés clene, to lye betwene,
  Made of threde and twyne;
None other house, but leves and bowes,
  To cover your hed and myne.
O myne harte swete, this evyll dyéte
  Sholde make you pale and wan;
Wherefore I to the wode will go,
  Alone, a banyshed man."

"Amonge the wylde dere, such an archères,
  As men say that ye be,
Ne may not fayle of good vitayle,
  Where is so grete plentè:
And water clere of the ryvére
  Shall be full swete to me;
With which in hele I shall ryght wele
  Endure, as ye shall see;
And, er we go, a bedde or two
  I can provyde anone;
For, in my mynde, of all mankynde
  I love but you alone."

"Lo yet, before, ye must do more,
  Yf ye wyll go with me:
As cut your here up by your ere;
  Your kyrtel by the knee;
With bowe in hande, for to withstande
  Your enemyes yf nede be:
And this same nyght before day-lyght,
  To wode-warde wyll I fle.
Yf that ye wyll all this fulfill,
  Do it shortely as ye can:
Els wyll I to the grene wode go,
  Alone, a banyshed man."

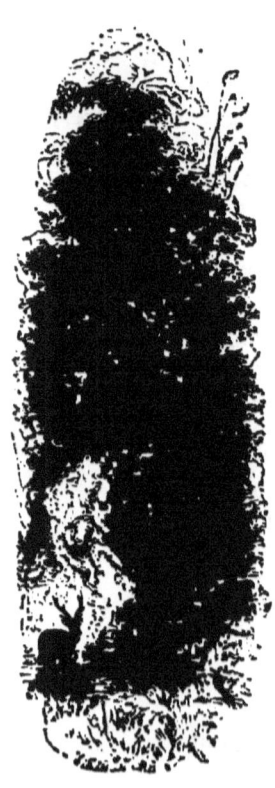

"I shall as nowe do more for you
  Than longeth to womanhede;
To short my here, a bowe to bere,
  To shote in tyme of nede.
O my sweet mother, before all other
  For you I have most drede:
But nowe, adue! I must ensue,
  Wher fortune doth me lede.
All this make ye: now let us fle;
  The day cometh fast upon;
For, in my mynde, of all mankynde
  I love but you alone."

"Nay, nay, not so; ye shall not go,
  And I shall tell ye why,—
Your appetyght is to be lyght
  Of love, I wele espy:
For, lyke as ye have sayed to me,
  In lyke wyse hardely
Ye wolde answére whosoever it were,
  In way of company.
It is sayd of olde, Sone hote, sone colde:
  And so is a womàn.
Wherfore I to the wode wy'll go,
  Alone, a banyshed man."

"Yf ye take hede, yett is no nede
  Such wordes to say by me;
For oft ye prayed, and longe assayed,
  Or I you loved, perdè:
And though that I of auncestry
  A barons daughter be,
Yet have you proved how I you loved,
  A squyer of lowe degre;
And ever shall, whatso befall;
  To yé therfore anone;
For, in my mynde, of all mankynde
  I love but you alone."

"A barons chylde to be begylde!
 It were a cursed dede;
To be felàwe with an outlawe!
 Almighty God forbede!
Yet better were, the pore squyère
 Alone to forest yede,
Than ye sholde say another day,
 That, by my wicked dede,
Ye were betrayd: wherfore, good mayd,
 The best redè that I can,
Is, that I to the grene wode go,
 Alone, a banyshed man."

"Whatever befall, I never shall
 Of this thyng you upbrayd:
But yf ye go, and leve me so,
 Than have ye me betrayd.
Remember wele, howe that ye dele;
 For, yf ye, as ye sayd,
Be so unkynde, to leve behynde,
 Your love, the Nut-brown Mayd,
Trust me truly, that I shall dy
 Sone after ye be gone;
For, in my mynde, of all mankynde
 I love but you alone."

"Yf that ye went, ye sholde repent;
 For in the forest nowe
I have purvayed me of a mayd,
 Whom I love more than you;
Another fayrère, than ever ye were,
 I dare it wele avowe;
And of you bothe eche sholde be wrothe
 With other, as I trowe:
It were myne ese, to lyve in pese;
 So wyll I, yf I can;
Wherfore I to the wode wyll go,
 Alone, a banyshed man."

"Though in the wode I undyrstode
  Ye had a paramour,
All this may nought remove my thought,
  But that I wyll be your:
And she shall fynde me soft, and kynde
  And courteys every hour;
Glad to fulfyll all that she wyll
  Commaunde me to my power:
For had ye, lo, an hundred mo,
  Of them I wolde be one;
For, in my mynde, of all mankynde
  I love but you alone."

"Myne owne dere love, I see the prove
  That ye be kynde and true;
Of mayde, and wyfe, in all my lyfe,
  The best that ever I knewe.
Be mery and glad, be no more sad,
  The case is chaunged newe;
For it were ruthe, that, for your truthe,
  Ye sholde have cause to rewe.
Be not dismayed; whatsoever I sayd
  To you, whan I began;
I wyll not to the grene wode go;
  I am no banyshed man."

"These tydings be more gladd to me,
  Than to be made a quene.
Yf I were sure they sholde endure:
  But it is often sene
Whan men wyll breke promyse, they speke
  The wordès on the splene.
Ye shape some wyle me to begyle,
  And stele from me, I wene:
Than were the case worse than it was,
  And I more wo-begone:
For, in my mynde, of all mankynde
  I love but you alone."

"Ye shall not nede farther to drede;
I wyll not dysparàge
You, (God defend!) syth ye descend
Of so grete a lynàge.
Nowe undyrstande; to Westmarlande,
Which is myne herytage,
I wyll you brynge; and with a rynge
By way of maryage
I wyll you take, and lady make,
As shortely as I can :
Thus have you won an erlys son
And not a banyshed man."

The reader may be interested in comparing some readings of the old ballad, as printed in Arnold's Chronicle, with those that occur in the "folio MS." of Dr. Percy. In—

Line 9, Arnold's Chron., to them ;   Percy, do them.
" 28, ... they peyne; . the payne.
" 50, ... moche; . . . grete.
" 79, ... ought; . . . nought.
" 81, ... loo; . . . . to.
" 98, ... whan; . . . what.
" 126, ... to bere and; . ready to.
" 136, ... ye; . . . . . I.
" 137, ... and; . . . . in.
" 158, ... ful; . . . . but.
" 159, ... ful; . . . . ryght.
" 162, ... and; . . . . or.

These examples will suffice to shew that very few changes were introduced in the "Reliques." The most important occurs in lines 21 and 22, which Percy prints:

Which, when her love came, her to prove,
To her to make his mone.

We retain the reading as we find it in Arnold. In the several editions of Arnold, there are also some variations, but none of them are of much importance; they are all given in a small reprint of the ballad, published in 1836, by Mr. Pickering: From one of them, Percy appears to have copied the two lines inserted above. In this reprint, the text is copied from the earliest edition of Arnold, "supposed" to have been printed about 1502; the variations are, chiefly, from the edition of 1521. The orthography varies with the various editions; we have, generally, followed Percy. As an example, we may observe, that in Arnold, the word which occurs so frequently is spelt "bannisshed,"

Here may ye se, that women be
  In love, meke, kynde, and stable:
Late never man reprove them than,
  Or call them variable;
But, rather, pray God that we may
  To them be comfortable;
Which sometyme proveth such as loveth,
  Yf they be charytable.
For syth men wolde that women sholde
  Be meke to them each one,
Moche more ought they to God obey,
  And serve but hym alone.

KEMPION.*

"Cum heir, cum heir, ye freely fee'd,
   And lay your head low on my knee;
The heaviest weird I will you read,
   That ever was read to gay ladye.

"O meikle dolour sall ye dree,
   And aye the salt seas o'er ye 'se swim;
And far mair dolour sall ye dree
   On Estmere crags, when ye them climb,

* See Appendix.

Kempion

"I weird ye to a fiery beast,
   And relieved sall ye never be,
Till Kempion, the kingis son,
   Cum to the crag, and thrice kiss thee."—

O meikle dolour did she dree,
   And aye the salt seas o'er she swam;
And far mair dolour did she dree
   On Estmere crags, when she them clamb:

And aye she cried for Kempion,
   Gin he would but come to her hand.
Now word has gane to Kempion,
   That sicken a beast was in his land.

"Now, by my sooth," said Kempion,
   "This fiery beast I'll gang and see."
"And by my sooth," said Segramour,
   "My ae brother, I'll gang wi' thee."

Then bigged hae they a bonny boat,
   And they hae set her to the sea;
But a mile before they reached the shore,
   Around them she gared the red fire flee.

"O Segramour, keep the boat afloat,
   And let her na the land o'er near;
For this wicked beast will sure gae mad,
   And set fire to a' the land and mair."—

Syne has he bent an arblast bow,
   And aimed an arrow at her head;
And swore if she didna quit the land,
   Wi' that same shaft to shoot her dead.

"O out of my stythe I winna rise,
   (And it is not for the awe o' thee,)
Till Kempion, the kingis son,
   Cum to the crag, and thrice kiss me."—

He has louted him o'er the dizzy crag,
   And gien the monster kisses ane;
Awa she gaed, and again she cam,
   The fieryest beast that ever was seen.

"O out o' my stythe I winna rise,
   (And not for a' thy bow nor thee,)
Till Kempion, the kingis son,
   Cum to the crag, and thrice kiss me."—

He's louted him o'er the Estmere crag,
   And he has gi'en her kisses twa:
Awa she gaed, and again she cam,
   The fieryest beast that ever you saw.

"O out of my den I winna rise,
   Nor flee it for the fear o' thee,
Till Kempion, that courteous knight,
   Cum to the crag, and thrice kiss me."

He's louted him o'er the lofty crag,
   And he has gi'en her kisses three:
Awa she gaed, and again she cam,
   The loveliest ladye e'er could be!

"And by my sooth," says Kempion,
   "My ain true love, (for this is she,)
They surely had a heart o' stane,
   Could put thee to such misery.

"O was it warwolf* in the wood?
   Or was it mermaid in the sea?
Or was it man or vile woman,
   My ain true love, that mis-shaped thee?"—

* Warwolf signifies a magician, possessing the power of transforming himself into a wolf, for the purpose of ravage and destruction.

"It wasna warwolf in the wood,
　Nor was it mermaid in the sea;
But it was my wicked step-mother,
　And wae and weary may she be!"—

"O, a heavier wierd shall light her on,
　Than ever fell on vile woman;
Her hair shall grow rough,
　And her teeth grow lang,
　And on her four feet shall she gang.

"None shall take pity her upon;
　In Wormeswood she aye shall wan;
And relieved shall she never be,
　Till St. Mungo come over the sea."—
And sighing, said that weary wight,
　"I doubt that day I'll never see!"

THE CHILD OF ELLE.*

On yonder hill a castle standes
  With walles and towres bedight,
And yonder lives the Child of Elle,
  A younge and comely knighte.

The Child of Elle to his garden went,
  And stood at his garden, pale, [page
Whan, lo! he beheld fair Emmelines
  Come trippinge downe the dale.

* See Appendix.

The Child of Elle he hyed him thence,
  Y-wis he stoode not stille,
And soone he mette faire Emmelines page
  Come climbing up the hille.

"Nowe Christe thee save, thou little foot-
  Nowe Christe thee save and see! [page,
Oh, tell me how does thy ladye gaye,
  And what may thy tydinges bee?"

"My lady she is all woe-begone,
  And the teares they falle from her eyne;
And aye she laments the deadlye feude
  Betweene her house and thine.

"And here shee sends thee a silken scarfe
  Bedewde with many a teare,
And biddes thee sometimes thinke on her,
  Who loved thee so deare.

"And here shee sends thee a ring of golde
  The last boone thou mayst have,
And biddes thee weare it for her sake,
  Whan she is layd in grave.

"For, ah! her gentle heart is broke,
  And in grave soone must shee bee. [love,
Sith her father hath chose her a new new
  And forbidde her to think of thee

"Her father hath brought her a carlish
  Sir John of the north countràye, [knighte,
And within three days shee must him
  Or he vowes he will her slaye." [wedde,

"Nowe hye thee backe, thou little foot-
  And greet thy ladye from mee, [page,
And tell her that I, her owne true love,
  Will dye, or sette her free.

The Child of Elle

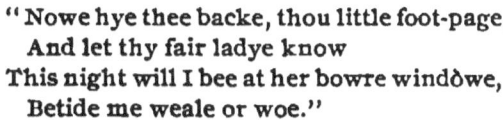

"Nowe hye thee backe, thou little foot-page,
  And let thy fair ladye know
This night will I bee at her bowre windòwe,
  Betide me weale or woe."

The boye he tripped, the boye he ranne,
  He neither stint ne stayd
Until he came to fair Emmelines bowre,
  Whan kneeling downe he sayd :

"O ladye, I've been with thy own true love,
  And he greets thee well by mee ;
This night will he be at thy bowre-windòwe,
  And dye or sette thee free."

Nowe day was gone and night was come,
  And all were fast asleepe,
All save the ladye Emmeline,
  Who sate in her bowre to weepe ;

And soone shee heard her true loves voice
  Lowe whispering at the walle :
"Awake, awake, my deare ladyè,
  Tis I thy true love call.

"Awake, awake, my ladye deare,
  Come, mount this faire palfràye ;
This ladder of ropes will lette thee downe,
  Ile carrye thee hence awaye."

"Nowe nay, nowe nay, thou gentle knighte,
  Nowe nay, this may not bee ;
For aye should I tint my maiden fame,
  If alone I should wend with thee."

"O ladye, thou with a knighte so true
  Mayst safelye wend alone,
To my ladye mother I will thee bringe,
  Where marriage shall make us one."

The Child of Elle

"My father he is a baron bolde,
  Of lynage proude and hye ;
And what would he saye if his daughter
  Awaye with a knighte should fly?

"Ah ! well I wot, he never would rest,
  Nor his meate should do him no goode,
Until he had slain thee, Child of Elle,
  And seene thy deare hearts bloode."

"O ladye, wert thou in thy saddle sette,
  And a little space him fro,
I would not care for thy cruel fathèr,
  Nor the worst that he could doe.

"O ladye, wert thou in thy saddle sette,
  And once without this walle,
I would not care for thy cruel fathèr,
  Nor the worst that might befalle."

Fair Emmeline sighed, fair Emmeline wept,
  And aye her heart was woe :
At length he seized her lilly-white hand,
  And downe the ladder he drewe :

And thrice he clasped her to his breste,
  And kist her tenderlìe :
The teares that fell from her fair eyes
  Ranne like the fountayne free.

Hee mounted himselfe on his stede so talle.
  And her on a fair palfràye,
And slung his bugle about his necke,
  And roundlye they rode away.

All this beheard her owne damsèlle,
  In her bed whereas shee ley,
Quoth shee : "My lord shall knowe of this,
  Soe I shall have golde and fee.

The Child of Elle

"Awake, awake, thou baron bolde!
  Awake, my noble dame!   [Elle
Your daughter is fledde with the Child of
  To doe the deede of shame."

The baron he woke, the baron he rose,
  And called his merrye men all:
"And come thou forth, Sir John the knighte,
  Thy ladye is carried to thrall."

Faire Emmeline scant had ridden a mile
  A mile forth of the towne,
When she was aware of her fathers men
  Come galloping over the downe:

And formost came the carlish knighte,
  Sir John of the north countràye:
"Nowe stop, nowe stop, thou false traitòure,
  Nor carry that ladye awaye.

"For she is come of hye linèage,
  And was of a ladye born,
And ill it beseems thee—a false churls sonne
  To carry her hence to scorne."

"Nowe loud thou lyest, Sir John the knighte,
  Nowe thou doest lye of mee;
A knighte me bred, and a ladye me bore,
  Soe never did none by thee.

"But light nowe downe, my ladye faire,
  Light downe, and hold my steed;
While I and this discourteous knighte
  Doe try this arduous deede.

"But light nowe downe, my deare ladyè,
  Light downe, and hold my horse;
While I and this discourteous knighte
  Doe trye our valours force."

Fair Emmeline sighed, fair Emmeline wept,
  And aye her heart was woe,
While twixt her love and the carlish knighte
  Past many a baneful blowe.

The Child of Elle hee fought soe well,
  As his weapon he waved amaine,
That soone he had slaine the carlish knighte,
  And layd him upon the plaine.

And nowe the baron and all his men
  Full fast approached nye:
Ah, what may ladye Emmeline doe!
  Twere nowe no boote to flye.

Her lover he put his horne to his mouth,
  And blew both loud and shrill,
And soone he saw his owne merry men
  Come ryding over the hill.

"Nowe hold thy hand, thou bold baròn,
  I pray thee hold thy hand,
Nor ruthless rend two gentle hearts
  Fast knit in true loves band.

"Thy daughter I have dearly loved
  Full long and many a day;
But with such love as holy kirke
  Hath freelye said wee may.

"O give consent, shee may be mine,
  And bless a faithfull paire:
My lands and livings are not small,
  My house and lineage faire:

"My mother she was an earls daughtèr,
  And a noble knighte my sire:"—
The baron he frowned and turn'd away
  With mickle dole and ire.

The Child of Elle

Fair Emmeline sighed, faire Emmeline wept,
  And did all tremblinge stand:
At length she sprang upon her knee,
  And held his lifted hand.

"Pardon, my lorde and father deare,
  This faire younge knighte and me:
Trust me, but for the carlish knighte,
  I never had fled from thee.

"Oft have you called your Emmeline
  Your darling and your joye;
O! let not then your harsh resolves
  Your Emmeline destroye."

The baron he stroakt his dark-brown cheeke,
  And turned his heade asyde
To wipe awaye the starting teare
  He proudly strave to hyde.

In deepe revolving thought he stoode,
  And mused a little space: [grounde,
Then raised faire Emmeline from the
  With many a fond embrace.*

* In the Scottish ballads, as we have intimated, the affair has a far less happy termination; the lover dying of his wounds, and the Lady Margaret of a broken heart:

> Lord William was buried in St. Maries kirk,
>   Lady Marg'ret in Maries quire;
> Out of the ladys grave grew a bonny red rose,
>   And out of the knights a brier.
>
> And they twa met, and they twa plat,
>   And fain they wad be near;
> And a' the warld might ken right weel,
>   They were twa lovers dear.
>
> But bye and rade the black Douglas,
>   And wow but he was rough!
> For he pulled up the bonny brier,
>   And flang'd in St. Maries loch.

"Here take her, Child of Elle,"—he sayd,
  And gave her lillye white hand;—
"Here take my deare and only child,
  And with her half my land:

"Thy father once mine honour wronged
  In days of youthful pride—
Do thou the injurye repayre
  In fondness for thy bride;

"And as thou love her, and hold her deare,
  Heaven prosper thee and thine!
And nowe my blessing wend wi' thee,
  My lovelye Emmeline!"

The Twa Brothers

THE TWA BROTHERS.*

There were twa brothers at the scule,
  And when they got awa'—
It 's "Will ye play at the stane-chucking,
  Or will ye play at the ba',
Or will ye gae up to yon hill head?
  And there we 'll warsell a fa'."

" I winna play at the stane-chucking,
  Nor will I play at the ba',
But I 'll gae up to yon bonnie green hill,
  And there we 'll warsell a fa'."

* See Appendix.

The Twa Brothers

They warsled up, they warsled down,
   Till John fell to the ground;
A dirk fell out of Williams pouch,
   And gave John a deadly wound.

"O lift me up upon your back,
   Tak me to yon well fair;
And wash my bluidy wounds o'er and o'er,
   And they'll ne'er bleed nae mair."

He's lifted his brother upon his back,
   Ta'en him to yon well fair;   [o'er,
He's washed his bluidy wounds o'er and
   But they bleed ay mair and mair.

"Tak ye aff my Holland sark,
   And rive it gair by gair,
And row it in my bluidy wounds,
   And they'll ne'er bleed nae mair."

He's taken aff his Holland sark,
   And torn it gair by gair;
He's row it in his bluidy wounds,
   But they bleed ay mair and mair.

"Tak now aff my green sleiding,
   And row me saftly in;
And tak me up to yon kirk style,
   Whare the grass grows fair and green."

He's taken aff the green sleiding,
   And rowed him softly in;
He's laid him down by yon kirk style,
   Whare the grass grows fair and green.

The Twa Brothers

"What will ye say to your father dear,
  When ye gae hame at e'en?"
"I 'll say ye 're lying at yon kirk style,
  Whare the grass grows fair and green."

"O no, O no, my brother dear,
  O you must not say so;
But say, that I 'm gane to a foreign land,
  Whare nae man does me know."

When he sat in his fathers chair
  He grew baith pale and wan.
"O what blude 's that upon your brow?
  O dear son, tell to me."

"It is the blude o' my gude gray steed—
  He wadna ride wi' me."
"O thy steeds blude was ne'er sae red,
  Nor e'er sae dear to me.

"O what blude 's that upon your cheek?
  O dear son, tell to me."
"It is the blude of my greyhound,
  He wadna hunt for me."

"O thy hounds blude was ne'er sae red,
  Nor e'er sae dear to me;
O what blude 's this upon your hand?
  O dear son, tell to me."

"It is the blude of my gay goss hawk
  He wadna flee for me."
"O thy hawks blude was ne'er sae red,
  Nor e'er sae dear to me;

"O what blude 's this upon your dirk?
  Dear Willie, tell to me."
"It is the blude of my ae brother,
  O, dule and wae is me!"

"O what will ye say to your father?
  Dear Willie, tell to me."
"I 'll saddle my steed, and awa I 'll ride,
  To dwell in some far countrie."

"O when will ye come hame again?
  Dear Willie, tell to me."
"When sun and mune leap on yon hill,
  And that will never be."

She turned hersel' right round about,
  And her heart burst into three:
"My ae best son is deid and gane,
  And my tother ane I 'll ne'er see."

The Beggar's Daughter

THE BEGGAR'S DAUGHTER OF BEDNALL GREEN.*

FITT THE FIRST.

Itt was a blind beggar, had long lost his sight,
He had a faire daughter most pleasant and bright:
And many a gallant brave suitor had shee,
For none was soe comelye as pretty Bessee.

And though shee was of favor most faire,
Yett seeing she was but a poor beggars heyre
Of ancyent housekeepers despised was shee,
Whose sonnes came as suitors to prettye Bessee.

* See Appendix.

The Beggar's Daughter

Wherefore in great sorrow faire Bessee did say,
"Good father, and mother, let me goe away
To seeke out my fortune, whereever itt bee."
The suite then they granted to pretty Bessee.

Then Bessee, that was of bewtye soe bright,
All cladd in gray russett, and late in the night,
From father and mother alone parted shee ;
Who sighed and sobbed for pretty Bessee.

Shee went till shee came to Stratford-le-Bow ;
Then knew shee not whither, nor which way to goe :
With teares shee lamented her hard destinie,
So sadd and soe heavy was pretty Bessee.

Shee kept on her journey untill it was day,
And went unto Rumford along the hye way ;
Where at the Queenes armes entertained was shee :
So faire and wel favoured was pretty Bessee.

Shee had not been there one month to an end,
But master and mistress and all was her friend:
And every brave gallant, that once did her see,
Was strait-way in love with pretty Bessee.

Great gifts they did send her of silver and gold,
And in their songs daylye her love was extold ;
Her bewtye was blazed in every degree ;
Soe faire and soe comelye was pretty Bessee.

The younge men of Rumford in her had their joy ;
Shee shew'd herself curteous, but never too coye ;
And at their commandment still wold she bee ;
Soe fayre and soe comlye was pretty Bessee.

Foure suitors att once unto her did goe ;
They craved her favor, but still she sayd "Noe ;
I would not wish gentles to marry with mee."
Yett ever they honored pretty Bessee.

The first of them was a gallant young knight,
And he came unto her disguisde in the night:
The second a gentleman of good degree,
Who wooed and sued for pretty Bessee.

A merchant of London, whose wealth was not small,
Was then the third suitor, and proper withall:
Her masters own sonne the fourth man must bee,
Who swore he would dye for pretty Bessee.

"And, if thou wilt marry with mee," quoth the knight,
"Ile make thee a lady with joy and delight;
My heart's so inthralled by thy faire bewtie,
Then grant me thy favour, my pretty Bessee."

The gentleman sayd, "Come, marry with mee,
In silks and in velvets my Bessee shall bee:
My heart lives distressed: O heare me," quoth hee;
"And grant me thy love, my pretty Bessee."

"Let me be thy husband," the merchant did say,
"Thou shalt live in London both gallant and gay;
My shippes shall bring home rych jewels for thee,
And I will for ever love pretty Bessee."

Then Bessee shee sighed, and thus shee did say,
"My father and mother I meane to obey;
First gett theyr good will, and be faithfull to mee,
And you shall enjoye your pretty Bessee."

To every one this answer shee made;
Wherefore unto her they joyfullye sayd,
"This thing to fulfill wee all doe agree;
But where dwells thy father, my pretty Bessee?"

"My father," quoth shee, "is plaine to be seene:
The silly blind beggar of Bednall-greene,
That daylye sits begging for charitie,
He is the good father of pretty Bessee.

The Beggar's Daughter

"His markes and his tokens are known full well;
He alwayes is led with a dogg and a bell:
A silly olde man, God knoweth, is hee,
Yett hee is the father of pretty Bessee."

"Nay then," quo' the merchant, "thou art not for mee;
"Nor," quo' the innholder, "my wiffe shalt not bee:"
"I lothe," sayd the gentle, "a beggars degree,
And therefore, adewe, my pretty Bessee!"

"Why then," quoth the knight, "hap better or worse,
I waighe not true love by the waight of the pursse,
And bewtye is bewtye in every degree;
Then welcome to me, my pretty Bessee.

"With thee to thy father forthwith will I goe."
"Nay soft," quoth his kinsmen, "it must not be soe;
A poor beggars daughter noe ladye shall bee,
Then take thy adewe of pretty Bessee."

But soone after this, by break of the day,
The knight had from Rumford stole Bessee away.
The younge men of Rumford, so sicke as may be,
Rode after to fetche againe pretty Bessee.

As swifte as the winde to ride they were seene,
Untill they came neare unto Bednall-greene;
And as the knight lighted most courteouslie
They all fought against him for pretty Bessee.

But rescew came presentlye over the plaine,
Or else the knight there for his love had been slaine.
This fray being ended, then strait he did see
His kinsmen come rayling at pretty Bessee.

Then spake the blind beggar, "Although I bee poore,
Yett rayle not against my child at my own doore:
Though shee be not decked in velvett and pearle,
Yett will I dropp angells with you for my girle.

The Beggar's Daughter

" And then, if my gold will better her birthe,
And equall the gold that you lay on the earth,
Then neyther rayle nor grudge you to see
The blind beggars daughter a lady to bee.

" Butt first I will heare, and have it well knowne,
The gold that you drop shall be all your owne."
With that they replyed, " Contented wee bee."
"Then here 's," quoth the beggar, "for pretty Bessee."

With that an angell he cast on the ground,
And dropped in angells full three thousand pound ;
And oftentimes itt was proved most plaine,
For the gentlemans one the beggar dropt twayne :

So as the place, wherein they did sitt,
With gold it was covered every whitt ;
The gentleman then having dropt all his store,
Sayd, " Now, beggar, hold, for I have noe more.

"Thou hast fulfilled thy promise arright."
"Then marry," quoth he, " my girle to the knight ;
And heere," quoth he, " I will now throwe you downe
A hundred pounds more to buy her a gowne."

The gentlemen all, that this treasure had seene,
Admired the beggar of Bednall-greene ;
And those that were her suitors before,
Their fleshe for very anger they tore.

Thus was their Bessee matched to a knight,
And made a ladye in others despite :
A fairer ladye there never was seene,
Than the blind beggars daughter of Bednall-greene.

But of her sumptuous marriage and feast,
What brave lords and knights thither were prest.
The second fitt shall set forth to your sight
With marveilous pleasure and wished delight.

The Beggar's Daughter

FITT THE SECOND.

Off a blind beggars daughter most fair and bright,
That late was betrothed unto a younge knight;
All the discourse thereof you may see;
But now comes the wedding of pretty Bessee.

Within a gallant palace most brave,
Adorned with all the cost they could have,
This wedding was kept most sumptuouslie,
And all for the love of pretty Bessee.

All kinds of dainties, and delicates sweete
Were brought to their banquet, as it was thought meete;
Partridge, and plover, and venison most free,
Against the brave wedding of pretty Bessee.

This wedding thro' England was spread, by report,
So that a great number did thither resort
Of nobles and gentles in every degree;
And all for the fame of pretty Bessee.

To church then went this gallant younge knight;
His bride followed after, a ladye most bright,
With troopes of ladyes, the like nere was seene
As went with sweete Bessee of Bednall-greene.

This marryage being solemnized then,
With musicke performed by the skilfullest men,
The nobles and gentles sate downe at that tyde,
Each one beholding the beautiful bryde.

But, after the sumptuous dinner was done,
To talke, and to reason a number begunn:
To talke of the blind beggars daughter most bright,
And what with his daughter he gave to the knight.

The Beggar's Daughter

Then spake the nobles, "Much marveil have wee,
The jolly blind beggar wee cannot here see."
"My lords," quoth the bride, "my father's so base,
Hee is loth with his presence these states to disgrace."

"The prayse of a woman in questyon to bringe
Before her own face were a flattering thinge;
Yett wee thinke thy fathers baseness," quoth they,
"Might by thy bewtye bee cleane put away."

They had noe sooner these pleasant words spoke,
But in comes the beggar cladd in a silke cloke:
A faire velvet capp, and a fether had hee:
And nowe a musicyan forsooth he would bee.

Hee had a daintye lute under his arme,
Hee touched the strings, which made such a charme,
Sayd, "Please you to heare any musicke of mee,
A song I will sing you of pretty Bessee."

With that his lute hee twanged straitway,
And thereon begann most sweetlye to play;
And after that lessons were playd two or three,
Hee straynd out this song most delicatelie.

"A poore beggars daughter did dwell on a greene,
Who for her bewtye might well bee a queene:
A blithe bonny lasse, and daintye was shee,
And many one called her pretty Bessee.

"Her father hee had noe goods, nor noe lands,
But begged for a penny all day with his hands;
And yett for her marriage hee gave thousands three,
And still hee hath somewhat for pretty Bessee.

"And if any one her birth doe disdaine,
Her father is ready, with might and with maine,
To proove shee is come of a noble degree:
Therefore let none floute att my prettye Bessee."

The Beggar's Daughter

With that the lords and companye round
With hearty laughter were readye to swound:
Att last said the lords, "Full well wee may see,
The bride and the beggar 's behoulden to thee."

With that the bride all blushing did rise,
With the faire water all in her brighte eyes:
"Pardon my father, grave nobles," quoth shee,
"That throughe blind affection thus doteth on mee."

"If this bee thy father," the nobles did say,
"Well may hee bee proud of this happy day;
Yett by his countenance well may wee see,
His birth with his fortune did never agree;

"And therefore, blind beggar, wee pray thee bewray,
(And looke that the truth to us thou doe say)
Thy birth and thy parentage, what itt may bee,
For the love that thou bearest to pretty Bessee."

"Then give me leave, nobles and gentles, each one,
A song more to sing, and then I'll begone,
And if that I do not winn your good report,
Then doe not give me a groat for my sport.

"Sir Simon de Montfort my subject shall bee:
Once chiefe of all the great barons was hee,
Yett fortune so cruelle this lorde did abase,
Nowe loste and forgotten are hee and his race.

"When the barons in armes did King Henrye oppose,
Sir Simon de Montfort their leader they chose:
A leader of courage undaunted was hee,
And oft-times hee made their enemyes flee.

"At length in the battle on Eveshame plaine
The barons were routed, and Montfort was slaine:
Most fatall that battel did prove unto thee,
Though thou wast not borne then, my pretty Bessee!

"Along with the nobles, that fell at that tyde,
His eldest sonne Henrye, who fought by his side,
Was felde by a blowe, hee receivde in the fight :
A blowe that deprivde him for ever of sight.

"Among the dead bodyes all lifelesse hee laye,
Till evening drewe on of the following daye,
When by a younge ladye discovered was hee ;—
And this was thy mother, my pretty Bessee.

"A barons faire daughter stept forth in the night,
To search for her father, who fell in the fight,
And seeing younge Montfort, where gasping hee laye,
Was moved with pitye, and brought him awaye.

"In secrette shee nurst him, and swaged his paine,
While hee through the realme was beleevd to be slaine :
At length his faire bride shee consented to bee,
And made him glad father of pretty Bessee.

"And nowe lest oure foes our lives sholde betraye,
Wee clothed ourselves in beggars arraye :
Her jewelles shee solde, and hither came wee :
All our comfort and care was our pretty Bessee.

"And here have wee lived in fortunes despite,
Though poore, yett contented with humble delighte :
Full forty winters thus have I beene
A silly blind beggar of Bednall-greene.

"And here, noble lordes, is ended the song
Of one, that once to your owne ranke did belong ;
And thus have you learned a secrette from mee,
That ne'er had been knowne, but for pretty Bessee."

Now when the faire companye every one,
Had heard the strange tale in the song hee had showne,
They all were amazed, as well they might bee,
Both at the blinde beggar, and the pretty Bessee.

With that the faire bride they all did embrace,
Saying, "Sure thou art come of an honourable
Thy father likewise is of noble degree,   [race,
And thou art well worthy a lady to bee."

Thus was the feast ended with joye and delighte,
A bridegroome most happy was the younge
In joy and felicitie long lived hee,   [knighte,
All with his faire ladye, the pretty Bessee.

From Oberon in fairye land,
  The king of ghosts and shadowes there,
Mad Robin I, at his command,
  Am sent to viewe the night-sports here.
      What revell route
      Is kept about,
  In every corner where I go,
    I will o'ersee, and merry bee,
  And make good sport, with ho, ho, ho!

More swift than lightening can I flye
  About this aery welkin soone,
And, in a minutes space, descrye
  Each thing that 's done belowe the moone,
      There 's not a hag
      Or ghost shall wag,
  Or cry, ware Goblins! where I go;
    But Robin I their feates will spy,
  And send them home, with ho, ho, ho!

* See Appendix.

Whene'er such wanderers I meete,
  As from their night-sports they trudge
With counterfeiting voice I greete,   [home;
  And call them on, with me to roam
      Thro' woods, thro' lakes,
      Thro' bogs, thro' brakes;
Or else, unseene, with them I go,
  All in the nicke, to play some tricke
And frolicke it, with ho, ho, ho!

Sometimes I meete them like a man;
  Sometimes, an ox, sometimes, a hound;
And to a horse I turn me can;
  To trip and trot about them round.
      But if, to ride,
      My backe they stride,
More swift than winde away I go,
  Ore hedge and lands, thro' pools and
I whirry, laughing, ho, ho, ho!   [ponds

When lads and lasses merry be,
  With possets and with juncates fine,
Unseene of all the company,
  I eat their cakes and sip their wine;
      And to make sport,
      I snore and snort;
And out the candles I do blow:
  The maids I kiss; they shrieke—Who's
I answer naught, but ho, ho, ho!   [this?

Yet now and then, the maids to please,
  At midnight I card up their wool;
And while they sleepe and take their ease,
  With wheel, to threads, their flax I pull.
      I grind at mill
      Their malt up still;
I dress their hemp, I spin their tow;
  If any 'wake, and would me take,
I wend me, laughing, ho, ho, ho!

Robin Good=Fellow

When house or harth doth sluttish lye,
  I pinch the maidens black and blue;
The bed-clothes from the bedd pull I
  And lay them naked all to view.
      'Twixt sleepe and wake,
      I do them take,
And on the key-cold floor them throw.
  If out they cry, then forth I fly,
  And loudly laugh out, ho, ho, ho!

When any need to borrowe aught,
  We lend them what they do require;
And for the use demand we nought;
  Our owne is all we do desire.
      If to repay,
      They do delay,
Abroad amongst them then I go,
  And night by night, I them affright
  With pinchings, dreames, and ho, ho, ho!

When lazie queans have nought to do,
  But study how to cog and lye;
To make debate and mischief too,
  'Twixt one another secretlye:
      I marke their gloze,
      And it disclose,
To them whom they have wronged so;
  When I have done, I get me gone,
  And leave them scolding, ho, ho, ho!

When men do traps and engins set
  In loope holes were the vermine creepe,
Who from their foldes and houses, get
  Their duckes and geese, their lambes and
      I spy the gin,   [sheepe:
      And enter in,
And seeme a vermine taken so:
  But when they there approach me neare,
  I leap out laughing, ho, ho, ho!

By wells and rills, in meadowes greene,
  We nightly dance our hey-day guise;
And to our fairye king and queene
  We chant our moon-light minstrelsies.
    When larks gin sing,
    Away we fling,
And babes new borne steale as we go,
  And elfe in bed we leave instead,
And wend us laughing, ho, ho, ho!

From hag-bred Merlin's time have I
  Thus nightly revelled to and fro;
And for my pranks men call me by
  The name of Robin Good-fellow.
    Fiends, ghosts, and sprites,
    Who haunt the nights,
The hags and goblins do me know;
  And beldames old my feates have told;
So *Vale, Vale;* ho, ho, ho!

Sir Patrick Spens 79

The king sits in Dunfermline town,
   Drinking the blude-red wine:
"O where will I get a skeely skipper
   To sail this new ship of mine?"

O up and spake an eldern knight,
   Sat at the kings right knee:
"Sir Patrick Spens is the best sailor
   That ever sailed the sea."

Our king has written a braid letter,
   And sealed it with his hand,
And sent it to Sir Patrick Spens,
   Was walking on the strand.

* See Appendix.

"To Noroway, to Noroway,
  To Noroway, o'er the faem;
The kings daughter of Noroway,
  'T is thou maun bring her hame!"

The first word that Sir Patrick read,
  Sae loud loud laughed he;
The neist word that Sir Patrick read,
  The tear blindit his e'e.

"O wha is this has done this deed,
  And tauld the king o' me,
To send us out at this time o' the year,
  To sail upon the sea?

"Be it wind, be it weet, be it hail, be it sleet,
  Our ship must sail the faem;
The kings daughter of Noroway
  'T is we must fetch her hame."

They hoysed their sails on Monenday morn,
  Wi' a' the speed they may:
They hae landed in Noroway
  Upon a Wodensday.

They hadna been a week, a week
  In Noroway, but twae,
When that the lords o' Noroway
  Began aloud to say:

"Ye Scottishmen spend a' our kings gowd
  And a' our queenis fee."—
"Ye lie, ye lie ye liars loud!
  Fu' loud I hear ye lie!

"For I hae brought as much white monie
  As gane my men and me,   [gowd
And I hae brought a half-fou o' gude red
  Out owre the sea wi' me.

"Make ready, make ready, my merrymen
  Our gude ship sails the morn."—   [a'!

Sir Patrick Spens

"Now, ever alake! my master dear,
  I fear a deadly storm.

"I saw the new moon, late yestreen,
  Wi' the auld moon in her arm;
And if we gang to sea, master,
  I fear we 'll come to harm."

They hadna sailed a league, a league,
  A league but barely three, [loud,
When the lift grew dark, and the wind blew
  And gurly grew the sea.

The ankers brak, and the topmasts lap,
  It was sic a deadly storm;
And the waves came o'er the broken ship
  Till a' her sides were torn.

"O where will I get a gude sailor
  To take my helm in hand,
Till I get up to the tall topmast
  To see if I can spy land?"

"O here am I, a sailor gude,
  To take the helm in hand,
Till you go up to the tall topmast—
  But I fear you 'll ne'er spy land."

He hadna gane a step, a step,
  A step, but barely ane,
When a boult flew out of our goodly ship,
  And the salt sea it came in.

"Gae fetch a web o' the silken claith,
  Another o' the twine,
And wap them into our ships side,
  And letna the sea come in."

They fetched a web o' the silken claith,
  Another o' the twine, [side;
And they wapped them roun' the gude ships
  But still the sea came in.

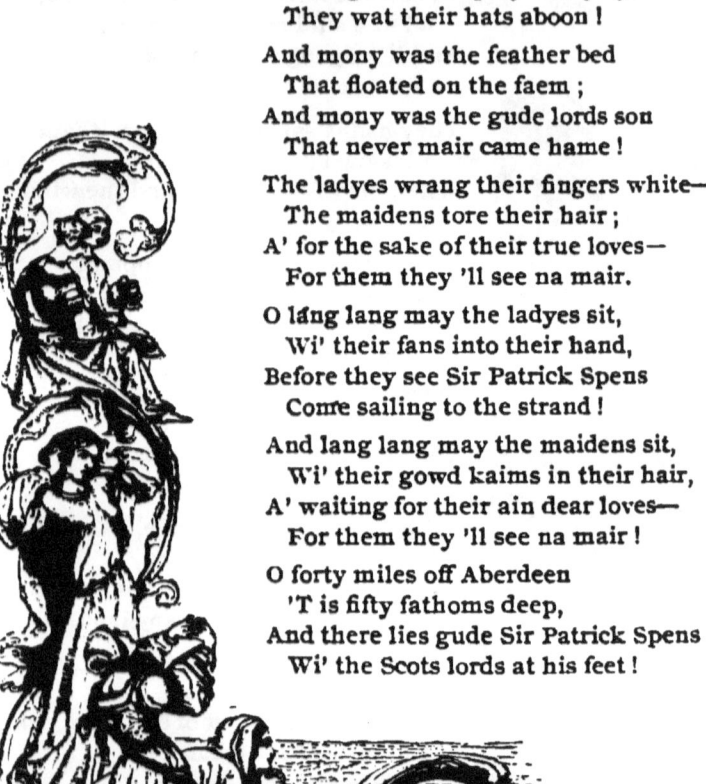

O laith laith were our gude Scots lords
    To weet their cork-heeled shoon,
But lang or a' the play was played
    They wat their hats aboon!

And mony was the feather bed
    That floated on the faem;
And mony was the gude lords son
    That never mair came hame!

The ladyes wrang their fingers white—
    The maidens tore their hair;
A' for the sake of their true loves—
    For them they 'll see na mair.

O lang lang may the ladyes sit,
    Wi' their fans into their hand,
Before they see Sir Patrick Spens
    Come sailing to the strand!

And lang lang may the maidens sit,
    Wi' their gowd kaims in their hair,
A' waiting for their ain dear loves—
    For them they 'll see na mair!

O forty miles off Aberdeen
    'T is fifty fathoms deep,
And there lies gude Sir Patrick Spens
    Wi' the Scots lords at his feet!

Gil Morrice

Gil Morrice was an erles son,
His name it waxed wide;
It was nae for his parentage,
Nor yet his meikle pride,
Bot for his dame, a lady gay,
Wha livd on Carrons side.

* See Appendix.

"Whar sall I get a bonny boy,
  That will win hose and shoen,
That will gae to Lord Barnards ha',
  And bid his lady come?

"And ye maun rin my errand, Willie,
  And ye maun rin wi' speid;
When ither boys gang on their feet,
  Ye sall ha' prancing steid."

"O, no! O, no! my master deir,
  I dar na for my life;
I'll no gae to the bauld barons,
  For to triest furth his wife."

"My bird Willie, my boy Willie,
  My deir Willie!" he said,
"How can ye strive against the streim?
  For I sall be obeyd."

"Bot O my master deir," he cryd,
  "In grene wode ye 're your lane;
Gi' owr sic thochts I wold ye red,
  For feir ye sold be tane."

"Haste! haste! I say, gae to the ha',
  Bid her come here wi' speid:
If ye refuse my hie command,
  I'll gar your body bleid.

"Gae bid her tak this gay mantel,
  'T is a' gowd but the hem;
Bid her come to the gude grene wode,
  Ein by hersel alane;

"And there it is, a silken sarke,
  Her ain hand sewd the sleeve;
And bid her come to Gil Morrice,
  Speir nae bauld barons leive."

Gil Morrice

"Yes! I will gae your black errand,
  Thoch it be to your cost:
Sen ye by me will nae be warnd,
  In it ye sall find frost.

"The baron he is a man o' micht,
  He neir cold bide to taunt;
And ye will see, before its nicht,
  Sma' cause ye ha' to vaunt.

"And sen I maun your errand rin,
  Sae sair against my will,
I 'se mak a vow, and keep it trow,
  It sall be done for ill!"

When he cam to the broken brig,
  He bent his bow and swam;
And when he cam to grass growing,
  Set down his feet and ran.

And when he cam to Barnards yeat,
  Wold neither chap nor ca',
Bot set his bent bow to his breist,
  And lichtly lap the wa'.

He wold na tell the man his errand,
  Thoch he stude at the yeat;
Bot streight into the ha' he cam,
  Whar they were set at meat.

"Hail! hail! my gentle sire and dame!
  My message winna wait,—
Dame, ye maun to the grene wode gae,
  Afore that it be late.

"Ye 're bidden tak this gay mantel,
  'T is a' gowd bot the hem;
Ye maun haste to the gude grene wode
  Ein by yoursell alane.

"And there it is, a silken sark,
  Your ain hand sewd the sleive:
Ye maun gae speik to Gil Morrice,
  Speir nae bauld barons leive."

The lady stamped wi' her foot,
  And winked wi' her eie;
Bot a' that shee cold say or do,
  Forbidden he wold nae be.

"It 's surely to my bower-woman,
  It neir cold be to me."—
"I brocht it to Lord Barnards lady,
  I trow that ye be shee."

Then up and spak the wylie nurse
  (The bairn upon her knee),
"If it be come from Gil Morrice,
  It 's deir welcum to me."

"Ye lie, ye lie, ye filthy nurse,
  Sae loud I heir ye lie;
I brocht it to Lord Barnards lady,
  I trow ye be nae shee."

Then up and spake the bauld baron,
  An angry man was he:
He has tane the table wi' his foot,
  Sae has he wi' his knee,
Till siller cup and mazer dish
  In flinders he gard flie.

"Gae bring a robe of your cleiding,
  Wi a' the haste ye can;
And I 'll gae to the gude grene wode,
  And speik wi your lemman."

"O bide at hame now, Lord Barnard!
  I warde ye bide at hame;
Neir wyte a man for violence,
  Wha neir wyte ye wi' nane!"

Gil Morrice

Gil Morrice sat in the grene wode
  He whistled and he sang:
"O, what meins a' the folk coming?
  My mother tarries long."*

The baron to the grene wode cam,
  Wi' meikle dule and care;
And there he first spyed Gil Morrice
  Kaming his yellow hair.

"Nae wonder, nae wonder, Gil Morrice,
  My lady loes thee weil;
The fairest part of my body
  Is blacker than thy heil.

"Yet neir the less now, Gil Morrice,
  For a' thy great bewtie,
Ye 'll rew the day ye eir was born;
  That heid shall gae wi' me!"

* The following are the stanzas alluded to in the Introductory Remarks. They are, obviously, emendations by "a modern hand":

    His hair was like the threeds of gold,
      Drawn frae Minervas loome:
    His lippes like roses drapping dew;
      His breath was a' perfume.

    His brow was like the mountain snae
      Gilt by the morning beam:
    His cheeks like living roses glow:
      His een like azure stream.

    The boy was clad in robes of grene,
      Sweete as the infant spring:
    And like the mavis on the bush,
      He gart the vallies ring.

The following verse occurs after the line "Kaming his yellow hair":

    That sweetly wavd around his face,
      That face beyond compare:
    He sang sae sweet it might dispel
      A' rage but fell despair.

Now he has drawn his trusty brand,
  And slaided owr the strae;
And thronch Gil Morrice fair body
  He gard the cauld iron gae.

And he has tane Gil Morrice heid,
  And set it on a speir;
The meinest man in a' his train,
  Has gotten that heid to beir.

And he has taen Gil Morrice up,
  Laid him across his steid;
The meinest man in a' his train,
  Has gotten that steid to lede.

The lady on the castle wa'
  Beheld baith dale and down;
And there she saw Gil Morrice heid
  Cum trailing to the toun.

"Better I loe that bluidy heid,
  Bot and that yellow hair,
Than Lord Barnard and a' his lands,
  As they lie here and there."

And she has taen her Gil Morrice,
  And kissed baith cheik and chin;
"I was ance as fou o' Gil Morrice,
  As the hip is o' the stane.

"I bore ye in my fathers house,
  Wi' meikle sin and shame;
I brocht ye up in the grene wode,
  Under the heavy rain.

"Oft have I by thy craddle sitten,
  And fondly seen thee sleip;
But now I maun gae 'bout thy grave
  A mothers teirs to weep!"

Gil Morrice

Again she kissd his bluidy cheik,
  Again his bluidy chin;
"O better I loed my son Morrice,
  Than a' my kyth and kin!"

"Awa, awa, ye ill woman,
  An ill dethe may ye die!
Gin I had kend he was your son,
  He had neir been slayne by me!"

"Obraid me not, my lord Barnard,
  Obraid me not for shame!
Wi' that same speir, O perce my heart,
  And save me frae my pain!

"Since naething but Gil Morrice head
  Thy jealous rage cold quell,
Let that same hand now tak her lyfe,
  That neir to thee did ill.

"To me nae after days nor nichts
  Will eir be saft or kind;
I 'll fill the air wi' heavy sichs,
  And greit till I be blind."

"Eneuch of bluid by me 's been spilt,
  Seek not your dethe frae me;
I 'd rather far it had been mysel,
  Than either him or thee.

"Wi' hopeless wae I hear your plaint,
  Sair, sair, I rue the deed—
That eir this cursed hand of mine
  Sold gar his body bleid!

"Dry up your teirs, my winsome dame,
  They neir can heal the wound;
Ye see his heid upon the spier,
  His hearts bluid on the ground.

"I curse the hand that did the deid,
　The heart that thocht the ill,
The feet that bare me wi' sic speid,
　The comlie youth to kill.

"I 'll aye lament for Gil Morrice,
　As gin he was my ain;
I 'll neir forget the dreiry day
　On which the youth was slain."

Sir Aldingar

SIR ALDINGAR.*

Our king hee kept a false stewàrde,
   Sir Aldingar they him call :
A falser stewarde than hee was one,
   Servde not in bower nor hall.

Hee wolde have layne by our comelye queene,
   Her deere worshippe to betraye :
Our queene shee was a good womàn,
   And evermore said him naye.

Sir Aldingar was wrothe in his mind,
   With her hee was never content,
Till traiterous meanes hee colde devyse,
   In a fyer to have her brent.

* See Appendix.

Sir Aldingar

There came a lazar to the Kings gate,
   A lazar both blinde and lame :
Hee tooke the lazar upon his backe,
   Him on the Queenes bedd has layne.

"Lye still, lazar, wheras thou lyest,
   Look thou goe not hence away :
Ile make thee a whole man and a sound
   In two howers of the day."

Then went him forth Sir Aldingar,
   And hyed him to our king :—
"If I might have grace, as I have space,
   Sad tydings I could bring."

"Say on, say on, Sir Aldingar,
   Say on the soothe to mee."
"Our queene hath chosen a newe, newe love,
   And shee will have none of thee!

"If shee had chosen a right good knight,
   The lesse had beene her shame ;
But shee hath chose her a lazar man,
   A lazar both blinde and lame."

"If this bee true, thou Aldingar,
   The tyding thou tellest to mee,
Then will I make thee a rich rich knight,
   Rich both of golde and fee.

"But if it be false, Sir Aldingar,
   As God nowe grant it bee !
Thy body, I sweare by the holye rood,
   Shall hang on the gallowes tree."

Hee brought our king to the Queenes cham-
   And opend to him the dore.   [ber,
"A lordlye love," King Harry says,
   "For our queene dame Elinore!

Sir Aldingar

"If thou were a man, as thou art none,
   Heere on my sword thou 'st dye ;
But a payre of new gallowes shall bee built,
   And there shalt thou hang on hye."

Forthe then hyed our king, I wysse,
   And an angry man was hee ;
And soon hee found Queene Elinore,
   That bride so bright of blee.

"Nowe God you save, our queene, madame,
   And Christ you save and see !
Heere you have chosen a newe newe love,
   And you will have none of mee !

"If you had chosen a right good knight,
   The lesse had been your shame ;
But you have chose you a lazar man,
   A lazar both blinde and lame ;

"Therfore a fyer there shall bee built,
   And brent all shalt thou bee !"
Nowe out alacke !" sayd our comelye queene,
   "Sir Aldingar 's false to mee."

"Nowe out alacke !" sayd our comelye queene,
   "My hart with griefe will brast:
I had thought swevens had never been true;
   I have proved them true at last.

"I dreamt in my sweven on Thursday eve,
   In my bed wheras I laye.
I dreamt a grype and a grimlie beast
   Had carryed my crowne awaye:

"My gorgett and my kirtle of golde,
   And all my faire head geere ;
And hee wolde worrye me with his tush
   And to his nest y-beare.

"Saving there came a little gray hawke,
　A merlin him they call,
Which untill the grounde did strike the grype,
　That dead hee downe did fall.

"Giffe I were a man, as nowe I am none,
　A battell wolde I prove,
To fight with that traitor Aldingar;
　Att him I cast my glove.

"Bot seeing Ime able noe battell to make,
　My liege, grant mee a knight
To fighte with that traitor Sir Aldingar,
　To maintaine mee in my righte."

"Nowe forty dayes I will give thee,
　To seeke thee a knight therin :
If thou finde not a knight in forty dayes
　Thy bodye it must brenn."

Then shee sent east, and shee sent west,
　By north and south bedeene ;
Bot never a champion colde shee finde,
　Wolde fighte with that knight soe keene.

Nowe twenty dayes were spent and gone,
　Noe helpe there might bee had :
Many a teare shed our comelye queene
　And aye her hart was sad.

Then came one of the Queenes damsèlles,
　And knelt upon her knee ;—
"Cheare up, cheare up, my gracious dame,
　I trust yet helpe may bee :

"And heere I will make mine avowe,
　And with the same mee binde ;
That never will I return to thee,
　Till I some helpe may finde !"

Sir Aldingar

Then forthe she rode on a faire palfrâye
  O'er hill and dale about;
Bot never a champion colde shee finde,
  Wolde fighte with that knight so stout.

And nowe the'daye drewe on apace,
  When our good queene must dye:
All woe-begone was that faire damsèlle,
  When she found no helpe was nye.

All woe-begone was that faire damsèlle,
  And the salt teares fell from her eye;
When lo! as shee rode by a rivers side,
  She mette with a tinye boye.

A tinye boye shee mette, God wot,
  All clad in mantle of golde:
Hee seemed noe more in mans likenèsse,
  Then a childe of four yeere old.

"Why grieve you, damselle faire," he sayd,
  "And what doth cause you moane?"
The damselle scant wolde deigne a looke,
  Bot fast shee pricked on.

"Yet turn againe, thou faire damsèlle,
  And greete thy queene from mee:
When bale is att hyest, boote is nyest,
  Nowe helpe enoughe may bee.

"Bid her remember what shee dreamt
  In her bedd, wheras shee lay;
How when the grype and the grimlie beast
  Wolde have carryed her crowne awaye.

"Even then there came a little gray hawke,
  And saved her from his clawes;
Then bidd the Queene be merry at hart,
  For heaven will fende her cause."

Back then rode that faire damsèlle.
   And her hart it lept for glee;
And when shee told her gracious dame
   A gladd woman then was shee.

Bot when the appointed daye was come,
   No helpe appeared nye;
Then woeful, woeful was her hart,
   And the teares stood in her eye.

And nowe a fyer was built of wood;
   And a stake was made of tree;
And nowe Queene Elinore forthe was led,
   A sorrowful sight to see.

Three times the herault he waved his hand,
   And three times spake on hye:
"Giffe any good knight will fende this dame,
   Come forthe, or shee must dye."

No knight stood forthe, no knight there came,
   No helpe appeared nye:
And nowe the fyer was lighted up,
   Queene Elinore shee must dye.

And nowe the fyer was lighted up,
   As hot as hot might be;
When riding upon a little white steed,
   The tinye boy they see.

"Away with that stake! away with those
   And loose our comelye queene: [brands!
I am come to fighte with Sir Aldingar,
   And prove him a traitor keene!"

Forthe then stoode Sir Aldingar,
   Bot when hee saw the chylde, [backe,
Hee laughed, and scoffed, and turned his
   And weened hee had been beguylde.

Sir Aldingar

"Nowe turne, nowe turn thee, Aldingar,
   And eyther fighte or flee :
I trust that I shall avenge the wronge,
   Though I am so small to see."

The boye pulld forthe a well good sworde
   So gilt it dazzled the ee :—
The first stroke stricken at Aldingar
   Smote off his leggs by the knee.

"Stand up ! stand up ! thou false traitòr,
   And fighte upon thy feete,
For and thou thrive, as thou beginst,
   Of height wee shall be meete !"

"A priest ! a priest !" sayes Aldingar,
   "While I am a man alive,—
A priest, a priest," sayes Aldingar,
   "Me for to houzle and shrive !

"I wolde have layne by our comelye queene,
   Bot shee wolde never consent ;
Then I thought to betraye her unto our king,
   In a fyer to have her brent.

"There came a lazar to the Kings gates,
   A lazar both blinde and lame ;
I tooke the lazar upon my backe,
   And on her bedd had him layne.

"Then ranne I to our comelye king,
   These tidings sore to tell.
Bot ever alacke !" sayes Aldingar,
   "Falsing never doth well :—

"Forgive ! forgive mee, Queene, madame,
   The short time I must live !"
"Nowe Christ forgive thee, Aldingar,
   As freely I forgive !"

"Here take thy queene, our King Harrye,
  And love her as thy life,
For never had a king in Christentye,
  A truer and fairer wife."

King Henrye ran to clasp his queene,
  And looséd her full sone;
Then turnd to look for the tinye boye;
  —The boye was vanisht and gone!

But first hee had touchd the lazar man,
  And stroakt him with his hand:
The lazar under the gallowes tree
  All whole and sounde did stand.

The lazar under the gallowes tree
  Was comelye, straight and tall;
King Henrye made him his head stewàrde
  To wayte within his hall.

SIR LANCELOT DU LAKE.*

When Arthur first in court began,
   And was approved king,
By force of armes great victorys won,
   And conquest home did bring.

Then into Britain straight hee came,
   Where fifty good and able
Knights, then repaired unto him,
   Which were of the Round Table:

* See Appendix.

And many justs and turnaments,
  Before him there were prest,
Wherein these knights did then excell
  And far surmount the rest;

But one Sir Lancelot du Lake,
  Who was approved well,
Hee, in his fights and deeds of armes,
  All others did excell.

When hee had rested him a while,
  To play, and game, and sport;
Hee thought hee wold approve himselfe
  In some adventurous sort.

Hee armèd rode in forrest wide,
  And met a damsell faire,
Who told him of adventures great,
  Wherto he gave good eare.

"Such wold I find," quoth Lancelot:
  "For that cause came I hither."
"Thou seemst," quoth shee, "a knight full good,
  And I will bring thee thither,

"Whereas a mighty knight doth dwell,
  That now is of great fame;
Therfore tell me what knight thou art,
  And what may bee thy name."

"My name is Lancelot du Lake."
  Quoth shee, "it likes me, then;
Here dwelles a knight who never was
  O'er-matcht of any man:

"Who hath in prison threescore knights
  And four, that hee hath bound;
Knights of King Arthurs court they bee,
  And of the Table Round."

Shee brought him to a river then,
    And also to a tree
Whereon a copper bason hung,
    His fellows shields to see.

Hee struck soe hard, the bason broke :—
    When Tarquine heard the sound,
Hee drove a horse before him straight,
    Whereon a knight was bound.

"Sir knight," then sayd Sir Lancelot,
    "Bring me that horse-load hither,
And lay him downe, and let him rest;
    We 'll try our force together;

"For, as I understand, thou hast,
    As far as thou art able,
Done great despite and shame unto
    The knights of the Round Table."

"If thou art of the Table Round,"
    Quoth Tarquine speedilye,
"Both thee and all thy fellowship
    I utterly defye."

"That 's over much," quoth Lancelot tho,
    "Defend thee by and by!"
They sett their spurs unto their steeds,
    And each at other flie.

They coucht their speares (their horses ran,
    As though there had been thunder),
And each struck then upon their shields,
    Wherewith they brake asunder.

Their horses backes brake under them;
    The knights they were astound :
To avoyd their horses they made haste
    To fight upon the ground.

Sir Lancelot du Lake

They tooke them to their shields full fast,
    Their swords they drew out then;
Wyth mighty strokes most eagerlye
    One at the other ran.

They wounded were, and bled full sore,
    For breath they both did stand;
And leaning on their swords awhile,
    Quoth Tarquine, "Hold thy hand,

"And tell to me what I shall aske."—
"Say on,"—quoth Lancelot tho:
"Thou art," quoth Tarquine, "the best
    That ever I did know;   [knight

"And like a knight that I did hate:
    Soe that thou bee not hee,
I will deliver all the rest,
    And eke accord wyth thee."

"That is well said," quoth Lancelot;
    "But sith it soe must bee,
What knight is that thou hatest so?
    I pray thee show to me."

"His name 's Sir Lancelot du Lake,
    Hee slew my brother deere;
Him I suspect of all the rest:
    I wold I had him here."

"Thy wish thou hast, but now unknowne:
    I am Lancelot du Lake,
Now of King Arthurs Table Round;
    King Hands son of Benwake;

"And I defye thee;—do thy worst."
    "Ha, ha!" quoth Tarquine tho,
"One of us two shall end our lives
    Before that we do go.

"If thou bee Lancelot du Lake,
  Then welcome shalt thou bee:
Wherfore see thou thyself defend,
  For now defye I thee."

They buckled then together so,
  Like unto wild boares rashing;
And wyth theire swords and shields they ran
  At one another slashing:

The ground besprinkled was wyth blood:
  Tarquine began to faint;
For hee had backt and bore his shield
  So low, hee did repent.*

* Several of the ancient ballads record similar fights between giants and the knights of King Arthur's Round Table. An "Ancient English Metrical Romance," printed by Ritson, entitled "Sir Ywaine and Sir Gawin," describes an encounter which led to a like result, —the delivering from prison sundry "fellowes" who, by the gallantry of their brother-in-arms, were "out of bales broght." We copy a few passages:

  Syr Ywaine rade into the playne,
  And the geant cum hym ogayne:—
  His levore was ful grete and lang,
  And himself ful mekyl and strang.
  He said: "What devil made the so balde
  For to cum heder out of thi halde?
  Who-so-ever the heder send
  Lufed the litel, so God me mend!
  Of the he wald be wroken fayn."
  "Do forth thi best!" said Sir Ywaine.
    *   *   *   *   *
  Sir Ywaine left his sper of hand,
  And strake obout him with his brand;
  And the geant, mekil of main,
  Strake ful fast to him ogayn.
    *   *   *   *   *
  Sethen with a stroke to him he stert,
  And smate the geant unto the hert;
  Ther was none other tale to tell,
  Bot fast unto the earth he fell,
  Als it had bene a hevy tre.
  Then might men in the kastel se
  Ful mekil mirth on ilka side,
  The yates kest thai open wyde.
    *   *   *   *   *

This soon espyde Sir Lancelot
  Hee leapt upon him then,
Hee pulld him downe upon his knee,
  And, rushing off his helm,

Forthwith hee strucke his necke in two;
  And, when hee had soe done,
From prison threescore knights and four
  Delivered everye one.

KING ARTHUR'S DEATH.*

On Trinity Monday in the morn,
  This sore battayle was doomed to be,
Where many a knight cryed, "Well-away!
  Alack, it was the more pitie!"

Ere the first crowing of the cock,
  When as the king in his bed lay,
He thought Sir Gawaine to him came,
  And there to him these wordes did say:

* See Appendix.

"Now, as you are mine unkle dear,
   And as you prize your life, this day,
O meet not with your foe in fight;
   Put off the battayle, if ye may;

"For Sir Launcelot is now in Fraunce,
   And with him many an hardy knight,
Who will within this moneth be back,
   And will assist ye in the fight."

The king then called his nobles all,
   Before the breaking of the day:
And told them how Sir Gawaine came,
   And there to him these wordes did say.

His nobles all this counsayle gave,
   That earlye in the morning, he
Shold send away an herauld at armes,
   To ask a parley fair and free.
                           [chose,
Then twelve good knightes King Arthur
   The best of all that with him were,
To parley with the foe in field,
   And make with him agreement fair.

The king he charged all his host,
   In readiness there for to be;
But no man shold no weapon sturre,
   Unless a sword drawn they shold see.

And Mordred on the other part,
   Twelve of his knights did likewise bring;
The best of all his company,
   To hold the parley with the king.

Sir Mordred also charged his host,
   In readiness there for to be;
But no man shold no weapon sturre,
   But if a sword drawn they shold see.

King Arthur's Death

For he durst not his unkle trust,
  Nor he his nephew, sothe to tell:
Alack! it was a woefull case,
  As ere in Christentye befell!

But when they were together met,
  And both to fair accordance brought,
And a months league between them set
  Before the battayle shold be fought,

An adder crept forth of a bush,   [knee;
  Stung one o' th' king's knights on the
Alack! it was a woefull chance,
  As ever was in Christentye!

When the knight found him wounded sore,
  And saw the wild-worm hanging there;
His sword he from his scabberd drew:
  A piteous case, as ye shall hear.

For when the two hostes saw the sword,
  They joyned battayle instanlye;
Till of so many noble knights,
  On one side there were left but three!

For all were slain that durst abide,
  And but some few that fled away:
Ay me! it was a bloody field
  As ere was fought on summers day!

Upon King Arthurs own partye,
  Only himself escaped there,
And Lukyn Duke of Gloster free,
  And the kings butler Bedevere.

And when the king beheld his knights,
  All dead and scattered on the mold,
The teares fast trickled down his face;
  That manly face in fight so bold!

"Now rest ye all, brave knights," he said,
  "So true and faithful to your trust:
And must ye then, ye valiant hearts,
  Be left to moulder into dust!

"Most loyal have ye been to me,
  Most true and faithful unto death:
And, oh! to rayse ye up again,
  How freely could I yield my breath!

"But see, the traitor's yet alive,
  Lo where he stalks among the dead!
Now bitterlye he shall abye;
  And vengeance fall upon his head."

"O stay, my liege," then sayd the duke;
  "O stay for love and charitie;
Remember what the vision spake,
  Nor meet your foe, if it may be."

"O stay me not, thou worthy wight,
  This debt my loyal knights I owe:
Betide me life, betide me death,
  I will avenge them of their foe."

Then strait he grasped his trusty spear,
  And on his horse then mounted he:
As his butler holpe him to his horse,
  His bowels gushed to his knee.

"Alas!" then sayd the noble king,
  "That I should live this sight to see!
To see this good knight here be slain,
  All for his love in helping me!"

He put his spear into his rest,
  And to Sir Mordred loud gan cry:
"Now set thyself upon thy guard,
  For, traitor, now thy death is nye."

Sir Mordred lifted up his sword,
    And fierce to meet the king ran he;
The king his spear he through him thrust;
    A fathom thorow his bodie.

When Mordred felt the stroke of death,
    And found that he was wounded so,
He thrust himself upon the spear,
    And struck the king a deadly blow.

Then grimly dyed Sir Mordred,
    Presently upon that tree;
And bloody streams ran from the king,
    Ere to the duke returned he.*

Sir Lukyn then he thus bespake,
    "Sir knight thou hast been faithfull tryde,
Now take my sword Excalibar,
    That hangs so freely by my syde:

" O take my sword Excalibar,
    And there into the river throw;
For here, henceforth, benethe this tree,
    All use of weapons I forego.

---

* Percy has printed also a ballad, entitled "The Legend of King Arthur," from his "ancient folio manuscript," in which the king relates his own history, describes the battle in which he fell, and mourns over his fate. Reference is thus made to the contest with Sir Mordred:

    And still I him pursued with speed
        Till at the last wee mett:
    Whereby an appointed day of fight
        Was there agreed and sett.

    Where we did fight, of mortal life
        Eche other to deprive,
    Till of a hundred thousand men
        Scarce one was left alive.

    There all the noble chivalrye
        Of Brittaine tooke their end.
    O see how fickle is their state
        That doe on feates depend!

"And fare thee well, thou trusty sword,
  A better neer had valiant knight,
With thee full oft, and many a day,
  Have I withstood my foe in fight.

"With this good fauchion in my hand,
  Oft have I reapd the bloody feelde;
But now the fatalle hour is come,
  That never more I may thee weelde."

The duke to the river side he went,
  And there his own sword in threw he;
But he kept back Excalibar,
  He kept it back in privitie.

For all of coleyne was the blade,
  And all the hilt of precious stone.
"And ever alack!" then sayd the knight,
  "Must such a sword away be thrown?"

Then back he came unto the king,
  Who sayd, "Sir Lukyn, what did ye see?"
"Nothing, my liege, save that the wind
  Blew o'er the waters fair and free."

"O go again," then said the king,
  "O good Sir Lukyn, go again;
Into the river throw my sword,
  Nor keep me lingering here in pain."

The duke then to the river went,
  And the kings scabberd in threw he;
But he kept back Excalibar,
  And hid it underneth a tree.

Then back he came to tell the king,
  Who sayd, "Sir Lukyn, saw ye ought?"—
"Nothing, my liege, save that the wind
  Now with the angry waters fought."

King Arthur's Death

"O Lukyn, Lukyn!" said the king,
  "Twice hast thou dealt deceitfully:
Alack, whom may we ever trust,
  When such a knight so false can be?

"Say, wouldst thou have thy master dead,
  All for a sword that wins thine eye?
Now go again, and throw it in,
  Or here the one of us shall dye."

The duke, all shent with this rebuke,
  No aunswer made unto the king;
But to the river took the sword,
  And threw it far as he could fling.

A hand and arm did meet the sword,
  And flourished three times in the air;
Then sunk benethe the renning streme,
  And of the duke was seen no mair.*

* In the romance of "Morte D'Arthur," as given by Mr. Ellis — "Specimens of Early English Metrical Romances,"—this incident is thus recorded: The knight having at length thrown into the water the good sword Excalibar,—

> There came an hand, withouten rest,
>   Out of the water, and fair it hent,
> And brandished as it should brast,
>   And sithe, as gleam away it went.
>
> To the king again went he there,
>   And said, "lief, sir, I saw a hand;
> Out of the water it came all bare,
>   And thrice brandished that rich brand."
>
> "Help me! soon were I thore!"
>   He led his lord unto the strand;
> A rich ship with masts and oar,
>   Full of ladies there they fand.
>
> The ladies that were fair and free,
>   Courteously the king gan they fong;
> And one that brightest was of blee,
>   Weeped sore and handes wrung.
>
> "Brother," she said, "woe is me,
>   From leeching hast thou been too long;
> I wot that greatly grieveth me,
>   For thy painis are full strong."

All sore astonied stood the duke;
  He stood as still as still mote be;
Then hastend back to tell the king,
  But he was gone from under the tree.

But to what place he cold not tell,
  For never after he did him spy;
But he saw a barge go from the land,
  And he heard ladyes howl and cry.

And whether the king were there, or not,
  He never knew, nor ever cold;
But from that sad and direfull day,
  He never more was seene on mold.

THE HEIRE OF LINNE.*
PART THE FIRST.

Lithe and listen, gentlemen,
  To sing a song I will beginne;
It is of a lord of faire Scotland,
  Which was the unthrifty heire of [Linne.

His father was a right good lord,
  His mother a lady of high degree:
But they, alas! were dead, him froe,
  And he lovd keeping companie.

To spend the daye with merry cheare,
  To drinke and revell every night,
To card and dice from eve to morne,
  It was, I ween, his hearts delighte.

See Appendix.

To ride, to runne, to rant, to roare,
    To alwaye spend and never spare,
I wott, an' it were the king himselfe,
    Of golde and fee he mote be bare.

Soe fares the unthrifty Lord of Linne
    Till all his golde is gone and spent;
And he maun sell his landes so broad,
    His house, and landes, and all his rent.

His father had a keen stewarde,
    And John o' the Scales was called he;
But John is become a gentel-man,
    And John has gott both golde and fee.

Sayes, "Welcome, welcome, Lord of Linne,
    Let nought disturb thy merry cheare;
If thou wilt sell thy landes soe broad,
    Good store of golde Ile give thee heere."

"My golde is gone, my money is spent;
    My lande nowe take it unto thee:
Give me the golde, good John o' the Scales,
    And thine for aye my lande shall be."

Then John he did him to record draw,
    And John he cast him a gods-pennie;
But for every pounde that John agreed,
    The lande, I wis, was well worth three.

Hee told him the golde upon the borde,
    He was right glad his lande to winne:
"The golde is thine, the lande is mine,
    And nowe Ile be the Lord of Linne."

Thus he hath sold his lande soe broad,
    Both hill and holt, and moore and fenne,
All but a poore and lonesome lodge,
    That stood far off in a lonely glenne.

The Heire of Linne

For soe he to his father hight.
"My sonne, when I am gonne," sayd he,
"Then thou wilt spend thy lande so broad,
And thou wilt spend thy golde so free;

"But sweare me nowe upon the roode,
That lonesome lodge thou 'lt never spend;
For when all the world doth frown on thee,
Thou there shalt find a faithful friend."

The heire of Linne is full of golde;
"And come with me, my friends," sayd he,
"Let's drinke, and rant, and merry make,
And he that spares, ne'er mote he thee."

They ranted, drank, and merry made,
Till all his golde it waxed thinne:
And then his friendes they slunk away;
They left the unthrifty heire of Linne.

He had never a penny left in his purse,
Never a penny left but three,
And one was brass, another was lead,
And another it was white money.

"Nowe, well-a-day," sayd the heire of Linne,
"Nowe well-a-day, and woe is me,
For when I was the Lord of Linne,
I never wanted golde nor fee.

"But many a trustye friend have I,
And why shold I feel dole or care?
Ile borrow of them all by turnes,
Soe need I not be never bare.

But one, I wis, was not at home;
Another had payd his golde away;
Another calld him thriftless loone,
And bade him sharpely wend his way.

"Nowe well-a-day," sayd the heire of Linne,
  "Nowe well-a-day, and woe is me!
For when I had my landes soe broad,
  On me they livd right merrilee.

"To beg my bread from door to door
  I wis, it were a brenning shame;
To rob and steal it were a sinne;
  To worke my limbs I cannot frame.

"Nowe Ile away to lonesome lodge,
  For there my father bade me wend;
When all the world shold frown on me,
  I there shold find a trusty friend."

PART THE SECOND.

Away then hyed the heire of Linne
  O'er hill and holt, and moore and fenne,
Untill he came to lonesome lodge
  That stood soe lowe in a lonely glenne.

Hee looked up, hee looked downe,
  In hope some comfort for to winne;
But bare and lothly were the walles:
  "It's sorry chear," quo' the heire of Linne.

The little windowe dim and darke
  Was hung with ivy, brere, and yewe;
No shimmering sunne heere ever shone;
  No halesome breeze heere ever blew.

No chair, ne table he mote spye,
  No chearful hearth, ne welcome bed;
Nought save a rope with renning noose,
  That dangling hung up o'er his head.

And over it, in broad letters,
  These words were written soe plain to see:
"Ah! gracelesse wretch, hast spent thine all,
  And brought thyself to penurie?

"All this my boding mind misgave,
   I therefore left this trustye friend:
Let it now sheeld thy foule disgrace,
   And all thy shame and sorrowes end."

Sorely shent wi' this rebuke,
   Sorely shent was the heire of Linne;
His heart, I wis, was near to brast
   With guilt and sorrowe, shame and sinne.

Never a word spake the heire of Linne,
   Never a word he spake but three:
"This is a trustye friend indeed,
   And is right welcome unto me."

Then round his necke the corde he drewe,
   And sprang aloft with his bodie;
When lo! the ceiling burst in twaine,
   And to the ground came tumbling he.

Astonyed lay the heire of Linne,
   Ne knewe if he were live or dead:
At length he looked, and sawe a bille,
   And in it a key of golde so redd.

Hee took the bille, and lookt it on,
   Strait good comfort found he there:
It told him of a hole in the wall,
   In which there stood three chests in-fere.

Two were full of the beaten golde,
   The third was full of white money,
And over them in broad letters
   These words were written soe plain to see:

"Once more, my sonne, I sett thee clere;
   Amend thy life and follies past;
For but thou amend thee of thy life,
   That rope must be thy end at last."

"And let it be," sayd the heire of Linne,
"And let it be, but if I amend;
For heere I will make mine avow,
This reade shall guide me to the end."

Away then went with a merry cheare,
Away then went the heire of Linne;
I wis he neither ceasd ne blanne
Till John o' the Scales house he did winne.

And when he came to John o' the Scales,
Up at the speere then looked he;
There sate three lords upon a rowe
Were drinking of the wine soe free.

And John himself sate at the bord-head
Because nowe Lord of Linne was he.
"I pray thee," he said, "good John o' the
One forty pence for to lend me." [Scales,

"Away, away, thou thriftless loone!
Away, away, this may not be;
For Christs curse on my head," he sayd,
"If ever I trust thee one pennie!"

Then bespake the heire of Linne,
To John o' the Scales wife then spake he:
"Madame, some almes on me bestowe,
I pray for sweet Saint Charitie."

"Away, away, thou thriftless loone!
I swear thou gettest no almes of me;
For if we shold hang any losel heere,
The first we wold beginne with thee."

Then bespake a good fellowe
Which sat at John o' the Scales his bord;
Sayd, "Turne againe, thou heire of Linne;
Some time thou wast a well good lord:

The Heire of Linne

"Some time a good fellowe thou hast been,
  And sparedst not thy golde and fee;
Therefore Ile lend thee forty pence,
  And other forty if need be.

"And ever, I pray thee, John o' the Scales,
  To let him sit in thy companie;
For well I wott thou hadst his lande,
  And a good bargaine it was to thee."

Up then spake him John o' the Scales,
  All wode he answerd him againe:
"Nowe Christs curse on my head," he sayd,
  But I did lose by that bargaine!

"And heere I proffer thee, heire of Linne,
  Before these lordes soe faire and free,
Thou shalt have it backe again better cheape
  By a hundred markes, than I had it of thee."

"I drawe you to record, lords," he sayd.
  With that he cast him a gods-pennie:
"Nowe by my fay!" sayd the heire of Linne,
  "And heere, good John, is thy money."

And he pulled forth three bagges of golde,
  And layd them down upon the bord:
All woe begone was John o' the Scales,
  Soe shent he cold say never a word.

He told him forth the good redd golde,
  He told it forth wi' mickle dinne.
"The golde is thine, the lande is mine,
  And now Ime againe the Lord of Linne,"

Sayes, "Have thou heere, thou good fellowe,
  Forty pence thou didst lend me:
Nowe I am againe the Lord of Linne,
  And forty pounds I will give thee.

"Ile make thee keeper of my forrest,
  Both of the wild deere and the tame;
For but I reward thy bounteous heart,
  I wis, good fellowe, I were to blame."

"Nowe well-a-day!" sayth Joan o' the
    Scales;
  "Nowe well-a-day! and woe is my life!
Yesterday I was Lady of Linne,
  Nowe Ime but John o' the Scales his wife."

"Nowe fare thee well," sayd the heire of
    Linne:
  "Farewell nowe, John o' the Scales," sayd
    he:
  "Christs curse light on me, if ever again
  I bring my landes in jeopardie!"

LORD SOULIS.*

Lord Soulis he sat in Hermitage Castle,
  And beside him Old Redcap sly;—
"Now, tell me, thou sprite, who art meikle of might
  The death that I must die."

"While thou shalt bear a charmed life,
  And hold that life of me,
'Gainst lance and arrow, sword and knife,
  I shall thy warrant be.

* See Appendix.

Lord Soulis

"Nor forged steel, nor hempen band,
   Shall e'er thy limbs confine,
Till threefold ropes of sifted sand
   Around thy body twine.

"If danger press fast, knock thrice on the [chest,
   With rusty padlocks bound;
Turn away your eyes, when the lid shall rise,
   And listen to the sound."

Lord Soulis he sat in Hermitage Castle,
   And Redcap was not by;
And he called on a page, who was witty and [sage,
   To go to the barmkin high.

"And look thou east, and look thou west,
   And quickly come tell to me,
What troopers haste along the waste,
   And what may their livery be."

He looked over fell, and he looked o'er flat,
   But nothing, I wist, he saw,
Save a pyot on a turret that sat
   Beside a corby craw.

The page he looked at the skrieh of day,
   But nothing, I wist, he saw,
Till a horseman gray, in the royal array,
   Rode down the Hazel-shaw.

"Say, why do you cross o'er moor and [moss?"
   So loudly cried the page;
"I tidings bring, from Scotland's King,
   To Soulis of Hermitage.

"He bids me tell that bloody warden,
   Oppressor of low and high,
If ever again his lieges complain,
   The cruel Soulis shall die."

By traitorous sleight they seized the knight,
  Before he rode or ran,
And through the key-stone of the vault
  They plunged him, both horse and man.

    *   *   *   *   *

O May she came, and May she gaed,
  By Goranberry green;
And May she was the fairest maid
  That ever yet was seen.

O May she came, and May she gaed,
  By Goranberry tower;
And who was it but cruel Lord Soulis
  That carried her from her bower?

He brought her to his castle gray,
  By Hermitage's side;
Says—"Be content, my lovely May,
  For thou shalt be my bride."

With her yellow hair, that glittered fair,
  She dried the trickling tear;
She sighed the name of Branxholm's heir,
  The youth that loved her dear,

" Now, be content, my bonny May,
  And take it for your hame;
Or ever and aye shall ye rue the day
  You heard Young Branxholm's name.

"O'er Branxholm tower, ere the morning hour,
  When the lift is like lead sae blue, [night,
The smoke shall roll white on the weary
  And the flame shall shine dimly through."

Syne he 's ca'd on him Ringan Red,
  A sturdy kemp was he;
From friend, or foe, in Border feid,
  Who never a foot would flee.

Red Ringan sped, and the spearmen led
  Up Goranberry slack ;
Ay, many a wight, unmatched in fight,
  Who never more came back.

And bloody set the westering sun,
  And bloody rose he up ;
But little thought young Branxholm's heir
  Where he that night should sup.

He shot the roebuck on the lee,
  The dun deer on the law ;
The glamour sure was in his ee
  When Ringan nigh did draw.

O'er heathy edge, through rustling sedge,
  He sped till day was set ;
And he thought it was his merry-men true,
  When he the spearmen met.

Far from relief, they seized the chief;
  His men were far away ;   [back
Through Hermitage slack they sent him
  To Soulis' castle gray ;
Syne onward fure for Branxholm tower
  Where all his merry-men lay.

"Now, welcome, noble Branxholm's heir !
  Thrice welcome," quoth Soulis, "to me !
Say, dost thou repair to my castle fair,
  My wedding guest to be ?
And lovely May deserves, per fay,
  A bride-man such as thee !"

And broad and bloody rose the sun,
  And on the barmkin shone,   [there,
When the page was aware of Red Ringan
  Who came riding all alone

Lord Soulis 125

To the gate of the tower Lord Soulis he
    As he lighted at the wall,   [speeds;
Says, "Where did ye stable my stalwart
    And where do they tarry all?"   [steeds,

"We stabled them sure, on the Tarras Muir;
    We stabled them sure," quoth he—
"Before we could cross the quaking moss
    They all were lost but me."

He clenched his fist, and he knocked on the
    And he heard a stifled groan;   [chest,
And at the third knock each rusty lock
    Did open one by one.

He turned away his eyes as the lid did rise,
    And he listened silentlie;   [low,
And he heard breathed slow, in murmurs
    "Beware of a coming tree!"

In muttering sound the rest was drowned,
    No other word heard he;
But slow as it rose, the lid did close
    With the rusty padlocks three.

    *   *   *   *

Now rose with Branxholm's ae brother
    The Teviot, high and low;
Bauld Walter by name, of meikle fame,
    For none could bend his bow.

O'er glen and glade, to Soulis there sped
    The fame of his array,
And that Teviotdale would soon assail
    His towers and castle gray.

With clenchèd fist, he knocked on the chest,
    And again he heard a groan;
And he raised his eyes as the lid did rise,
    But answer heard he none.

The charm was broke, when the spirit spoke,
  And it murmured sullenlie,—
"Shut fast the door, and for evermore
  Commit to me the key.

"Alas! that ever thou raisedst thine eyes,
  Thine eyes to look on me!
Till seven years are o'er, return no more,
  For here thou must not be"

Think not but Soulis was wae to yield
  His warlock chamber o'er;
He took the keys from the rusty lock,
  That never were ta'en before.

He threw them o'er his left shoulder,
  With meikle care and pain;
And he bade it keep them fathoms deep,
  Till he returned again.

And still, when seven years are o'er,
  Is heard the jarring sound;
When slowly opes the charmed door
  Of the chamber under ground.

And some within the chamber door
  Have cast a curious eye;
But none dare tell, for the spirits in hell,
  The fearful sights they spy.

* * * * *

When Soulis thought on his merry-men now,
  A woful wight was he;   [pine,
Says, "Vengeance is mine, and I will not re-
  But Branxholm's heir shall die!"

Says, "What would you do, young Branxholm,
  Gin ye had me, as I have thee?"—
"I would take you to the good greenwood
  And gar your ain hand wale the tree."

" Now shall thine ain hand wale the tree,
   For all thy mirth and meikle pride;
And May shall choose, if my love she refuse,
   A scrog bush thee beside."

They carried him to the good greenwood
   Where the green pines grew in a row;
And they heard the cry, from the branches
   Of the hungry carrion crow.   [high,

They carried him on from tree to tree.
   The spiry boughs below;
" Say, shall it be thine, on the tapering pine
   To feed the hooded crow?"

" The fir-tops fall by Branxholm wall
   When the night blast stirs the tree,
And it shall not be mine to die on the pine
   I loved in infancie."

Young Branxholm turned him and oft looked
   And aye he passed from tree to tree; [back,
Young Branxholm peep'd, and puirly spake,
   " O sic a death is no for me!"

And next they passed the aspin gray,
   Its leaves were rustling mournfullie; [gay!
" Now choose thee, choose thee, Branxholm
   Say, wilt thou never choose the tree?"—

" More dear to me is the aspin gray.
   More dear than any other tree;   [made,
For, beneath the shade that its branches
   Have pass'd the vows of my love and me."

Young Branxholm peep'd, and puirly spake,
   Until he did his ain men see,
With witches' hazel in each steel cap,
   In scorn of Soulis' gramarye;
Then shoulder-height for glee he lap,—
   " Methinks I spye a coming tree!"—

Lord Soulis

"Ay, many may come, but few return,"
  Quo' Soulis, the lord of gramarye;
"No warrior's hand in fair Scotland
  Shall ever dint a wound on me!"—

"Now, by my sooth," quo' bold Walter,
  "If that be true we soon shall see."—
His bent bow he drew, and his arrow was true,
  But never a wound or scar had he.

Then up bespake him true Thomas,
  He was the lord of Ersyltoun;
"The wizard's spell no steel can quell
  Till once your lances bear him down."—

They bore him down with lances bright,
  But never a wound or scar had he;
With hempen bands they bound him tight,
  Both hands and feet, on the Nine-stane lee.

That wizard accurst, the bands he burst:
  They mouldered at his magic spell;
And neck and heel, in the forged steel,
  They bound him against the charms of hell.

That wizard accurst, the bands he burst:
  No forged steel his charms could bide;
Then up bespake him true Thomas,
  "We'll bind him yet, whate'er betide."

The black spae-book from his breast he took,
  Impressed with many a warlock spell;
And the book it was wrote by Michael Scott
  Who held in awe the fiends of hell.

They buried it deep, where his bones they sleep,
  That mortal man might never it see;
But Thomas did save it from the grave
  When he returned from Faërie.

The black spae-book from his breast he took,
  And turned the leaves with curious hand;
No ropes, did he find, the wizard could bind
  But threefold ropes of sifted sand.

They sifted the sand from the Nine-stane burn,
  And shaped the ropes sae curiouslie;
But the ropes would neither twist nor twine
  For Thomas true and his gramarye.

The black spae-book from his breast he took,
  And again he turn'd it with his hand;
And he bade each lad of Teviot add
  The barley chaff to the sifted sand.

The barley chaff to the sifted sand
  They added still by handfuls nine:
But Redcap sly unseen was by,
  And the ropes would neither twist nor twine.

And still beside the Nine-stane burn,
  Ribbed like the sand at mark of sea,
The ropes that would not twist nor turn,
  Shaped of the sifted sand you see.

The black spae-book true Thomas he took,
  Again its magic leaves he spread;
And he found that to quell the powerful spell,
  The wizard must be boiled in lead.*

---

* "The tradition concerning the death of Lord Soulis," writes Sir Walter Scott," is not without a parallel in the real history of Scotland." Melville, of Glenbure, Sheriff of the Mearns, was detested by the barons of his country. Reiterated complaints of his conduct having been made to James I., the monarch answered, in a moment of unguarded impatience, "Sorrow gin the sheriff were sodden, and supped in broo!" The words were construed literally. The barons prepared a fire and a boiling cauldron into which they plunged the unlucky sheriff.

On a circle of stones they placed the pot,
  On a circle of stones but barely nine;
They heated it red and fiery hot,
  Till the burnished brass did glimmer and shine.

They roll'd him up in a sheet of lead,
  A sheet of lead for a funeral pall;
They plunged him in the cauldron red,
  And melted him, lead, and bones, and all.

At the Skelf-hill, the cauldron still
  The men of Liddesdale can show;
And on the spot, where they boil'd the pot,
  The spreat and the deer-hair ne'er shall grow.

LORD THOMAS AND FAIR ANNET.*

Lord Thomas and fair Annet
  Sate a' day on a hill;
Whan night was cum, and sun was sett,
  They had not talkt their fill.

Lord Thomas said a word in jest,
  Fair Annet took it ill:
"A'! I will nevir wed a wife
  Against my ain friends' will."

* See Appendix.

"Gif ye wull nevir wed a wife,
    A wife wull neir wed ye."
Sae he is hame to tell his mither,
    And knelt upon his knee:

"O rede, O rede, mither," he says,
    "A gude rede gie to me,
O sall I tak the nut-browne bride,
    And let faire Annet be?"

"The nut-browne bride has gowd and gear,
    Fair Annet she has gat nane;
And the little beauty fair Annet has,
    O it wull soon be gane!"

And he has till his brother gane:
    "Now, brother, rede ye me;
A' sall I marrie the nut-browne bride,
    And let fair Annet be?"

"The nut-browne bride has oxen, brother,
    The nut-browne bride has kye;
I wad hae ye marrie the nut-browne bride,
    And cast fair Annet bye."

"Her oxen may dye i' the house, Billie,
    And her kye into the byre;
And I sall hae nothing to my sell,
    Bot a fat fadge bye the fyre."

And he has till his sister gane:
    "Now, sister, rede ye me;
O sall I marrie the nut-browne bride,
    And set fair Annet free?"

"Ise rede ye tak fair Annet, Thomas,
    And let the browne bride alane,
Lest you should sigh, and say, Alace!
    What is this we brought hame?"

"No, I will take my mithers counsel,
  And marrie me owt o' hand;
And I will tak the nut-browne bride:
  Fair Annet may leive the land."

Up then rose fair Annets father
  Twa hours or it wer day,
And he is gane into the bower,
  Wherein fair Annet lay.

"Rise up, rise up, fair Annet," he says,
  "Put on your silken sheene;
Let us gae to St. Maries kirke,
  And see that rich weddeen."—

"My maides gae to my dressing-roome,
  And dress to me my hair;
Whair-eir ye laid a plait before,
  See ye lay ten times mair.

"My maids, gae to my dressing-room,
  And dress to me my smock;
The one half is o' the holland fine,
  The other o' needle-work."

The horse fair Annet rade upon
  He amblit like the wind,
Wi' siller he was shod before,
  Wi' burning gowd behind.

Four and twantye siller bells
  Wer a' tyed till his mane,
And yae tift o' the norland wind,
  They tinkled ane by ane.

Four and twantye gay gude knichts
  Rade by fair Annets side,
And four and twantye fair ladies,
  As gin she had bin a bride.

And whan she cam to Maries kirk,
    She sat on Maries stean:
The cleading that fair Annet hap on
    It skinkled in their een.

And whan she cam into the kirk,
    She shimmerd like the sun;
The belt that was about her waist,
    Was a' wi' pearles bedone.

She sat her by the nut-browne bride,
    And her een they wer sae clear,
Lord Thomas he clean forgat the bride
    When fair Annet she drew near.

He had a rose into his hand,
    And he gave it kisses three,
And reaching by the nut-browne bride,
    Laid it on fair Annets knee.

Up than spak the nut-browne bride,
    She spak wi' meikle spite:
"And whair gat ye that rose-water,
    That does mak ye sae white?"

"O I did get the rose-water
    Whair ye wull neir get nane,
For I did get that very rose-water
    Into my mithers wame."

The bride she drew a long bodkin
    Frae out her gay head-gear,
And strake fair Annet unto the heart,
    That word she nevir spak mair.

Lord Thomas he saw fair Annet wex pale,
    And marvelit what mote be:
But whan he saw her dear hearts blude,
    A' wode-wroth wexed he.

Lord Thomas and Fair Annet

He drew his dagger that was sae sharp,
  That was sae sharp and meet,
And drave it into the nut-browne bride,
  That fell deid at his feit.

"Now stay for me, dear Annet," he sed,
  "Now stay, my dear!" he cryd,—
Then strake the dagger untill his heart,
  And fell deid by her side.*

Lord Thomas was buried without kirk-wa;
  Fair Annet within the quiere;
And o' the tane thair grew a birk,
  The other a bonne briere.

* In Jamieson's ballad of "Sweet Willie and Fair Annie," the spirit of the lady, who dies of a broken heart, is made to visit the bridal bed of her betrayer:

  When night was come, and day was gone,
    And a' men boun to bed,
  Sweet Willie and the nut-browne bride
    In their chamber were laid,

  They werena weel lyen down,
    And scarcely fa'n asleep,
  Whan up and stands she, Fair Annie,
    Just up at Willie's feet.

  "Weel brook ye o' your brown brown bride,
    Between ye and the wa';
  And sae will I o' my winding sheet,
    That suits me best ava'.

  "Weel brook ye o' your brown brown bride,
    Between ye and the stock;
  And sae will I o' my black black kist,
    That has neither key nor lock.

  "Weel brook ye o' your brown brown bride,
    And o' your bridal bed;
  And sae will I o' the cald cald mools,
    That soon will hap my head."

  Sae Willie raise, put on his claes,
    Drew till him his hose and shoon,
  And he is on to Annie's bower,
    By the lei light o' the moon.
    *   *   *   *   *

  The lasten bower that he came till,
    O heavy was his care!
  The waxen lights were burning bright,
    And Fair Annie strceket there.

And ay they grew, and ay they threw,
As they wad faine be neare;
And by this ye may ken right well,
They were twa luvers deare.

¹ See Appendix.

FAUSE FOODRAGE.*

King Easter has courted her for her
  King Wester for her fee, [lands,
King Honour for her comelye face,
  And for her fair bodie.

They had not been four months mar-
  As I have heard them tell, [ried,
Until the nobles of the land
  Against them did rebel.

And they cast kevils them amang,
  And kevils them between;
And they cast kevils them amang,
  Wha suld gae kill the king.

* See Appendix.

O some said yea, and some said nay,
  Their words did not agree;
Till up and got him, Fause Foodrage,
  And swore it suld be he.

When bells were rung, and mass was sung,
  And a' men bound to bed,
King Honour and his gay ladye
  In a hie chamber were laid.

Then up and raise him, Fause Foodrage,
  When a' were fast asleep,
And slew the porter in his lodge,
  That watch and ward did keep.

O four and twenty silver keys
  Hung hie upon a pin;
And aye, as ae door he did unlock,
  He has fastened it him behind.

Then up and raise him, King Honour,
  Says—" What means a' this din?
Or what's the matter, Fause Foodrage,
  Or wha has loot you in?"—

" O ye my errand weel sall learn,
  Before that I depart."—
Then drew a knife, baith lang and sharp,
  And pierced him to the heart.

Then up and got the queen hersell,
  And fell low down on her knee:
" O spare my life, now, Fause Foodrage!
  For I never injured thee.

" O spare my life, now, Fause Foodrage!
  Until I lighter be!
And see gin it be lad or lass,
  King Honour has left wi' me."

Fause Foodrage

"O gin it be a lass," he says,
  "Weel nursed it sall be;
But gin it be a lad bairn,
  He sall be hangéd hie.

"I winna spare for his tender age
  Nor yet for his hie hie kin;
But soon as e'er he born is,
  He sall mount the gallows pin."—

O four-and-twenty valiant knights
  Were set the queen to guard;
And four stood aye at her bouir door,
  To keep both watch and ward.

But when the time drew near an end,
  That she suld lighter be,
She cast about to find a wile,
  To set her body free.

O she has birled these merry young men
  With the ale but and the wine,
Until they were a' deadly drunk
  As any wild-wood swine.

"O narrow, narrow, is this window,
  And big, big, am I grown!"—
Yet through the might of our Ladye,
  Out at it she has gone.

She wandered up, she wandered down,
  She wandered out and in;
And, at last, into the very swine's stythe,
  The queen brought forth a son.

Then they cast kevils them amang,
  Which suld gae seek the queen;
And the kevil fell upon Wise William,
  And he sent his wife for him.

Fause Foodrage

O when she saw Wise William's wife,
  The queen fell on her knee:
"Win up, win up, madam!" she says:
  "What needs this courtesie?"—

"O out o' this I winna ris
  Till a boon ye grant to me;
To change your lass for this lad bairn,
  King Honour left me wi'.

And ye maun learn my gay goss-hawk
  Right weel to breast a steed;
And I sall learn your turtle dow
  As weel to write and read.

"And ye maun learn my gay goss-hawk
  To wield baith bow and brand;
And I sall learn your turtle dow
  To lay gowd wi' her hand.

"At kirk and market when we meet,
  We'll dare make nae avowe,
But—Dame, how does my gay goss-hawk?
  —Madame, how does my dow?"*

---

* "This metaphorical language," says Scott, "was customary among the northern nations. In 925, King Adelstein sent an embassy to Harald Harfager, King of Norway, the chief of which presented that prince with a sword. As it was presented by the point, the Norwegian chief, in receiving it, unwarily laid hold of the hilt. The English ambassador declared, in the name of his master, that he accepted the act as a deed of homage. The Norwegian prince, resolving to circumvent his rival by a similar artifice, sent, next summer, an embassy to Adelstein, the chief of which presented Haco, the son of Harald, to the English prince; and, placing him on his knees, made the following declaration:—"*Haraldus, Normanorum Rex, amice te salutat; albamque hanc* avem *bene institutam mittit, utque melius deinceps erudias, postulat.*" The king received young Haco on his knees, which the Norwegian accepted, in the name of his master, as a declaration of inferiority; according to the proverb, "*Is minor semper habetur, qui alterius filium educat.*"

Fause Foodrage

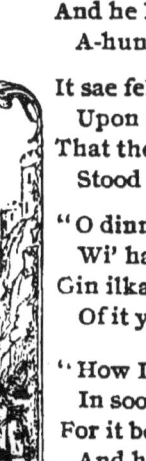

When days were gane, and years came on,
  Wise William he thought lang;
And he has ta'en King Honour's son
  A-hunting for to gang.

It sae fell out, at this hunting,
  Upon a simmer's day,
That they came by a fair castell,
  Stood on a sunny brae.

"O dinna ye see that bonny castell,
  Wi' halls and towers sae fair?
Gin ilka man had back his ain,
  Of it you suld be heir."—

"How I suld be heir of that castell,
  In sooth, I canna see;
For it belangs to Fause Foodrage,
  And he is na kin to me."—

"O gin ye suld kill him, Fause Foodrage,
  You would do but what was right;
For, I wot, he killed your father dear,
  Or ever ye saw the light.

"And gin ye suld kill him, Fause Foodrage,
  There is no man durst you blame;
For he keeps your mother a prisoner,
  And she daurna take ye hame."—

The boy stared wild like a grey goss hawk,
  Says,—"What may a' this mean?"
"My boy, ye are King Honour's son,
  And your mother 's our lawful queen."

"O gin I be King Honour's son,
  By our Ladye I swear,
This night I will that traitor slay,
  And relieve my mother dear!"

He has set his bent bow to his breast,
  And leaped the castell wa';
And soon he has seized on Fause Foodrage,
  Wha loud for help 'gan ca'.

"O haud your tongue, now, Fause Foodrage,
  Frae me ye shanna flee;"—
Syne pierced him through the fause, fause heart,
  And set his mother free.

And he has rewarded Wise William,
  Wi' the best half of his land;
And sae has he the turtle dow,
  Wi' the truth o' his right hand.

Genevieve

All thoughts, all passions, all delights,
Whatever stirs this mortal frame,
All are but ministers of Love,
    And feed his sacred flame.

Oft in my waking dreams do I
Live o'er again that happy hour,
When midway on the mount I lay,
    Beside the ruined tower.

* See Appendix.

Genevieve

The moonshine, stealing o'er the scene,
Had blended with the lights of eve;
And she was there, my hope, my joy,
    My own dear Genevieve!

She leaned against the armed man,
The statue of the armed knight;
She stood and listened to my lay,
    Amid the lingering light.

Few sorrows hath she of her own,
My hope! my joy! my Genevieve!
She loves me best whene'er I sing
    The songs that make her grieve.

I played a soft and doleful air,
I sang an old and moving story—
An old rude song, that suited well
    That ruin wild and hoary.

She listened with a flitting blush,
With downcast eyes and modest grace;
For well she knew I could not choose,
    But gaze upon her face.

I told her of the knight that wore
Upon his shield a burning brand;
And that for ten long years he wooed
    The Lady of the Land.

I told her how he pined: and ah!
The deep, the low, the pleading tone
With which I sang another's love,
    Interpreted my own.

She listened with a flitting blush,
With downcast eyes, and modest grace;
And she forgave me, that I gazed
    Too fondly on her face!

Genevieve

But when I told the cruel scorn
That crazed that bold and lovely knight,
And that he crossed the mountain-woods,
    Nor rested day nor night;

That sometimes from the savage den,
And sometimes from the darksome shade,
And sometimes starting up at once
    In green and sunny glade,—

There came and looked him in the face
An angel beautiful and bright;
And that he knew it was a fiend;
    This miserable knight!

And that, unknowing what he did,
He leaped amid a murderous band,
And saved from outrage worse than death
    The Lady of the Land;—

And how she wept, and clasped his knees;
And how she tended him in vain—
And ever strove to expiate
    The scorn that crazed his brain;—

And that she nursed him in a cave;
And how his madness went away,
When on the yellow forest-leaves
    A dying man he lay;—

His dying words—but when I reached
That tenderest strain of all the ditty,
My faltering voice and pausing harp
    Disturbed her soul with pity!

All impulses of soul and sense
Had thrilled my guileless Genevieve;
The music and the doleful tale,
    The rich and balmy eve;

And hopes, and fears that kindle hope,
An undistinguishable throng,
And gentle wishes long subdued,
    Subdued and cherished long!

She wept with pity and delight,
She blushed with love, and virgin shame;
And, like the murmur of a dream,
    I heard her breathe my name.

Her bosom heaved—she stepped aside,
As conscious of my look she stept—
Then suddenly, with timorous eye
    She fled to me and wept.

She half enclosed me with her arms,
She pressed me with a meek embrace;
And, bending back her head, looked up,
    And gazed upon my face.

'T was partly love, and partly fear,
And partly 't was a bashful art,
That I might rather feel, than see,
    The swelling of her heart.

I calmed her fears, and she was calm,
And told her love with virgin pride;
And so I won my Genevieve,
    My bright and beauteous bride.

FAIR MARGARET AND SWEET WILLIAM.*

As it fell out on a long summer's day,
   Two lovers they sat on a hill;
They sat together that long summer's day,
   And could not talk their fill.

"I see no harm by you, Margaret,
   And you see none by me;
Before to-morrow at eight o' the clock
   A rich wedding you shall see."

Fair Margaret sat in her bower-window,
   Combing her yellow hair;
There she spyed sweet William and his bride,
   As they were a riding near.

* See Appendix.

Then down she layd her ivory combe,
    And braided her hair in twain:—
She went alive out of her bower,
    But ne'er came alive in 't again.

When day was gone, and night was come,
    And all men fast asleep,
Then came the spirit of fair Marg'ret,
    And stood at William's feet.

"Are you awake, sweet William?" she said;
    "Or, sweet William, are you asleep?
God give you joy of your gay bride-bed,
    And me of my winding sheet."

When day was come, and night was gone,
    And all men waked from sleep,
Sweet William to his ladye sayd,
    "My dear, I have cause to weep;

"I dreamt a dream, my dear ladye,
    Such dreams are never good:
I dreamt my bower was full of red wine,
    And my bride-bed full of blood."—

"Such dreams, such dreams, my honoured sir,
    They never do prove good:
To dream thy bower was full of red wine,
    And thy bride-bed full of blood."

He called up his merry men all,
    By one, by two, and by three;
Saying, "I'll away to fair Marg'ret's bower,
    By the leave of my ladye."

And when he came to fair Marg'ret's bower,
    He knocked at the ring;
And who so ready as her seven brethren
    To let sweet William in.

Fair Margaret and Sweet William

Then he turned up the covering-sheet,—
"Pray let me see the dead:
Methinks she looks all pale and wan,
She hath lost her cherry red.

"I'll do more for thee, Margaret,
Than any of thy kin;
For I will kiss thy pale wan lips,
Though a smile I cannot win."

With that bespake the seven brethren,
Making most piteous mone;
"You may go kiss your jolly brown bride,
And let our sister alone."

"If I do kiss my jolly brown bride,
I do but what is right;
I ne'er made a vow to yonder poor corpse
By day, nor yet by night.*

* The following are the concluding stanzas of Jamieson's ballad, "Sweet Willie and Fair Annie":

> Pale Willie grew, wae was his heart,
> And sair he sighed wi' teen:
> "Oh Annie! had I kent thy worth,
> Ere it o'er late had been!
>
> "It's I will kiss your bonny cheek,
> And I will kiss your chin;
> And I will kiss your clay cald lip;
> But I'll never kiss woman again.
>
> "And that I was in love outdone,
> Sall ne'er be said o' me;
> For as ye 've died for me, Aunie,
> Sae will I do for thee!
>
> "The day ye deal at Annie's burial,
> The bread but and the wine;
> Before the morn at twall o'clock,
> They'll deal the same at mine."
>
> The tane was buried in Mary's kirk,
> The tither in Mary's quire;
> And out o' the tane there grew a birk,
> And out o' the tither a brier.
>
> And ay they grew, and ay they drew,
> Untill they twa did meet:
> And every one that past them by,
> Said, "Thae's twa lovers sweet."

Fair Margaret and Sweet William

"Deal on, deal on, my merry men all,
   Deal on your cake and your wine;
For whatever is dealt at her funeral to-day
   Shall be dealt to-morrow at mine."

Fair Margaret dyed to-day, to-day,
   Sweet William dyed the morrow:
Fair Margaret dyed for pure true love,
   Sweet William dyed for sorrow.

Margaret was buryed in the lower chancel,
   And William in the higher:
Out of her brest there sprang a rose,
   And out of his a briar.

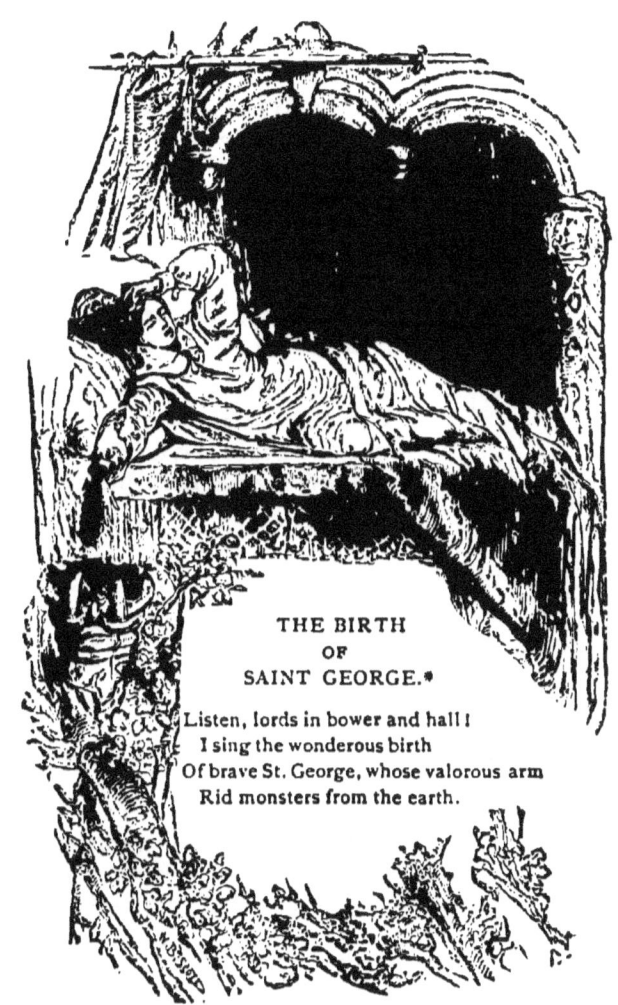

THE BIRTH
OF
SAINT GEORGE.*

Listen, lords in bower and hall!
I sing the wonderous birth
Of brave St. George, whose valorous arm
Rid monsters from the earth.

* See Appendix.

Distressèd ladies to relieve
  He travelled many a day;
In honour of the christian faith,
  Which shall endure for aye.

In Coventry sometime did dwell
  A knight of worthy fame,
High steward of this noble realme,
  Lord Albert was his name:

He had to wife a princely dame,
  Whose beauty did excell,—
This virtuous lady, being with child,
  In sudden sadness fell:

For thirty nights, no sooner sleep
  Had closed her wakeful eyes,
But, lo! a foul and fearful dream
  Her fancy would surprise:—

She dreamt a dragon fierce and fell
  Conceived within her womb,
Whose mortal fangs her body rent
  Ere he to life could come!

All woe-begone, and sad was she,
  She nourisht constant woe;
Yet strove to hide it from her lord,
  Lest he should sorrow know.

In vain she strove; her tender lord,
  Who watched her slightest look,
Discovered soon her secret pain,
  And soon that pain partook.

And when to him the fearful cause
  She weeping did impart,
With kindest speech he strove to heal
  The anguish of her heart.

The Birth of St. George

"Be comforted, my lady dear,
  Those pearly drops refrain;
Betide me weal, betide me woe,
  I'll try to ease thy pain.

"And for this foul and fearful dream,
  That causeth all thy woe,
Trust me I'll travel far away,
  But I'll the meaning knowe."

Then giving many a fond embrace,
  And shedding many a teare,
To the weïrd lady of the woods,
  He purposed to repaire.

To the weïrd lady of the woods,
  Full long and many a day,
Through lonely shades and thickets rough
  He winds his weary way.

At length he reached a dreary dell
  With dismal yews o'erhung;
Where cypress spred its mournful boughs,
  And pois'nous nightshade sprung.

No chearful gleams here pierced the gloom,
  He hears no chearful sound;
But shrill night-ravens' yelling scream,
  And serpents hissing round.

The shriek of fiends and damned ghosts
  Ran howling through his ear:
A chilling horror froze his heart,
  Though all unused to fear.

Three times he strives to win his way,
  And pierce those sickly dews:
Three times to bear his trembling corse
  His knocking knees refuse.

The Birth of St. George

At length upon his beating breast
  He signs the holy crosse;
And, rouzing up his wonted might,
  He treads th' unhallowed mosse.

Beneath a pendant craggy cliff,
  All vaulted like a grave,
And opening in the solid rock,
  He found the inchanted cave.

An iron gate closed up the mouth,
  All hideous and forlorne;
And, fastened by a silver chain,
  Near hung a brazed horne.

Then offering up a secret prayer,
  Three times he blowes amaine:
Three times a deepe and hollow sound
  Did answer him againe.

"Sir Knight, thy lady beares a son,
  Who, like a dragon bright,
Shall prove most dreadful to his foes,
  And terrible in fight.

"His name, advanced in future times,
  On banners shall be worn:
But, lo! thy lady's life must passe
  Before he can be born."

All sore opprest with fear and doubt
  Long time Lord Albert stood;
At length he winds his doubtful way
  Back through the dreary wood.

Eager to clasp his lovely dame,
  Then fast he travels back;
But when he reached his castle gate,
  His gate was hung with black.

The Birth of St. George

In every court and hall he found,
  A sullen silence reigne;
Save where, amid the lonely towers,
  He heard her maidens 'plaine;

And bitterly lament and weep,
  With many a grievous grone:
Then sore his bleeding heart misgave,
  His lady's life was gone.

With faultering step he enters in,
  Yet half affraid to goe;
With trembling voice asks why they grieve,
  Yet fears the cause to knowe.

"Three times the sun hath rose and set,"
  They said, then stopt to weep,
"Since heaven hath laid thy lady deare
  In death's eternal sleep.

"For, ah! in travail sore she fell,
  So sore that she must dye;
Unless some shrewd and cunning leech
  Could ease her presentlye.

"But when a cunning leech was fet,
  Too soon declaréd he,
She, or her babe must lose its life;
  Both savéd could not be.

"'Now take my life,' thy lady said;
  'My little infant save:
And O! commend me to my lord,
  When I am laid in grave.

"'O! tell him how that precious babe
  Cost him a tender wife;
And teach my son to lisp her name,
  Who died to save his life.'

"Then calling still upon thy name,
  And praying still for thee,
Without repining or complaint,
  Her gentle soul did flee."

What tongue can paint Lord Albert's woe,—
  The bitter tears he shed,—
The bitter pangs that wrung his heart,
  To find his lady dead!

He beat his breast, he tore his hair,
  And, shedding many a tear,
At length he askt to see his son—
  The son that cost so dear.

New sorrowe seized the damsells all:
  At length they faultering say:—
"Alas, my lord! how shall we tell?
  Thy son is stoln away.

" Fair as the sweetest flower of spring,
  Such was his infant mien:
And on his little body stampt,
  Three wonderous marks were seen:

" A blood-red cross was on his arm;
  A dragon on his breast;
A little garter all of gold
  Was round his leg exprest.

"Three carefull nurses we provide,
  Our little lord to keep:
One gave him sucke, one gave him food,
  And one did lull to sleep.

"But, lo! all in the dead of night,
  We heard a fearful sound;
Loud thunder clapt; the castle shook;
  And lightning flasht around.

The Birth of St. George

"Dead with affright at first we lay;
  But rousing up anon,
We ran to see our little lord—
  Our little lord was gone!

"But how or where we could not tell;
  For, lying on the ground,
In deep and magic slumbers laid,
  The nurses there we found."

"O grief on grief!" Lord Albert said:
  No more his tongue cou'd say,
When falling in a deadly swoone,
  Long time he lifeless lay.

At length restored to life and sense,
  He nourisht endless woe;
No future joy his heart could taste,
  No future comfort know.

So withers on the mountain top
  A fair and stately oake,
Whose vigorous arms are torn away
  By some rude thunder-stroke.

At length his castle irksome grew,
  He loathes his wonted home;
His native country he forsakes,
  In foreign lands to roame.

There up and downe he wandered far,
  Clad in a palmer's gown,
Till his brown locks grew white as wool,
  His beard as thistle down.

At length, all wearied, down in death
  He laid his reverend head.—
Meantime amid the lonely wilds
  His little son was bred.

The Birth of St. George

There the weïrd lady of the woods
  Had borne him far away;
And trained him up in feates of armes,
  And every martial play.

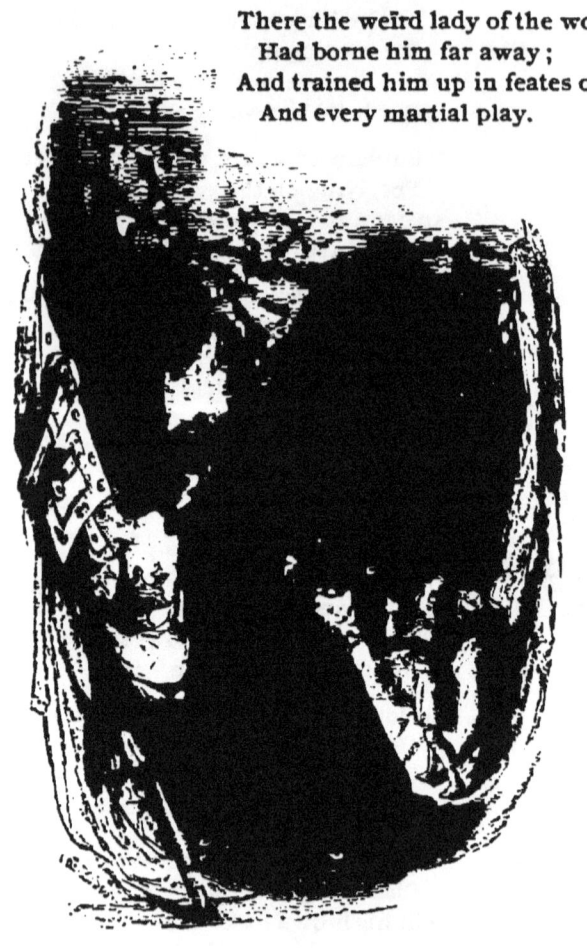

THE MERMAID.*

On Jura's heath how sweetly swell
    The murmurs of the mountain bee!
How softly mourns the writhed shell,
    Of Jura's shore, its parent sea!

But softer, floating o'er the deep,
    The mermaid's sweet sea-soothing lay,
That charmed the dancing waves to sleep,
    Before the bark of Colonsay.

* See Appendix.

The Mermaid

Aloft the purple pennons wave,
    As parting gay from Crinan's shore,
From Morven's wars the seamen brave
    Their gallant chieftain homeward bore.

In youth's gay bloom, the brave Macphail
    Still blamed the lingering bark's delay;
For her he chid the flagging sail,
    The lovely Maid of Colonsay.

And "raise," he cried, "the song of love,
    The maiden sung with tearful smile,
When first, o'er Jura's hills to rove,
    We left afar the lonely isle!—

"When on this ring of ruby red
    Shall die," she said, "the crimson hue,
Know that thy favourite fair is dead,
    Or proves to thee and love untrue."

Now, lightly poised, the rising oar
    Disperses wide the foamy spray,
And, echoing far o'er Crinan's shore,
    Resounds the song of Colonsay.

"Softly blow, thou western breeze,
    Softly rustle through the sail:
Soothe to rest the furrowy seas,
    Before my love, sweet western gale!

"Where the wave is tinged with red,
    And the russet sea-leaves grow,
Mariners, with prudent dread,
    Shun the shelving reefs below.

"As you pass through Jura's sound,
    Bend your course by Scarba's shore,
Shun, O shun, the gulf profound,
    Where Corrivrekin's surges roar!

"If, from that unbottomed deep,
  With wrinkled form and wreathed train,
O'er the verge of Scarba's steep,
  The sea-snake heave his snowy mane,

"Unwarp, unwind his oozy coils,
  Sea-green sisters of the main,
And, in the gulf where ocean boils,
  The unwieldy, wallowing monster chain.

"Softly blow, thou western breeze,
  Softly rustle through the sail!
Soothe to rest the furrowed seas,
  Before my love, sweet western gale!"

Thus all to soothe the chieftain's woe,
  Far from the maid he loved so dear,
The song arose so soft and slow,
  He seemed her parting sigh to hear.

The lonely deck he paces o'er,
  Impatient for the rising day,
And still from Crinan's moonlight shore,
  He turns his eyes to Colonsay.

The moonbeams crisp the curling surge,
  That streaks with foam the ocean green:
While forward still the rowers urge
  Their course, a female form was seen.

That sea-maid's form, of pearly light,
  Was whiter than the downy spray,
And round her bosom, heaving bright,
  Her glossy yellow ringlets play.

Borne on a foamy-crested wave,
  She reached amain the bounding prow,
Then clasping fast the chieftain brave,
  She, plunging, sought the deep below.

The Mermaid

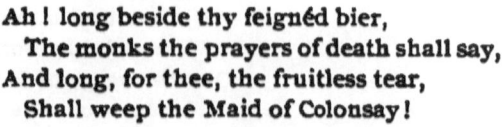

Ah! long beside thy feignéd bier,
   The monks the prayers of death shall say,
And long, for thee, the fruitless tear,
   Shall weep the Maid of Colonsay!

But downwards, like a powerless corse,
   The eddying waves the chieftain bear;
He only heard the moaning hoarse
   Of waters, murmuring in his ear.

The murmurs sink by slow degrees;
   No more the surges round him rave;
Lulled by the music of the seas,
   He lies within a coral cave.

In dreamy mood reclines he long,
   Nor dares his trancéd eyes unclose;
Till, warbling wild, the sea-maid's song,
   Far in the crystal cavern rose:

Soft as that harp's unseen control,
   In morning dreams which lovers hear,
Whose strains steal sweetly o'er the soul,
   But never reach the waking ear.

As sunbeams through the tepid air,
   When clouds dissolve the dews unseen,
Smile on the flowers that bloom more fair,
   And fields that glow with livelier green;

So melting soft the music fell;
   It seemed to soothe the fluttering spray—
"Say, heardst thou not these wild notes swell?
   Ah! 't is the song of Colonsay."

Like one that from a fearful dream
   Awakes, the morning light to view,
And joys to see the purple beam,
   Yet fears to find the vision true,—

The Mermaid

He heard that strain, so wildly sweet,
  Which bade his torpid languor fly;
He feared some spell had bound his feet,
  And hardly dared his limbs to try.

"This yellow sand, this sparry cave,
  Shall bend thy soul to beauty's sway;
Canst thou the maiden of the wave
  Compare to her of Colonsay?"

Roused by that voice of silver sound,
  From the paved floor he lightly sprung,
And glancing wild his eyes around,
  Where the fair nymph her tresses wrung,

No form he saw of mortal mould;
  It shone like ocean's snowy foam;
Her ringlets waved in living gold,
  Her mirror crystal, pearl her comb.

Her pearly comb the siren took,
  And careless bound her tresses wild;
Still o'er the mirror stole her look,
  As on the wondering youth she smiled.

Like music from the greenwood tree,
  Again she raised the melting lay:—
"Fair warrior, wilt thou dwell with me,
  And leave the Maid of Colonsay?

"Fair is the crystal hall for me,
  With rubies and with emeralds set;
And sweet the music of the sea
  Shall sing, when we for love are met.

"How sweet to dance with gliding feet,
  Along the level tide so green;
Responsive to the cadence sweet,
  That breathes along the moonlight scene!

" And soft the music of the main
   Rings from the motley tortoise-shell;
While moonbeams, o'er the watery plain,
   Seem trembling in its fitful swell.

" How sweet, when billows heave their head,
   And shake their snowy crests on high,
Serene in Ocean's sapphire-bed,
   Beneath the tumbling surge to lie;

"To trace, with tranquil step, the deep,
   Where pearly drops of frozen dew,
In concave shells, unconscious, sleep,
   Or shine with lustre, silvery blue!

" Then shall the summer sun, from far,
   Pour through the wave a softer ray;
While diamonds, in a bower of spar,
   At eve shall shed a brighter day.

" Nor stormy wind, nor wintry gale,
   That o'er the angry ocean sweep,
Shall e'er our coral groves assail,
   Calm in the bosom of the deep.

" Through the green meads beneath the sea,
   Enamoured, we shall fondly stray;
Then, gentle warrior, dwell with me,
   And leave the Maid of Colonsay!"

"Though bright thy locks of glistering
   Fair maiden of the foamy main!   [gold,
Thy life-blood is the water cold,
   While mine beats high in every vein.

" If I beneath thy sparry cave,
   Should in thy snowy arms recline,
Inconstant as the restless wave,
   My heart would grow as cold as thine."

The Mermaid

As cygnet down, proud swelled her breast,
  Her eye confessed the pearly tear;
His hand she to her bosom pressed—
  " Is there no heart for rapture here?

" These limbs, sprung from the lucid sea,
  Does no warm blood their currents fill;
No heart-pulse riot, wild and free,
  To joy, to love's delirious thrill? "

" Though all the splendour of the sea
  Around thy faultless beauty shine,
That heart that riots wild and free,
  Can hold no sympathy with mine.

" These sparkling eyes, so wild and gay,
  They swim not in the light of love:
The beauteous Maid of Colonsay,
  Her eyes are milder than the dove!

" Even now, within the lonely isle,
  Her eyes are dim with tears for me;
And canst thou think that siren smile
  Can lure my soul to dwell with thee? "

An oozy film her limbs o'erspread;
  Unfolds in length her scaly train:
She tossed, in proud disdain, her head,
  And lashed, with webbéd fin, the main.

" Dwell here alone! " the mermaid cried,
  " And view far off the sea-nymphs play;
Thy prison wall, the azure tide,
  Shall bar thy steps from Colonsay.

" Whene'er, like Ocean's scaly brood,
  I cleave with rapid fin, the wave,
Far from the daughter of the flood,
  Conceal thee in this coral cave.

"I feel my former soul return;
  It kindles at thy cold disdain:
And has a mortal dared to spurn
  A daughter of the foamy main?"

She fled; around the crystal cave
  The rolling waves resume their road;
On the broad portal idly rave,
  But enter not the nymph's abode.

And many a weary night went by,
  As in the lonely cave he lay;
And many a sun rolled through the sky,
  And poured its beams on Colonsay.

And oft, beneath the silver moon,
  He heard afar the mermaid sing,
And oft, to many a melting tune,
  The shell-formed lyres of ocean ring.

And when the moon went down the sky,
  Still rose, in dreams, his native plain,
And oft he thought his love was by,
  And charmed him with some tender strain.

And heart-sick oft he waked to weep,
  When ceased that voice of silver sound;
And thought to plunge him in the deep,
  That walled his crystal cavern round.

But still the ring of ruby red,
  Retained its vivid crimson hue;
And each despairing accent fled,
  To find his gentle love so true.

When seven long lonely months were gone,
  The mermaid to his cavern came;
No more mis-shapen from the zone,
  But like a maid of mortal frame.

The Mermaid

"O give to me that ruby ring,
  That on thy finger glances gay,
And thou shalt hear the mermaid sing
  The song thou lov'st of Colonsay."

"This ruby ring, of crimson grain,
  Shall on thy finger glitter gay,
If thou wilt bear me through the main,
  Again to visit Colonsay."

"Except thou quit thy former love,
  Content to dwell for aye with me,
Thy scorn my finny frame might move,
  To tear thy limbs amid the sea."

"Then bear me swift along the main,
  The lonely isle again to see;
And when I here return again,
  I plight my faith to dwell with thee."

An oozy film her limbs o'erspread,
  While slow unfolds her scaly train,
With gluey fangs her hands were clad,
  She lashed, with webbéd fin, the main.

He grasps the mermaid's scaly sides,
  As, with broad fin, she oars her way;
Beneath the silent moon she glides,
  That sweetly sleeps on Colonsay.

Proud swells her heart! she deems, at last,
  To lure him with her silver tongue,
And, as the shelving rocks she passed,
  She raised her voice, and sweetly sung.

In softer sweeter strains she sung,
  Slow gliding o'er the moonlight bay,
When light to land the chieftain sprung,
  To hail the Maid of Colonsay.

The Mermaid

O sad the mermaid's gay notes fell,
    And sadly sink remote at sea!
So sadly mourns the writhéd shell
    Of Jura's shore, its parent sea.

And ever, as the year returns,
    The charm-bound sailors know the day;
For sadly still the mermaid mourns
    The lovely Chief of Colonsay.

LORD ULLIN'S DAUGHTER.*

A chieftain, to the Highlands bound,
  Cries, "Boatman, do not tarry!
And I'll give thee a silver pound
  To row us o'er the ferry."—

"Now, who be ye would cross Lochgyle,
  This dark and stormy water?"
"O, I'm the chief of Ulva's Isle,
  And this Lord Ullin's daughter.

* See Appendix.

"And fast before her father's men,
   Three days we 've fled together;
For should he find us in the glen,
   My blood would stain the heather.

"His horsemen hard behind us ride;
   Should they our steps discover,
Then who will cheer my bonny bride,
   When they have slain her lover?"

Out spoke the hardy Highland wight,
   "I 'll go, my chief—I 'm ready:—
It is not for your silver bright,
   But for your winsome lady:

"And, by my word! the bonny bird
   In danger shall not tarry;
So, though the waves are raging white,
   I 'll row you o'er the ferry."

By this the storm grew loud apace,
   The water-wraith was shrieking;
And in the scowl of heaven each face
   Grew dark as they were speaking.

But still as wilder blew the wind,
   And as the night grew drearer,
Adown the glen rode arméd men;
   Their trampling sounded nearer.

"O haste thee, haste!" the lady cries,
   "Though tempests round us gather;
I 'll meet the raging of the skies,
   But not an angry father."

The boat has left a stormy land,
   A stormy sea before her,—
When, Oh! too strong for human hand
   The tempest gather'd o'er her.

Lord Ullin's Daughter

And still they row'd amidst the roar
  Of waters fast prevailing:
Lord Ullin reached that fatal shore,
  His wrath was changed to wailing.

For sore dismay'd, through storm and
  His child he did discover; [shade,
One lovely hand she stretch'd for aid,
  And one was round her lover.

"Come back! come back!" he cried in
  "Across this stormy water; [grief,
And I'll forgive your Highland chief.
  My daughter! Oh! my daughter!"—*

---

* In a ballad, entitled "Duncan," printed by Herd, are some vigorous and beautiful stanzas, which describe the meeting of the lover and the uncle of a lady who has been taken from her "old home":

  "The rose I pluckt o' right is mine,
    Our hearts together grew
  Like twa sweet roses on ae stalk;
    Frae hate to love they flew."

He stampt his foot upo' the ground,
  And thus in wrath did say,
"God strike my saul, if frae this field,
  We baith in life shall gae."

He wav'd his hand, the pipers play'd,
  The targets clatter'd round;
And now between the meeting faes
  Was little space of ground.

But wha is she that runs sae fast?
  Her feet nae stap they find;
Sae swiftly rides the milky cloud,
  Upo' the summer's wind.

Her face a mantle screen'd afore,
  She show'd of lily hue;
Sae frae the grey mist breaks the sun,
  To drink the morning dew.

"Alack! my friends; what sight is this?
  O stap your rage," she cry'd;
"Whar love with honey'd lips should be,
  Mak not a breach sae wide."

  *   *   *   *   *

'T was vain; the loud waves lash'd the
Return or aid preventing:— [shore,
The waters wild went o'er his child,
And he was left lamenting.

SIR AGILTHORN.*

Oh! gentle huntsman, softly tread,
  And softly wind thy bugle-horn;
Nor rudely break the silence shed
  Around the grave of Agilthorn!

Oh! gentle huntsman, if a tear
  E'er dimmed for others' woe thine eyes,
Thou 'lt surely dew, with drops sincere,
  The sod where Lady Eva lies.

* See Appendix.

Yon crumbling chapel's sainted bound
 Their hands and hearts beheld them plight;
Long held yon towers, with ivy crowned,
 The beauteous dame and gallant knight.

Alas! the hour of bliss is past,
 For hark! the din of discord rings;
War's clarion sounds, Joy hears the blast,
 And trembling plies his radiant wings.

And must sad Eva lose her lord?
 And must he seek the martial plain?
Oh! see she brings his casque and sword!
 Oh! hark, she pours her plaintive strain!

"Blessed is the village damsel's fate,
 Though poor and low her station be;
Safe from the cares which haunt the great,
 Safe from the cares which torture me!

"No doubting fear, no cruel pain,
 No dread suspense her breast alarms;
No tyrant honour rules her swain,
 And tears him from her folding arms.

"She, careless wandering 'midst the rocks,
 In pleasing toil consumes the day;
And tends her goats, or feeds her flocks,
 Or joins her rustic lover's lay.

"Though hard her couch, each sorrow flies
 The pillow which supports her head;
She sleeps, nor fears at morn her eyes
 Shall wake, to mourn a husband dead.

"Hush, impious fears! the good and brave,
 Heaven's arm will guard from danger free;
When death with thousands gluts the grave,
 His dart, my love, shall glance from thee;

Sir Agiltborn

"While thine shall fly direct and sure,
    This buckler every blow repel;
This casque from wounds that face secure,
    Where all the loves and graces dwell.

"This glittering scarf, with tenderest care,
    My hands in happier moments wove;
Cursed be the wretch, whose sword shall tear
    The spell-bound work of wedded love!

"Lo! on thy falchion keen and bright,
    I shed a trembling consort's tears;
Oh! when their traces meet thy sight,
    Remember wretched Eva's fears!

"Think how thy lips she fondly pressed,
    Think how she wept—compelled to part;
Think, every wound which scars thy breast,
    Is doubly marked on Eva's heart!"—

"O thou! my mistress, wife, and friend!"—
    Thus Agilthorn with sighs began;
"Thy fond complaints my bosom rend,
    Thy tears my fainting soul unman:

"In pity cease, my gentle dame,
    Such sweetness and such grief to join!
Lest I forget the voice of Fame,
    And only list to Love's and thine.

"Flow, flow, my tears, unbounded gush!
    Rise, rise, my sobs, I set ye free:
Bleed, bleed, my heart! I need not blush
    To own that life is dear to me.

"The wretch whose lips have pressed the
    The bitter bowl of pain and woe,   [bowl,
May careless reach his mortal goal,
    May boldly meet the final blow:

Sir Agilthorn

"His hopes destroyed, his comfort wrecked,
  A happier life he hopes to find;
But what can I in heaven expect,
  Beyond the bliss I leave behind?

"Oh, no! the joys of yonder skies,
  To prosperous love present no charms;
My heaven is placed in Eva's eyes,
  My paradise in Eva's arms.

"Yet mark me, sweet! if Heaven's command
  Hath doomed my fall in martial strife,
Oh! let not anguish tempt thy hand
  To rashly break the thread of life!

"No! let our boy thy care engross,
  Let him thy stay, thy comfort be;
Supply his luckless father's loss,
  And love him for thyself and me.

"So may oblivion soon efface
  The grief which clouds this fatal morn;
And soon thy cheeks afford no trace
  Of tears which fall for Agilthorn!"

He said; and couched his quivering lance:
  He said; and braced his moony shield:—
Sealed a last kiss, threw a last glance,
  Then spurred his steed to Flodden Field.

But Eva, of all joy bereft,
  Stood rooted at the castle gate,
And viewed the prints his courser left,
  While hurrying at the call of fate.

Forebodings sad her bosom told,
  The steed which bore him thence so light,
Her longing eyes would ne'er behold
  Again bring home her own true knight.

Sir Agiltborn

While many a sigh her bosom heaves,
  She thus addressed her orphan page :—
"Dear youth, if e'er my love relieved
  The sorrows of thy infant age :

"If e'er I taught thy locks to play,
  Luxuriant round thy blooming face;
If e'er I wiped thy tears away,
  And bade them yield to smiles their place :

"Oh! speed thee, swift as steed can bear,
  Where Flodden groans with heaps of dead;
And o'er the combat, home repair,
  And tell me how my lord has sped.

"Till thou return'st each hour 's an age,
  An age employed in doubt and pain;
Oh! haste thee, haste, my little foot-page,
  Oh! haste and soon return again."

"Now lady dear, thy grief assuage,
  Good tidings soon shall ease thy pain;
I 'll haste, I 'll haste, thy little foot-page,
  I 'll haste, and soon return again."

Then Osway bade his courser fly;
  But still, while hapless Eva wept,
Time scarcely seemed his wings to ply,
  So slow the tedious moments crept.

And oft she kissed her baby's cheek,
  Who slumbered on her throbbing breast :
And now she bade the warder speak,
  And now she lulled her child to rest.

"Good warder, say, what meets thy sight?
  What se'st from the castle tower?"
"Nought but the rocks of Elginbright,
  Nought but the shades of Forest-Bower."

"Oh, pretty babe! thy mother's joy,
    Pledge of the purest, fondest flame,
To-morrow's sun, dear helpless boy,
    May see thee bear an orphan's name.

"Perhaps, e'en now, some Scottish sword
    The life-blood of thy father drains;
Perhaps, e'en now, that heart is gored,
    Whose streams supplied thy little veins.

"O warder, from the castle tower,
    Now say what objects meet thy sight?"
"None but the shades of Forest-Bower,
    None but the rocks of Elginbright."

"Smil'st thou, my babe? so smiled thy sire,
    When gazing on his Eva's face;
His eyes shot beams of gentle fire,
    And joyed such beams in mine to trace.

"Sleep, sleep, my babe! of care devoid:
    Thy mother breathes this fervent vow—
Oh, never be thy soul employed
    On thoughts so sad as hers are now!

"Now warder, warder, speak again!
    What se'st thou from the turret's height?"
"Oh, lady, speeding o'er the plain,
    The little foot-page appears in sight!"

Quick beat her heart, short grew her breath;
    Close to her breast the babe she drew—
"Now, Heaven," she cried, "for life or death!"
    And forth to meet the page she flew.

"And is thy lord from danger free?
    And is the deadly combat o'er?"—
In silence Osway bent his knee,
    And laid a scarf her feet before.

Sir Agiltborn

The well-known scarf with blood was stained,
  And tears from Osway's eyelids fell;
Too truly Eva's heart explained,
  What meant those silent tears to tell.

"Come, come, my babe!" she wildly cried,
  "We needs must seek the field of woe:
Come, come, my babe! cast fear aside!
  To dig thy father's gave we go."

"Stay, lady, stay! a storm impends;
  Lo! threatening clouds the sky o'erspread;
The thunder roars, the rain descends,
  And lightning streaks the heavens with red.

"Hark, hark! the winds tempestuous rave!
  Oh! be thy dread intent resigned!
Or, if resolved the storm to brave,
  Be this dear infant left behind!"

"No, no! with me the baby stays!
  With me he lives; with me he dies!
Flash, lightnings, flash! your friendly blaze
  Will shew me where my warrior lies."

O see she roams the bloody field,
  And wildly shrieks her husband's name:
O see she stops and eyes a shield,
  A heart the symbol, wrapt in flame.

His armour broke in many a place,
  A knight lay stretched that shield beside;
She raised his vizor, kissed his face,
  Then on his bosom sunk and died.

Huntsman, their rustic grave behold:
  'T is here, at night, the fairy king.
Where sleeps the fair, where sleeps the bold,
  Oft forms his light fantastic ring.

'T is here, at eve, each village youth
  With freshest flowers the turf adorns;
'T is here he swears eternal truth,
  By Eva's faith and Agilthorn's.

And here the virgins sadly tell,
  Each seated by her shepherd's side,
How brave the gallant warrior fell,
  How true his lovely lady died.

Ah! gentle huntsman, pitying hear,
  And mourn the gentle lovers' doom!
Oh! gentle huntsman, drop a tear,
  And dew the turf of Eva's tomb.

So ne'er may fate thy hopes oppose;
  So ne'er may grief to thee be known;
They who can weep for others' woes,
  Should ne'er have cause to weep their
    own.

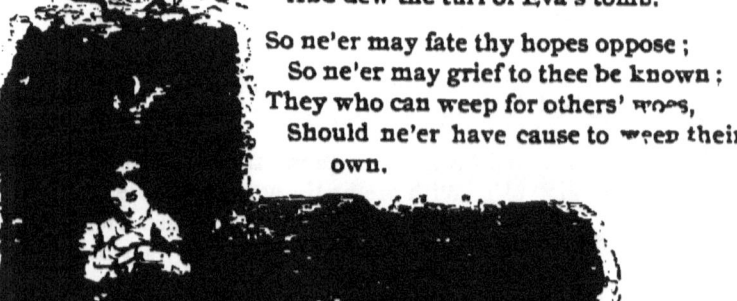

JOHNIE OF BREADISLEE.*

Johnie rose up in a May morning,
  Called for water to wash his hands—
"Gar loose to me the gude graie dogs,
  That are bound wi' iron bands."

When Johnie's mother gat word o' that,
  Her hands for dule she wrang—
"O Johnie! for my benison,
  To the greenwood dinna gang!

* See Appendix.

"Eneugh ye hae o' gude wheat bread,
　And eneugh o' the blude-red wine;
And, therefore, for nae venison, Johnie,
　I pray thee, stir frae hame."

But Johnie's busk't up his gude bend bow,
　His arrows, ane by ane;
And he has gane to Durrisdeer,
　To hunt the dun deer down.

As he came down by Merriemass,
　And in by the benty line,
There has he espied a deer lying
　Aneath a bush of ling.

Johnie he shot, and the dun deer lap,
　And he wounded her on the side;
But, atween the water and the brae,
　His hounds they laid her pride.

And Johnie has bryttled the deer sae weel,
　That he's had out her liver and lungs;
And wi' these he has feasted his bluidy
　As if they had been earl's sons.　[hounds,

They eat sae much o' the venison,
　And drank sae much o' the blude,
That Johnie and a' his bluidy hounds,
　Fell asleep as they had been dead.

And by there came a silly auld carle,
　An ill death mote he die!
For he's awa to Hislinton,
　Where the seven foresters did lie.

"What news, what news, ye gray headed
　What news bring ye to me?"　　[carle,
"I bring nae news," said the gray headed
　"Save what these eyes did see.　[carle,

" As I came down by Merriemass,
　And down among the scroggs,

Johnie of Breadislee

The bonniest childe that ever I saw,
  Lay sleeping amang his dogs.
"The shirt that was upon his back
  Was o' the holland fine;
The doublet which was over that
  Was o' the lincome twine.

"The buttons that were on his sleeve
  Were o' the goud sae gude:
The gude graie hounds he lay amang,
  Their mouths were dyed wi' blude."
Then out and spak the first forester,
  The heid man ower them a'—
"If this be Johnie o' Breadislee,
  Nae nearer will we draw."

But up and spak the sixth forester
  (His sister's son was he),
"If this be Johnie o' Breadislee,
  We soon shall gar him die!"
The first flight of arrows the foresters shot,
  They wounded him on the knee;
And out and spak the seventh forester,
  "The next will gar him die."

Johnie 's set his back against an aik,
  His fute against a stane;
And he has slain the seven foresters,
  He has slain them a' but ane.

He has broke three ribs in that ane's side,
  But and his collar bane;
He 's laid him twa-fald ower his steed,
  Bade him carry the tidings hame.

"O is there nae a bonnie bird,
  Can sing as I can say?—
Could flee away to my mother's bower,
  And tell to fetch Johnie away?"

The starling flew to his mother's window
  It whistled and it sang;   [stane,
And aye the ower word o' the tune
  Was—" Johnie tarries lang!"

They made a rod o' the hazel bush,
  Another o' the slae-thorn tree,
And mony, mony were the men
  At fetching o'er Johnie.

Then out and spak his auld mother,
  And fast her tears did fa'—
" Ye wad nae be warned, my son Johnie,
  Frae the hunting to bide awa'.

"Aft hae I brought to Breadislee,
  The less gear and the mair;
But I ne'er brought to Breadislee,
  What grieved my heart sae sair.

"But wae betide that silly auld carle,
  An ill death shall he die!
For the highest tree in Merriemass
  Shall be his morning's fee."

Now Johnie's gude bend bow is broke,
  And his gude graie dogs are slain;
And his bodie lies dead in Durrisdeer,
  And his hunting it is done.

THE DOWIE DENS OF YARROW.*

Late at e'en, drinking the wine,
    And ere they paid the lawing,
They set a combat them between,
    To fight it in the dawing.

"O stay at hame, my noble lord!
    O stay at hame, my marrow!
My cruel brother will you betray
    On the dowie houms of Yarrow."—

* See Appendix.

The Dowie Dens of Yarrow

"O fare ye weel, my ladye gaye!
　O fare ye weel, my Sarah!
For I maun gae, though I ne'er return
　Frae the dowie banks o' Yarrow."

She kissed his cheek, she kaimed his hair,
　As oft she had done before, O;
She belted him with his noble brand,
　And he's away to Yarrow.

As he gaed up the Tennies bank,
　I wot he gaed wi' sorrow,
Till, down in a den, he spied nine armed men,
　On the dowie houms of Yarrow.

"O! come ye here to part your land,
　The bonnie forest thorough?
Or come ye here to wield your brand,
　On the dowie houms of Yarrow?"—

"I come not here to part my land,
　And neither to beg nor borrow;
I come to wield my noble brand,
　On the bonnie banks of Yarrow."

"If I see all, ye're nine to ane,
　And that's an unequal marrow;
Yet will I fight while lasts my brand,
　On the bonnie banks of Yarrow."

Four has he hurt, and five has slain,
　On the bonnie braes of Yarrow;
Till that stubborn knight came him behind,
　And ran his body thorough.

"Gae hame, gae hame, good brother John,
　And tell your sister Sarah
To come and lift her leafu' lord;
　He's sleeping sound on Yarrow."—

The Dowie Dens of Yarrow

"Yest'reen I dreamed a dolefu' dream;*
I fear there will be sorrow!
I dreamed I pu'd the heather green,
Wi' my true love, on Yarrow.

"O gentle wind, that bloweth south,
From where my love repaireth,
Convey a kiss from his dear mouth,
And tell me how he fareth!

"But in the glen strive arméd men;
They 've wrought me dole and sorrow;
They 've slain—the comeliest knight
they 've slain,
He bleeding lies on Yarrow."

As she sped down yon high high hill,
She gaed wi' dole and sorrow;
And in the den spied ten slain men,
On the dowie banks of Yarrow.

* The following is the fragment given by Mr. Herd, "to the tune of Leaderhaughs and Yarrow":

"I dream'd a dreary dream last night;
God keep us a' frae sorrow;
I dream'd I pu'd the birk sae green,
Wi' my true luve on Yarrow."

"I 'll read your dream, my sister dear,
I 'll tell you a' your sorrow;
You pu'd the birk wi' your true love;
He 's kill'd, he 's kill'd, on Yarrow."

"O gentle wind, that bloweth south,
To where my luve repaireth,
Convey a kiss from his dear mouth,
And tell me how he fareth.

"But o'er yon glen run arméd men,
Have wrought me dule and sorrow;
They 've slain, they 've slain, ta comeliest swain,
He bleeding lies on Yarrow."

The Dowie Dens of Yarrow

She kissed his cheek, she kaimed his hair,
  She searched his wounds all thorough;
She kissed them till her lips grew red,
  On the dowie houms of Yarrow.

"Now haud your tongue, my daughter dear!
  For a' this breeds but sorrow;
I 'll wed thee to a better lord
  Than him ye lost on Yarrow."

"O haud your tongue, my father dear;
  Ye mind me but of sorrow;
A fairer rose did never bloom
  Than now lies cropped on Yarrow."

The Bonnie Bairns

THE BONNIE BAIRNS.*

The lady she walk'd in yon wild wood
  Aneath the hollin tree,
And she was aware of two bonnie bairns
  Were running at her knee.

* See Appendix

The tane it pull'd a red, red rose,
  With a hand as soft as silk;
The other, it pull'd the lily pale,
  With a hand mair white than milk.

"Now, why pull ye the red rose, fair bairns?
  And why the white lily?"
"O we sue wi' them at the seat of grace,
  For the soul of thee, ladie!"

"O bide wi' me, my twa bonnie bairns!
  I'll cleid ye rich and fine;
And all for the blaeberries of the wood,
  Yese hae white bread and wine."

She heard a voice, a sweet low voice,
  Say, "Weans, ye tarry long"—   [bairn,
She stretch'd her hand to the youngest
  "Kiss me before ye gang."

She sought to take a lily hand,
  And kiss a rosie chin—
"O, nought sae pure can bide the touch
  Of a hand red-wet wi' sin!"

The stars were shooting to and fro,
  And wild fire fill'd the air,
As that lady followed thae bonnie bairns
  For three lang hours and mair.

"O! where dwell ye, my ain sweet bairns?
  I'm woe and weary grown!"
"O! lady, we live where woe never is,
  In a land to flesh unknown."

There came a shape which seem'd to her
  As a rainbow 'mang the rain;
And sair these sweet babes pled for her,
  And they pled and pled in vain.

The Bonnie Bairns

"And O! and O!" said the youngest babe,
  "My mother maun come in":
"And O! and O!" said the eldest babe,
  "Wash her twa hands frae sin."

"And O! and O!" said the youngest babe,
  "She nursed me on her knee":
"And O! and O!" said the eldest babe,
  "She's a mither yet to me."*

* The following is Motherwell's copy, referred to in the Introduction, and is thus prefaced:—"A small fragment of this ballad appeared in the introductory note to the ballad of Lady Anne, printed in the Border Minstrelsy, vol. ii. Through the kindness of a friend we are now enabled to give the ballad in a complete state. Like many other ancient pieces of a similar description, it has a burden of no meaning and much childishness; the repetition of which, at the end of the first and third lines of every stanza, has been omitted. The reader, however, has a right to have the ballad as we received it; and therefore he may, in the first of the places pointed out, insert, ' Three, three, and three by three;' and in the second, ' Three, three, and thirty-three;' which will give him it entire and unmutilated."

She leaned her back unto a thorn'
And there she had her two babes born.

She took frae 'bout her ribbon-belt
And there she bound them hand and foot.

She has ta'en out her wee pen-knife
And there she ended baith their life.

She has howked a hole baith deep and wide,
She has put them in baith side by side.

She has cover'd them o'er with a marble stone,
Thinking she would gang maiden hame.

As she was walking by her father's castle wa',
She saw twa pretty babes playing at the ba'.

"O bonny bairns, gin ye were mine,
I would dress you up in satin fine!

"O I would dress you in the silk
And wash you ay in morning milk!"

"O cruel mother! we were thine,
And thou made us to wear the twine.

'O cursed mother! heaven is high,
And that's where thou 'll ne'er win nigh

"O cursed mother! hell is deep,
And there thou 'll enter step by step."

"And O! and O!" said the babes baith,
  "Take her where waters rin,
And white as the milk of her white breast,
  Wash her twa hands frae sin."

GLENFINLAS.*

"O hone a rie'! O hone a rie'!
  The pride of Albin's line is o'er,
And fall'n Glenartney's stateliest tree;
  We ne'er shall see Lord Ronald more!'

* See Appendix.

O, sprung from great Macgillianore,
   The chief that never fear'd a foe,
How matchless was thy broad claymore,
   How deadly thine unerring bow!

Well can the Saxon widows tell,
   How, on the Teith's resounding shore,
The boldest Lowland warriors fell,
   As down from Lenny's pass you bore.

But o'er his hills, in festal day,
   How blazed Lord Ronald's beltane-tree,
While youths and maids the light strathspey
   So nimbly danced with Highland glee!

Cheer'd by the strength of Ronald's shell,
   E'en age forgot his tresses hoar;
But now the loud lament we swell,
   O ne'er to see Lord Ronald more!

From distant isles a chieftain came,
   The joys of Ronald's halls to find,
And chase with him the dark-brown game,
   That bounds o'er Albin's hills of wind.

'Twas Moy; whom in Columba's isle
   The seer's prophetic spirit found,
As, with a minstrel's fire the while,
   He waked his harp's harmonious sound.

Full many a spell to him was known,
   Which wandering spirits shrink to hear;
And many a lay of potent tone,
   Was never meant for mortal ear.

For there, 't is said, in mystic mood,
   High converse with the dead they hold,
And oft espy the fated shroud,
   That shall the future corpse enfold.

Glenfinlas

O so it fell, that on a day,
    To rouse the red deer from their den,
The Chiefs have ta'en their distant way,
    And scoured the deep Glenfinlas glen.

No vassals wait their sports to aid,
    To watch their safety, deck their board;
Their simple dress, the Highland plaid,
    Their trusty guard, the Highland sword.

Three summer days, through brake and dell,
    Their whistling shafts successful flew;
And still, when dewy evening fell,
    The quarry to their hut they drew.

In grey Glenfinlas' deepest nook
    The solitary cabin stood,
Fast by Moneira's sullen brook,
    Which murmurs through that lonely wood.

Soft fell the night, the sky was calm,
    When three successive days had flown;
And summer mist in dewy balm
    Steep'd heathy bank, and mossy stone

The moon, half-hid in silvery flakes,
    Afar her dubious radiance shed,
Quivering on Katrine's distant lakes,
    And resting on Benledi's head.

Now in their hut, in social guise,
    Their silvan fare the Chiefs enjoy;
And pleasure laughs in Ronald's eyes,
    As many a pledge he quaffs to Moy.

"What lack we here to crown our bliss,
    While thus the pulse of joy beats high?
What, but fair woman's yielding kiss,
    Her panting breath and melting eye?

"To chase the deer of yonder shades,
　This morning left their father's pile
The fairest of our mountain maids,
　The daughters of the proud Glengyle.

"Long have I sought sweet Mary's heart,
　And dropp'd the tear, and heaved the sigh;
But vain the lover's wily art,
　Beneath a sister's watchful eye.

"But thou may'st teach that guardian fair,
　While far with Mary I am flown,
Of other hearts to cease her care,
　And find it hard to guard her own.

"Touch but thy harp, thou soon shalt see
　The lovely Flora of Glengyle,
Unmindful of her charge and me,
　Hang on thy notes, 'twixt tear and smile.

" Or, if she choose a melting tale,
　All underneath the greenwood bough,
Will good St. Ornan's rule prevail,
　Stern huntsman of the rigid brow?"—

"Since Enrick's fight, since Morna's death,
　No more on me shall rapture rise,
Responsive to the panting breath,
　Or yielding kiss, or melting eyes.

"E'en then, when o'er the heath of woe,
　Where sunk my hopes of love and fame,
I bade my harp's wild wailings flow,
　On me the Seer's sad spirit came.

" The last dread curse of angry heaven,
　With ghastly sights and sounds of woe,
To dash each glimpse of joy was given—
　The gift, the future ill to know.

"The bark thou saw'st, yon summer morn,
  So gaily part from Oban's bay,
My eye beheld her dash'd and torn,
  Far on the rocky Colonsay.

"Thy Fergus too—thy sister's son, [power,
  Thou saw'st, with pride, the gallant's
As marching 'gainst the Lord of Downe,
  He left the skirts of huge Benmore.

"Thou only saw'st their tartans wave,
  As down Benvoirlich's side they wound,
Heard'st but the pibroch, answering brave
  To many a target clanking round.

"I heard the groans, I mark'd the tears,
  I saw the wound his bosom bore,
When on the serried Saxon spears
  He pour'd his clan's resistless roar.

"And thou, who bidst me think of bliss,
  And bidst my heart awake to glee,
And court, like thee, the wanton kiss—
  That heart, O Ronald, bleeds for thee!

"I see the death-damps chill thy brow;
  I hear thy Warning Spirit cry; [now...
The corpse-lights dance—they're gone, and
  No more is given to gifted eye!"—

"Alone enjoy thy dreary dreams,
  Sad prophet of the evil hour!
Say, should we scorn joy's transient beams,
  Because to-morrow's storm may lour?

"Or false, or sooth, thy words of woe,
  Clangillian's Chieftain ne'er shall fear;
His blood shall bound at rapture's glow,
  Though doom'd to stain the Saxon spear.

"E'en now, to meet me in yon dell,
  My Mary's buskins brush the dew."
He spoke, nor bade the Chief farewell,
  But call'd his dogs, and gay withdrew.

Within an hour return'd each hound;
  In rush'd the rousers of the deer;
They howl'd in melancholy sound,
  Then closely couch'd beside the seer.

No Ronald yet; though midnight came,
  And sad were Moy's prophetic dreams,
As, bending o'er the dying flame,
  He fed the watch-fire's quivering gleams.

Sudden the hounds erect their ears,
  And sudden cease their moaning howl;
Close press'd to Moy, they mark their fears
  By shivering limbs, and stifled growl.

Untouch'd, the harp began to ring,
  As softly, slowly, oped the door;
And shook responsive every string,
  As light a footstep press'd the floor.

And by the watch-fire's glimmering light,
  Close by the minstrel's side was seen
An huntress maid, in beauty bright,
  All dropping wet her robes of green.

All dropping wet her garments seem;
  Chill'd was her cheek, her bosom bare,
As, bending o'er the dying gleam,
  She wrung the moisture from her hair.

With maiden blush she softly said,
  "O gentle huntsman, hast thou seen,
In deep Glenfinlas' moonlight glade,
  A lovely maid in vest of green:

Glenfinlas

"With her a Chief in Highland pride;
His shoulders bear the hunter's bow,
The mountain dirk adorns his side,
Far on the wind his tartans flow?"—

"And who art thou? and who are they?"
All ghastly gazing, Moy replied:
"And why, beneath the moon's pale ray,
Dare ye thus roam Glenfinlas' side?"—

"Where wild Loch Katrine pours her tide,
Blue, dark, and deep, round many an isle,
Our father's towers o'erhang her side,
The castle of the bold Glengyle.

"To chase the dun Glenfinlas deer,
Our woodland course this morn we bore,
And haply met, while wandering here,
The son of great Macgillianore.

"O aid me, then, to seek the pair,
Whom, loitering in the woods, I lost;
Alone, I dare not venture there, [ghost."—
Where walks, they say, the shrieking

"Yes, many a shrieking ghost walks there;
Then first, my own sad vow to keep,
Here will I pour my midnight prayer,
Which still must rise when mortals sleep."—

"O first, for pity's gentle sake,
Guide a lone wanderer on her way!
For I must cross the haunted brake,
And reach my father's towers ere day."—

"First, three times tell each Ave-bead,
And thrice a Pater-noster say;
Then kiss with me the holy rede;
So shall we safely wend our way."—

"O shame to knighthood, strange and foul!
  Go, doff the bonnet from thy brow,
And shroud thee in the monkish cowl,
  Which best befits thy sullen vow.

"Not so, by high Dunlathmon's fire,
  Thy heart was froze to love and joy,
When gaily rung thy raptured lyre,
  To wanton Morna's melting eye."

Wild stared the minstrel's eyes of flame,
  And high his sable locks arose,
And quick his colour went and came,
  As fear and rage alternate rose.

"And thou! when by the blazing oak
  I lay, to her and love resign'd,
Say, rode ye on the eddying smoke,
  Or sail'd ye on the midnight wind!

"Not thine a race of mortal blood,
  Nor old Glengyle's pretended line;
Thy dame, the Lady of the Flood,
  Thy sire, the Monarch of the Mine."

He mutter'd thrice St. Oran's rhyme,
  And thrice St. Fillan's* powerful prayer;
Then turn'd him to the eastern clime,
  And sternly shook his coal-black hair.

And, bending o'er his harp, he flung
  His wildest witch-notes on the wind;
And loud, and high, and strange, they rung,
  As many a magic change they find.

* In a note to Marmion, we are told that St. Fillan was a Scottish saint of some reputation, whose wells and springs are still places of pilgrimage and offering:

"St. Fillan's blessed well,
Whose spring can frenzied dreams dispel,
And the crazed brain restore."

Tall wax'd the Spirit's altering form,
  Till to the roof her stature grew;
Then, mingling with the rising storm,
  With one wild yell away she flew.

Rain beats, hail rattles, whirlwinds tear:
  The slender hut in fragments flew;
But not a lock of Moy's loose hair
  Was waved by wind, or wet by dew.

Wild mingling with the howling gale,
  Loud bursts of ghastly laughter rise;
High o'er the minstrel's head they sail,
  And die amid the northern skies.

The voice of thunder shook the wood,
  As ceased the more than mortal yell;
And, spattering foul, a shower of blood
  Upon the hissing firebrands fell.

Next dropp'd from high a mangled arm;
  The fingers strain'd an half-drawn blade:
And last, the life-blood streaming warm,
  Torn from the trunk, a gasping head.

Oft o'er that head, in battling field,
  Stream'd the proud crest of high Benmore;
That arm the broad claymore could wield,
  Which dyed the Teith with Saxon gore.

Woe to Moneira's sullen rills!
  Woe to Glenfinlas' dreary glen!
There never son of Albin's hills
  Shall draw the hunter's shaft agen!

E'en the tired pilgrim's burning feet
  At noon shall shun that sheltering den,
Lest, journeying in their rage, he meet
  The wayward Ladies of the Glen.

And we—behind the Chieftain's shield,
  No more shall we in safety dwell;
None leads the people to the field—
  And we the loud lament must swell.

O hone a rie'! O hone a rie'!
  The pride of Albin's line is o'er!
And fall'n Glenartney's stateliest tree;
  We ne'er shall see Lord Ronald more!

THE GAY GOSS HAWK

"O waly, waly, my gay goss-hawk,
  Gin your feathering be sheen!"—
"And waly, waly, my master dear,
  Gin ye look pale and lean!

"O have ye tint, at tournament,
  Your sword, or yet your spear?
    Or mourn ye for the Southern lass,
      Whom ye may not win near?"—

"I have not tint, at tournament,
  My sword, nor yet my spear;
But sair I mourn for my true love,
  Wi' mony a bitter tear,

* See Appendix.

The Gay Goss-hawk

"But weel's me on ye, my gay goss-hawk,
  Ye can baith speak and flee;
Ye sall carry a letter to my love,
  Bring an answer back to me."—

"But how sall I your true love find,
  Or how suld I her know?
I bear a tongue ne'er wi' her spake,
  An eye that ne'er her saw."—

"O weel sall ye my true love ken,
  Sae sune as ye her see;
For, of a' the flowers of fair England,
  The fairest flower is she.

"The red, that's on my true love's cheek
  Is like blood-drops on the snaw;
The white, that is on her breast bare,
  Like the down o' the white sea-maw.

"And even at my love's bour-door
  There grows a flowering birk;
And ye maun sit and sing thereon
  As she gangs to the kirk.

"And four-and-twenty fair ladyes
  Will to the mass repair;
But weel may ye my ladye ken,
  The fairest ladye there."

Lord William has written a love-letter,
  Put it under his pinion gray;
And he is awa to Southern land
  As fast as wings can gae.

And even at the ladye's bour
  There grew a flowering birk;
And he sat down and sung thereon
  As she gaed to the kirk.

The Gay Goss-Hawk

And weel he kent that ladye fair
  Amang her maidens free;   [ing,
For the flower, that springs in May morn-
  Was not sae sweet as she.

He lighted at the ladye's yate,
  And sat him on a pin;
And sang fu' sweet the notes o' love,
  Till a' was cosh within.

And first he sang a low low note,
  And syne he sang a clear;
And aye the o'erword o' the sang
  Was—"Your love can no win here."—

"Feast on, feast on, my maidens a',
  The wine flows you amang,
While I gang to my shot-window,
  And hear yon bonny bird's sang.

"Sing on, sing on, my bonny bird,
  The sang ye sung yestreen;
For weel I ken, by your sweet singing,
  Ye are frae my true love sen."

O first he sang a merry sang,
  And syne he sang a grave;
And syne he pick'd his feathers gray,
  To her the letter gave.

"Have there a letter from Lord William;
  He says he's sent ye three;
He canna wait your love langer,
  But for your sake he'll die."—

"Gae bid him bake his bridal bread,
  And brew his bridal ale;
And I shall meet him at Mary's kirk,
  Lang, lang ere it be stale."

The Gay Goss-Hawk

The lady 's gane to her chamber,
   And a moanfu' woman was she;
As gin she had ta'en a sudden brash,
   And were about to die.

"A boon, a boon, my father deir,
   A boon I beg of thee!"
"Ask not that haughty Scottish lord,
   For him you ne'er shall see.

"But, for your honest asking else,
   Weel granted it shall be."—
"Then, gin I die in Southern land,
   In Scotland gar bury me.

"And the first kirk that ye come to,
   Ye 's gar the mass be sung;
And the next kirk that ye come to,
   Ye 's gar the bells be rung.

"And when ye come to St. Mary's kirk,
   Ye 's tarry there till night."
And so her father pledg'd his word,
   And so his promise plight.

She has ta'en her to her bigly bour
   As fast as she could fare;
And she has drank a sleepy draught,
   That she had mix'd wi' care.

And pale, pale grew her rosy cheek,
   That was sae bright of blee,
And she seem'd to be as surely dead
   As any one could be.

Then spake her cruel step-minnie,
   "Tak ye the burning lead,
And drap a drap on her bosome,
   To try if she be dead."

The Gay Goss-Hawk

They took a drap o' boiling lead,
  They drapp'd it on her breast;
"Alas! alas!" her father cried,
  "She's dead without the priest."

She neither chatter'd with her teeth,
  Nor shiver'd with her chin;
"Alas! alas!" her father cried,
  "There is nae breath within."

Then up arose her seven brethren,
  And hew'd to her a bier;
They hew'd it frae the solid aik,
  Laid it o'er wi' silver clear.

Then up and gat her seven sisters,
  And sewed to her a kell;
And every steek that they put in
  Sewed to a siller bell.

The first Scots kirk that they cam to,
  They garr'd the bells be rung;
The next Scots kirk that they cam to,
  They garr'd the mass be sung.

But when they cam to St. Mary's kirk,
  There stude spearmen all on a raw;
And up and started Lord William,
  The chieftane amang the a'.

"Set down, set down the bier," he said;
  "Let me look her upon":   [hand,
But as soon as Lord William touch'd her
  Her colour began to come.

She brightened like the lily flower,
  Till her pale colour was gone
With rosy cheek, and ruby lip,
  She smiled her love upon.

"A morsel of your bread, my lord,
   And one glass of your wine;
For I hae fasted these three lang days,
   All for your sake and mine.—

"Gae hame, gae hame, my seven bauld
    brothers!
Gae hame and blaw your horn!
I trow ye wad hae gi'en me the skaith,
   But I 've gi'en you the scorn.

"Commend me to my grey father,
   That wished my saul gude rest;
But wae be to my cruel step-dame,
   Garr'd burn me on the breast."—

"Ah! woe to you, you light woman!
   An ill death may ye die!
For we left father and sisters at hame
   Breaking their hearts for thee."

COLIN AND LUCY.*

Of Leinster, fam'd for maidens fair,
   Bright Lucy was the grace;
Nor e'er did Liffy's limpid stream
   Reflect so fair a face.

* See Appendix.

Till luckless love and pining care
  Impair'd her rosy hue,
Her coral lip, and damask cheek,
  And eyes of glossy blue.

Oh! have you seen a lily pale,
  When beating rains descend?
So droop'd the slow-consuming maid;
  Her life now near its end.

By Lucy warn'd, of flattering swains
  Take heed, ye easy fair:
Of vengeance due to broken vows,
  Ye perjured swains beware.

Three times, all in the dead of night,
  A bell was heard to ring;
And at her window, shrieking thrice,
  The raven flapp'd his wing.

Too well the love-lorn maiden knew
  The solemn boding sound;
And thus, in dying words, bespoke
  The virgins weeping round.

"I hear a voice you cannot hear,
  Which says, I must not stay:
I see a hand you cannot see,
  Which beckons me away.

"By a false heart, and broken vows,
  In early youth I die.
Am I to blame, because his bride
  Is thrice as rich as I?

"Ah Colin! give not her thy vows;
  Vows due to me alone;
Nor thou, fond maid, receive his kiss,
  Nor think him all thy own.

Colin and Lucy

"To-morrow in the church to wed,
  Impatient, both prepare;
But know, fond maid, and know, false man,
  That Lucy will be there.

"Then, bear my corse, ye comrades, bear,
  The bridegroom blithe to meet;
He in his wedding-trim so gay,
  I in my winding-sheet."

She spoke, she died;—her corse was borne,
  The bridegroom blithe to meet
He in his wedding-trim so gay,
  She in her winding-sheet.

Then what were perjured Colin's thoughts?
  How were those nuptials kept?
The bride-men flock'd round Lucy dead,
  And all the village wept.

Confusion, shame, remorse, despair,
  At once his bosom swell:
The damps of death bedew'd his brow,
  He shook, he groan'd, he fell.

From the vain bride (ah, bride no more!)
  The varying crimson fled,
When, strétch'd before her rival's corse,
  She saw her husband dead.

Then to his Lucy's new-made grave,
  Convey'd by trembling swains,
One mould with her, beneath one sod,
  For ever he remains.

Oft at their grave the constant hind
  And plighted maid are seen;
With garlands gay, and true-love knots,
  They deck the sacred green.

But, swain forsworn, whoe'er thou art,
This hallow'd spot forbear;
Remember Colin's dreadful fate,
And fear to meet him there.

KATHARINE JANFARIE.*

There was a may, and a weel-far'd may,
  Lived high up in yon glen :
Her name was Katharine Janfarie,
  She was courted by mony men.

Up then came Lord Lauderdale,
  Up frae the Lawland Border;
And he has come to court this may,
  A' mounted in good order.

* See Appendix.

He told na her father, he told na her mother,
    And he told na ane o' her kin ;
But he whisper'd the bonnie lassie hersell,
    And has her favour won.

But out then came Lord Lochinvar,
    Out frae the English Border,
All for to court this bonny may,
    Weel mounted, and in order.

He told her father, he told her mother,
    And a' the lave o' her kin ;
But he told na the bonny may hersell,
    Till on her wedding e'en.

She sent to the Lord o' Lauderdale,
    Gin he wad come and see ;
And he has sent word back again,
    Weel answer'd she suld be.

And he has sent a messenger
    Right quickly through the land,
And raised mony an armed man
    To be at his command.

The bride looked out at a high window,
    Beheld baith dale and down,
And she was aware of her first true love,
    With riders mony a one.

She scoffed him, and scorned him,
    Upon her wedding day ;
And said—"It was the Fairy court
    To see him in array !

"O come ye here to fight, young lord,
    Or come ye here to play?
Or come ye here to drink good wine
    Upon the wedding day ?"—

Katharine Janfarie

"I come na here to fight," he said,
  "I come na here to play;
I 'll but lead a dance wi' the bonnie bride,
  And mount, and go my way."

It is a glass of the blood-red wine
  Was filled up them between,
And aye she drank to Lauderdale,
  Wha her true love had been.

He 's ta'en her by the milk-white hand,
  And by the grass-green sleeve;
He 's mounted her hie behind himself,
  At her kinsmen speir'd na leave.*

"Now take your bride, Lord Lochinvar!
  Now take her if you may!
But, if you take your bride again,
  We 'll call it but foul play."

There were four-and-twenty bonnie boys,
  A' clad in Johnstone grey;
They said they would take the bride again,
  By the strong hand, if they may.

Some o' them were right willing men,
  But they were na willing a';
And four-and-twenty Leader lads
  Bid them mount and ride awa'.

Then whingers flew frae gentles' sides,
  And swords flew frae the shea's,
And red and rosy was the blood
  Ran down the lily braes.

* ["One touch to her hand, and one word in her ear,
When they reach'd the hall door, and the charger stood near;
So light to the croupe the fair lady he swung,
So light to the saddle before her he sprung!
'She is won! we are gone, over bank, bush, and scaur;
They 'll have fleet steeds that follow,' quoth young Lochinvar."
                                                    Marmion.]

The blood ran down by Caddon bank,
  And down by Caddon brae;
And, sighing, said the bonny bride—
  "O wae's me for foul play!"

My blessing on your heart, sweet thing!
  Wae to your wilfu' will!
There's mony a gallant gentleman
  Whae's bluid ye have garr'd to spill.

Now a' you lords of fair England,
  And that dwell by the English Border,
Come never here to seek a wife,
  For fear of sic disorder.

They'll haik ye up, and settle ye bye,
  Till on your wedding day;
Then gie ye frogs instead of fish,
  And play ye foul, foul play.

RUDIGER.*

Bright on the mountain's healthy slope
　The day's last splendours shine,
And, rich with many a radiant hue,
　Gleam gaily on the Rhine.

* See Appendix.

And many a one from Waldhurst's walls
  Along the river stroll'd,
As ruffling o'er the pleasant stream
  The ev'ning gales came cold.

So as they stray'd a swan they saw
  Sail stately up and strong,
And by a silver chain he drew
  A little boat along,—

Whose streamer to the gentle breeze
  Long floating flutter'd light,
Beneath whose crimson canopy
  There lay reclin'd a knight.

With arching crest and swelling breast
  On sail'd the stately swan,
And lightly up the parting tide
  The little boat came on.

And onward to the shore they drew,
  Where having left the knight,
The little boat adown the stream
  Fell soon beyond the sight.

Was never a knight in Waldhurst's walls
  Could with this stranger vie;
Was never a youth at aught esteem'd
  When Rudiger was by.

Was never a maid in Waldhurst's walls
  Might match with Margaret;
Her cheek was fair, her eyes were dark,
  Her silken locks like jet.

And many a rich and noble youth
  Had strove to win the fair;
But never a rich and noble youth
  Could rival Rudiger.

At every tilt and tourney he
　Still bore away the prize;
For knightly feats superior still,
　And knightly courtesies.

His gallant feats, his looks, his love,
　Soon won the willing fair;
And soon did Margaret become
　The wife of Rudiger.

Like morning dreams of happiness
　Fast roll'd the months away;
For he was kind and she was kind,
　And who so blest as they?

Yet Rudiger would sometimes sit
　Absorb'd in silent thought,
And his dark downward eye would seem
　With anxious meaning fraught:

But soon he rais'd his looks again,
　And smil'd his cares away,
And mid the hall of gaiety
　Was none like him so gay.

And onward roll'd the waning months—
　The hour appointed came,
And Margaret her Rudiger
　Hail'd with a father's name.

But silently did Rudiger
　The little infant see;
And darkly on the babe he gaz'd,—
　A gloomy man was he.

And when to bless the little babe
　The holy Father came,
To cleanse the stains of sin away
　In Christ's redeeming name,

Then did the cheek of Rudiger
  Assume a death-pale hue,
And on his clammy forehead stood
  The cold convulsive dew;

And falt'ring in his speech he bade
  The Priest the rites delay,
Till he could, to right health restor'd,
  Enjoy the festive day.

When o'er the many-tinted sky
  He saw the day decline,
He called upon his Margaret
  To walk beside the Rhine;

"And we will take the little babe,
  For soft the breeze that blows,
And the mild murmurs of the stream
  Will lull him to repose."*

And so together forth they went;
  The ev'ning breeze was mild,
And Rudiger upon his arm
  Pillow'd the little child.

* "Now who can judge this to be other than one of those spirits that are named Incubi?" says Thomas Heywood, in his "Notes to the Hierarchies of the Blessed Angels," a poem printed by Adam Islip in 1635. "I have adopted his story," writes Southey, "but not his solution, making the unknown soldier not an evil spirit, but one who had purchased happiness of a malevolent being, by the promised sacrifice of his first-born child." Southey has borrowed themes of other ballads from this quaint old writer; one in particular, "Donica," who moved about the world many years after she was dead, eating and drinking, "although very sparingly," and indicating the absence of the soul only by "a deep paleness on her countenance." At length a magician coming by where she was, in the company of other virgins, as soon as he beheld her he said, "Fair maids, why keep you company with this dead virgin, whom you suppose to be alive?" when taking away the magic charm which was hid under her arm, the body fell down lifeless and without motion.

Rudiger

And many a one from Waldhurst's walls
  Along the banks did roam;
But soon the evening wind came cold,
  And all betook them home.

Yet Rudiger in silent mood
  Along the banks would roam,
Nor aught could Margaret prevail
  To turn his footsteps home.

"Oh turn thee, turn thee, Rudiger!
  The rising mists behold,
The ev'ning wind is damp and chill,
  The little babe is cold!"

"Now hush thee, hush thee, Margaret,
  The mists will do no harm,
And from the wind the little babe
  Lies shelter'd on my arm."

"Oh turn thee, turn thee, Rudiger!
  Why onward wilt thou roam?
The moon is up, the night is cold,
  And we are far from home."

He answer'd not, for now he saw
  A swan come sailing strong,
And by a silver chain he drew
  A little boat along.

To shore they came, and to the boat
  Fast leapt he with the child,
And in leapt Margaret—breathless now,
  And pale with fear and wild.

With arching crest and swelling breast
  On sail'd the stately swan,
And lightly down the rapid tide
  The little boat went on.

The full-orb'd moon, that beam'd around
   Pale splendour through the night,
Cast through the crimson canopy
   A dim discolour'd light;

And swiftly down the hurrying stream
   In silence still they sail,
And the long streamer flutt'ring fast
   Flapp'd to the heavy gale.

And he was mute in sullen thought,
   And she was mute with fear;
Nor sound but of the parting tide
   Broke on the list'ning ear.

The little babe began to cry,
   Then Marg'ret rais'd her head,
And with a quick and hollow voice
   "Give me the child!" she said.

"Now hush thee, hush thee, Margaret,
   Nor my poor heart distress!
I do but pay perforce the price
   Of former happiness.

"And hush thee, too, my little babe!
   Thy cries so feeble cease:
Lie still, lie still;—a little while
   And thou shalt be at peace."

So as he spake to land they drew,
   And swift he stept on shore,
And him behind did Margaret
   Close follow evermore.

It was a place all desolate,
   Nor house nor tree was there;
And there a rocky mountain rose,
   Barren, and bleak, and bare.

And at its base a cavern yawn'd,
  No eye its depth might view,
For in the moonbeam shining round
  That darkness darker grew.

Cold horror crept through Margaret's blood,
  Her heart it paus'd with fear,
When Rudiger approach'd the cave,
  And cried, "Lo, I am here!"

A deep sepulchral sound the cave
  Return'd, "Lo, I am here!"
And black from out the cavern gloom
  Two giant arms appear.

And Rudiger approach'd, and held
  The little infant nigh:
Then Margaret shriek'd, and gather'd then
  New pow'rs from agony.

And round the baby fast and close
  Her trembling arms she folds,
And with a strong convulsive grasp
  The little infant holds.*

---

* Several of the translated ballads of Jamieson, Lewis, and others, record incidents of a similar character. When Southey borrowed the story, it was comparatively new to the English reader. It would be easy to quote many illustrative examples. Jamieson publishes one—from the Danish—entitled "The Merman and Marstig's Daughter," in which occurs the following stanza,—the wedlock being followed by the drowning of the fair May:

> "The priest before the altar stood;
>   'O what for a good naight may this be?'
> The May leugh till herself, and said,
>   'God gif that gude knight were for me!'"
>
> *   *   *   *

A translation, apparently of the same ballad, has been made by Mr. Charles Mackay; it is entitled "The Wild Water-man, or the Fate of the Vain Maiden"; the following is the "moral":

> "I warn you maidens, whoever you be,
> Beware, beware of vanity;
> Maidens, I warn you all I can,
> Beware of the wild, wild water-man."

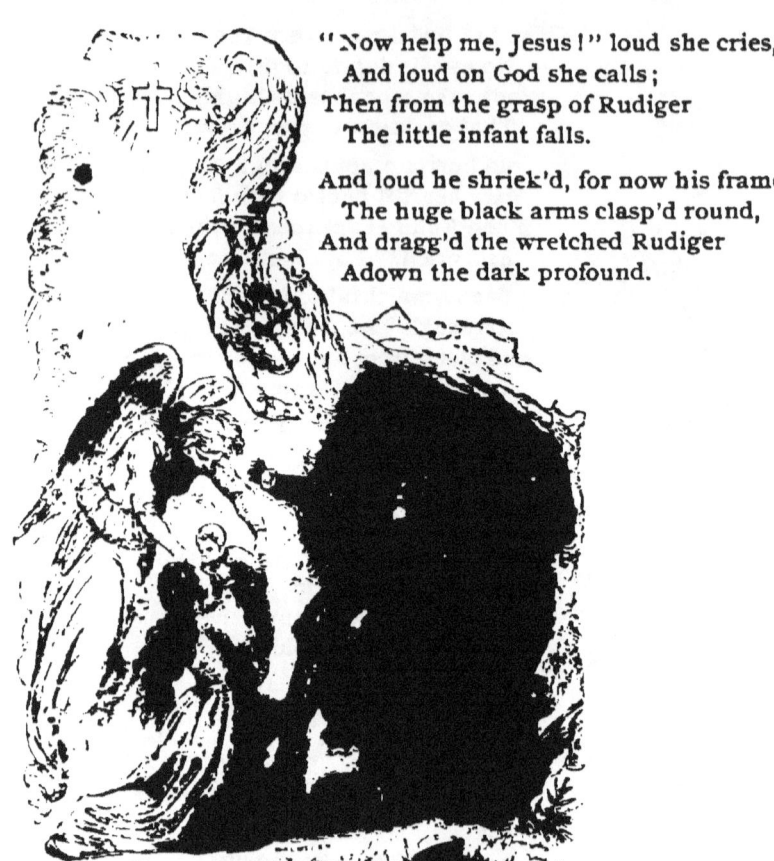

"Now help me, Jesus!" loud she cries,
    And loud on God she calls;
Then from the grasp of Rudiger
    The little infant falls.

And loud he shriek'd, for now his frame,
    The huge black arms clasp'd round,
And dragg'd the wretched Rudiger
    Adown the dark profound.

THE EVE OF ST. JOHN.*

The Baron of Smaylho'me rose with day,
  He spurr'd his courser on,
Without stop or stay, down the rocky way,
  That leads to Brotherstone.

He went not with the bold Buccleuch,
  His banner broad to rear;
He went not 'gainst the English yew,
  To lift the Scottish spear.

* See Appendix.

Yet his plate-jack was brac'd, his helmet was
  lac'd,
 And his vaunt-brace of proof he wore;
At his saddle-gerthe was a good steel sperthe,
 Full ten pound weight and more.

The baron return'd in three days' space,
 And his looks were sad and sour;
And weary was his courser's pace,
 As he reach'd his rocky tower.

He came not from where Ancram Moor
 Ran red with English blood;   [cleuch,
Where the Douglas true, and the bold Buc-
 'Gainst keen Lord Evers stood.

Yet was his helmet hack'd and hew'd,
 His acton pierced and tore,
His axe and his dagger with blood imbrued,—
 But it was not English gore.

He lighted at the Chapellage,
 He held him close and still;
And he whistled thrice for his little foot-page,
 His name was English Will.

"Come thou hither, my little foot-page,
 Come hither to my knee;
Though thou art young, and tender of age,
 I think thou art true to me.

"Come, tell me all that thou has seen,
 And look thou tell me true!
Since I from Smaylho'me tower have been,
 What did thy lady do?"—

"My lady, each night, sought the lonely light,
 That burns on the wild Watchfold;
For, from height to height, the beacons bright
 Of the English foemen told.

"The bittern clamour'd from the moss,
  The wind blew loud and shrill;
Yet the craggy pathway she did cross,
  To the eiry Beacon Hill.

"I watch'd her steps, and silent came
  Where she sat her on a stone;—
No watchman stood by the dreary flame
  It burned all alone.

"The second night I kept her in sight,
  Till to the fire she came,
And, by Mary's might! an armed knight
  Stood by the lonely flame.

"And many a word that warlike lord
  Did speak to my lady there;
But the rain fell fast, and loud blew the blast,
  And I heard not what they were.

"The third night there the sky was fair,
  And the mountain blast was still,
As again I watch'd the secret pair,
  On the lonesome Beacon Hill.

"And I heard her name the midnight hour,
  And name this holy eve;
And say:' Come this night to thy lady's bower;
  Ask no bold baron's leave.

"' He lifts his spear with the bold Buccleuch;
  His lady is all alone;
The door she'll undo to her knight so true,
  On the eve of good St. John.'—

"' I cannot come; I must not come;
  I dare not come to thee;
On the eve of St. John I must wander alone:
  In thy bower I may not be.'—

The Eve of St. John

" 'Now, out on thee, faint-hearted knight!
Thou shouldst not say me nay;
For the eve is sweet, and, when lovers meet,
. Is worth the whole summer's day.

" 'And I'll chain the blood-hound,
And the warder shall not sound,
And rushes shall be strew'd on the stair;
So, by the black rood-stone, and by holy St. John,
I conjure thee, my love, to be there!'—

" 'Though the blood-hound may be mute,
And the rush beneath my foot,
And the warder his bugle should not blow,
There sleepeth a priest in the chamber to the [east,
And my footstep he would know.'—

" 'O fear not the priest, who sleepeth to the [east!
For to Dryburgh the way he has ta'en;
And there to say mass, till three days do pass,
For the soul of a knight that is slayne.'—

"He turn'd him around, and grimly he [frown'd
Then he laugh'd right scornfully—
'He who says mass-rite for the soul of that [knight,
May as well say mass for me:

" 'At the midnight hour,
When bad spirits have power,
In thy chamber will I be.'—
With that he was gone, and my lady left alone,
And no more did I see."

Then changed, I trow, was that bold Baron's [brow,
From the dark to the blood-red high—
"Now, tell me the mien of the knight thou hast seen,
For, by Mary, he shall die!"—

"His arms shone bright, in the beacon's red
  His plume it was scarlet and blue ; [light!
On his shield was a hound,
In a silver leash bound,
  And his crest was a branch of the yew."—

"Thou liest, thou liest, thou little foot-page,
  Loud dost thou lie to me !
For that knight is cold,
And low laid in the mould,
  All under the Eildon-tree."—

"Yet hear but my word, my noble lord !
  For I heard her name his name ;
And that lady bright she called the knight
  Sir Richard of Coldinghame."—

The bold Baron's brow then changed, I trow,
  From high blood-red to pale—
" The grave is deep and dark—
And the corpse is stiff and stark—
  So I may not trust thy tale.

"Where fair Tweed flows round holy Melrose,
  And Eildon slopes to the plain,
Full three nights ago, by some secret foe,
  That gay gallant was slain.

" The varying light deceived thy sight,
  And the wild winds drown'd the name ;
For the Dryburgh bells ring,
And the white monks do sing,
  For Sir Richard of Coldinghame !"

He pass'd the court-gate,
And he oped the tower-gate,
  And he mounted the narrow stair,
To the bartizan seat,
Where, with maids that on her wait,
  He found his lady fair.

The Eve of St. John

That lady sat in mournful mood:
  Look'd over hill and vale;
Over Tweed's fair flood, and Mertoun's wood,
  And all down Teviotdale.

"Now hail, now hail, thou lady bright!"—
"Now hail, thou Baron true!
What news, what news, from Ancram fight?
  What news from the bold Buccleuch?"—

"The Ancram Moor is red with gore,
  For many a southern fell;
And Buccleuch has charged us, evermore,
  To watch our beacons well."—

The lady blush'd red, but nothing she said:
  Nor added the Baron a word:
Then she stepp'd down the stair to her cham- [ber fair,
  And so did her moody lord.

In sleep the lady mourn'd,
  And the Baron toss'd and turn'd,
    And oft to himself he said,—
"The worms around him creep,
  And his bloody grave is deep . . .
    It cannot give up the dead!"—

It was near the ringing of matin-bell,
  The night was well nigh done,
When a heavy sleep on that Baron fell,
  On the eve of good St. John.

The lady look'd through the chamber fair,
  By the light of a dying flame;
And she was aware of a knight stood there—
  Sir Richard of Coldinghame!

"Alas! away, away!" she cried,
  "For the holy Virgin's sake!"—
"Lady, I know who sleeps by thy side;
  But, lady, he will not awake.

"By Eildon-tree, for long nights three,
　In bloody grave have I lain;　　[me,
The mass and the death-prayer are said for
　But, lady, they are said in vain.

"By the Baron's brand, near Tweed's fair
　Most foully slain, I fell;　　[strand,
And my restless sprite on the beacon's
　For a space is doomed to dwell. [height,

"At our trysting-place, for a certain space,
　I must wander to and fro;　　[bower,
But I had not had power to come to thy
　Hadst thou not conjured me so."—

Love master'd fear—her brow she cross'd;
　"How, Richard, hast thou sped?
And art thou saved, or art thou lost?"—
　The vision shook his head!

"Who spilleth life shall forfeit life;
　So bid thy lord believe:
That lawless love is guilt above,
　This awful sign receive."

He laid his left palm on an oaken beam,
　His right upon her hand;
The lady shrunk, and fainting sunk,
　For it scorch'd like a fiery brand.

The sable score of fingers four
　Remains on that board impress'd;
And for evermore that lady wore
　A covering on her wrist.*

---

* The circumstance of the "nun who never saw the day" is not entirely imaginary. Neither is the incident of the lady wearing a covering on the wrist to conceal the "sable score of fingers four." Sir Walter says it is "founded on an Irish tradition." The circumstance referred to is not of a remote date. We have ourselves seen the bracelet said to have been thus used—and worn until death betrayed the secret of the wearer.

The Eve of St. John

There is a nun in Dryburgh bower,
  Ne'er looks upon the sun;
There is a monk in Melrose tower,
  He speaketh word to none.

That nun, who ne'er beholds the day,
  That monk who speaks to none—
That nun was Smaylho'me's Lady gay,
  That monk the bold Baron.

BARTHRAM'S DIRGE. *

They shot him dead at the Nine-Stone Rig,
  Beside the Headless Cross.
And they left him lying in his blood,
  Upon the moor and moss.

They made a bier of the broken bough,
  The sauch and the aspin gray,
And they bore him to the Lady Chapel,
  And waked him there all day.

A lady came to that lonely bower,
  And threw her robes aside;
She tore her ling long yellow hair,
  And knelt at Barthram's side.

* See Appendix.

She bathed him in the Lady-Well,
  His wounds so deep and sair ;
And she plaited a garland for his breast,
  And a garland for his hair.

They rowed him in a lily-sheet
  And bare him to his earth ;
And the Gray Friars sung the dead man's mass,
  As they pass'd the Chapel Garth.

They buried him at the mirk midnigt,
  When the dew fell cold and still,
When the aspin gray forgot to play,
  And the mist clung to the hill.

They dug his grave but a bare foot deep,
  By the edge of the Nine-Stone Burn,
And they covered him o'er with the heather-flower,
  The moss and the lady fern.

A Gray Friar staid upon the grave,
  And sang till the morning tide ;
And a friar shall sing for Barthram's soul,
  While the Headless Cross shall bide.

Sir Cauline.*

THE FIRST PART.

In Ireland, ferr over the sea,
  There dwelleth a bonnye kinge;
And with him a young and comlye knighte,
  Men call him Sir Cauline.

The kinge had a ladye to his daughter,
  In fashyon she hath no peere;
And princely wightes that ladye wooed
  To be theyr wedded feere.

* See Appendix.

Sir Cauline loveth her best of all,
  But nothing durst he saye;
Ne descreeve his counsayl to no man,
  But deerlye he lovde this may.

Till on a daye it so beffell,
  Great dill to him was dight;
The maydens love removde his mynd,
  To care-bed went the knighte,

One while he spred his armes him fro,
  One while he spred them nye:
And aye, "But I winne that ladye's love
  For dole now I mun dye."

And whan our parish-masse was done,
  Our kinge was bowne to dyne:
He sayes, "Where is Sir Cauline,
  That is wont to serve the wyne?"

Then aunswerde him a courteous knighte,
  And fast his handes gan wringe:
"Sir Cauline is sicke, and like to dye
  Without a good leechinge."

"Fetche me downe my daughter deere,
  She is a leeche fulle fine: [bread,
Goe take him doughe, and the baken
And serve him with the wyne soe red;
  Lothe I were him to tine."

Fair Christabelle to his chaumber goes,
  Her maydens followyng nye: [lord?"
"O well," she sayth, "how doth my
  "O sicke, thou fayr ladye."

"Nowe ryse up wightlye, man for shame,
  Never lye soe cowardlee;
For it is told in my father's halle,
  You dye for love of mee."

"Fayre ladye, it is for your love
  That all this dill I drye:
For if you wold comfort me with a kisse,
  Then were I brought from bale to blisse,
  No lenger wold I lye."

"Sir knighte, my father is a kinge,
  I am his only heire;
Alas! and well you knowe, syr knighte,
  I never can be youre fere."

"O ladye, thou art a kinges daughter,
  And I am not thy peere;
But let me doe some deedes of armes
  To be your bacheleere."

"Some deedes of arms if thou wilt doe,
  My bacheleere to bee,
But ever and aye my heart wold rue
  Giff harm shold happe to thee.

"Upon Eldridge hill there groweth a
  Upon the mores brodinge;   [thorne
And dare ye, syr knighte, wake there all
  Untill the fayre morninge?   [nighte,

"For the Eldridge knighte, so mickle of
  Will examine you beforne;   [mighte,
And never man bare life awaye,
  But he did him scath and scorne.

"That knighte he is a fond paynim,
  And large of limb and bone;
And but if heaven may be thy speede,
  Thy life it is but gone."

"Nowe on the Eldridge hilles Ile walke,
  For thy sake, faire ladye;
And Ile either bring you a ready token,
  Or Ile never more you see."

The lady is gone to her own chambere,
  Her maydens following bright:
Sir Cauline lope from care-bed soone,
And to the Eldridge hills is gone,
  For to wake there all night.

Unto midnight, that the moone did rise
  He walked up and downe:
Then a lightsome bugle heard he blowe,
  Over the bents soe browne;
Quoth hee, "If cryance come till my heart,
  I am far from any good towne."

And soone he spyde on the mores so broad,
  A furyous wight and fell;
A ladye bright his brydle led,
  Clad in a fayre kyrtell;

And soe fast he called on Sir Cauline,
  "O man, I rede thee flye,
For 'but' if cryance comes till my heart,
  I weene but thou mun dye."

He sayth, "No cryance comes till my heart,
  Nor in fayth, I wyll not flee;
For, cause thou minged not Christ before,
  The less me dreaded thee."

The Eldridge knighte he pricked his steed;
  Sir Cauline bold abode:
Then either shooke his trusty speare,
And the timber these two children bare
  Soe soone in sunder slode.

Then tooke they out theyr two good swordes,
  And layden on full faste,
Till helme and hawberke, mail and sheelde,
  They all were well-nye brast.

Sir Cauline

The Eldridge knight was mickle of might,
  And stiffe in stower did stande,
But Sir Cauline with a backward stroke,
  He smote off his right hand;
That soone he with paine and lacke of bloud
  Fell downe on that lay-land.

Then up Sir Cauline lift his brande
  All over his head so hye:
" And here I sweare by the holy roode
  Nowe, caytiffe, thou shalt dye."

Then up and came that ladye brighte
  Fast wringing of her hande:
" For the mayden's love, that most you love,
  Withhold that deadly brande:

" For the mayden's love, that most you love,
  Now smyte no more I praye;
And aye whatever thou wilt, my lord,
  He shall thy hests obaye."

" Now sweare to mee, thou Eldridge knighte,
  And here on this lay-land,
That thou wilt believe on Christ his laye,
  And thereto plight thy hand:

" And that thou never on Eldridge come
  To sporte, gamon, or playe,
And that thou here give up thy armes
  Until thy dying daye."

The Eldridge knighte gave up his armes
  With many a sorrowfulle sighe;
And sware to obey Sir Cauline's hest,
  Till the tyme that he shold dye.

And he then up, and the Eldridge knighte
  Sett him in his saddle anone,
And the Eldridge knighte and his ladye
  To theyr castle are they gone.

Then he tooke up the bloudy hand,
　That was so large of bone,
And on it he founde five rings of gold
　Of knightes that had he slone.

Then he tooke up the Eldridge sworde,
　As hard as any flint ;
And he tooke off those ringes five,
　As bright as fyre and brent.

Home then pricked Sir Cauline
　As light as leafe on tree ;
I-wys he neither stint ne blanne,
　Till he his ladye see.

Then downe he knelt upon his knee
　Before that ladye gay ;
"O ladye, I have bin on the Eldridge hills ;
　These tokens I bring away."

"Now welcome, welcome, Sir Cauline,
　Thrice welcome unto mee ;
For now I perceive thou art a true knighte,
　Of valour bolde and free."

"O ladye, I am thy own true knighte,
　Thy hests for to obaye ;
And mought I hope to winne thy love !"
　Ne more his tonge colde say.

The lady blushed scarlette redde,
　And fette a gentill sighe :
"Alas ! sir knighte, how may this bee,
　For my degree's soe highe ?

"But sith thou hast hight, thou comely
　To be my bacheleere,　　　　[youth,
Ile promise if thee I may not wedde,
　I will have none other fere."

Sir Cauline

Then shee held forthe her lilly-white hand
   Towards that knighte so free;
He gave to it one gentill kisse,—
His heart was brought from bale to blisse,
   The teares sterte from his ee.

"But keep my counsayl, Sir Cauline,
   Ne let no man it knowe;
For and ever my father sholde it ken,
   I wot he wolde us sloe."

From that day forthe that ladye fayre
   Lovde Sir Cauline, the knighte:
From that day forthe he only joyde
   Whan shee was in his sight.

Yea, and oftentimes they mette
   Within a fayre arboure,
Where they in love and sweet daliaunce
   Past manye a pleasaunt houre.

PART THE SECOND.

Everye white will have its blacke,
   And everye sweete its sowre:
This founde the Ladye Christabelle
   In an untimely howre.

Far so it befelle, as Sir Cauline
   Was with that ladye faire,
The kinge, her father, walked forthe
   To take the evenyng aire:

And into the arboure as he went
   To rest his wearye fect,
He found his daughter and Sir Cauline
   There sette in daliaunce sweet.

The kinge hee sterted forthe, i-wys,
  And an angrye man was hee:
"Nowe, traytoure, thou shalt hange or drawe,
  And rewe shall thy ladye."

Then forthe Sir Cauline he was ledde,
  And throwne in dungeon deepe;
And the ladye into a towre so hye,
  There left to wayle and weepe.

The queene she was Sir Cauline's friend,
  And to the kinge sayd shee:
"I praye you save Sir Cauline's life,
  And let him banisht bee."

"Now, dame, that traytoure shall be sent
  Across the salt sea fome:
But here I will make thee a band,
If ever he come within this land,
  A foule deathe is his doome."

All woebegone was that gentil knight
  To parte from his ladye;
And many a time he sighed sore,
  And cast a wistfulle eye:
"Faire Christabelle, from thee to parte,
  Farre lever had I dye."

Fair Christabelle, that ladye bright,
  Was had forthe of the towre;
But ever shee droopeth in her minde,
As nipt by an ungentle winde
  Doth some faire lillye flowre.

And ever shee doth lament and weepe
  To tint her lover soe:
"Sir Cauline, thou little think'st on mee,
  But I will still be true."

Sir Cauline

Manye a kinge, and manye a duke,
And lorde of high degree,
Did sue to that fayre ladye of love;
But never shee wolde them nee.

When manye a daye was past and gone,
Ne comfort she colde finde,
The kynge proclaimed a tourneament,
To cheere his daughter's mind:

And there came lords, and there came knights,
Fro manye a farre countrye,
To break a spere for theyr ladyes love
Before that faire ladye.

And manye a ladye there was sette
In purple and in palle:
But fair Christabelle soe woe-begone
Was the fayrest of them all.

Then manye a knight was mickle of might
Before his ladye gaye;
But a stranger wight, whom no man knewe,
He wan the prize eche daye.*

---

* Sir Cauline is here made to act up to the genuine spirit of perfect chivalry. In old romances no incident is of more frequent occurrence than this, of knights already distinguished for feats of arms laying aside their wonted cognizances, and, under the semblance of strange knights, manfully performing right valiant deeds. How often does the renowned Arthur, under such circumstances, exclaim, "O, Jesu! what knyte is that arrayed all in greene (or as the case may be)? He justeth myghtely!" The Emperor of Almaine, in like manner, after the timely succour afforded him by Syr Gowhter, is anxious to learn the name of his modest but unknown deliverer:

"Now dere God," said the Emperor,
"Whence com the knyght that is so styfe and stoure,
And al araide in rede,
Both hors, armour, and his stede?
A thousand Sarezyns he hath made blede,
And beteen hem to dethe,
That heder is com to helpe me,
And yesterday in black was he."

His acton it was all of blacke,
  His hewberke, and his sheelde,
Ne noe man wist whence he did come,
Ne noe man knewe where he did gone,
  When they came from the feelde.

And now three days were prestlye past
  In feates of chivalrye,
When lo upon the fourth morninge
  A sorrowfulle sight they see.

A hugye giaunt stiffe and starke,
  All foule of limbe and lere;
Two goggling eyen like fire farden,
  A mouthe from eare to eare.

Before him came a dwarffe full lowe,
  That waited on his knee;
And at his backe five heads he bare,
  All wan and pale of blee.

"Sir," quoth the dwarffe, and louted lowe,
  "Behold that hend Soldain!
Behold these heads I beare with me!
  They are kings which he hath slain.

"The Eldridge knight is his own cousine,
  Whom a knight of thine hath shent:
And hee is come to avenge his wrong,
And to thee, all thy knightes among,
  Defiance here hath sent.

"But yette he will appease his wrath
  Thy daughter's love to winne;
And but thou yeelde him that fayre mayd,
  Thy halls and towers must brenne.

"Thy head, sir king, must goe with mee,
  Or else thy daughter deere;
Or else within these lists soe broad
  Thou must finde him a peere."

The king he turned him round aboute,
  And in his heart was woe:
"Is there never a knighte of my round table
  This matter will undergoe?

"Is there never a knighte amongst yee all
  Will fight for my daughter and mee?
Whoever will fight yon grimme soldan,
  Right fair his meede shall bee.

"For hee shall have my broad lay-lands,
  And of my crowne be heyre;
And he shall winne fayre Christabelle
  To be his wedded fere."

But every knighte of his round table
  Did stand both still and pale:
For whenever they lookt on the grim soldan,
  It made their hearts to quail.

All woe-begone was that fayre ladye,
  When she sawe no helpe was nye:
She cast her thought on her owne true-love,
  And the teares gusht from her eye.

Up then sterte the stranger knighte,
  Sayd: "Ladye, be not affrayd;
Ile fight for thee with this grimme soldan,
  Thoughe he be unmacklye made.

"And if thou wilt lend me the Eldridge
  That lyeth within thy bowre,   [sworde,
I trust in Christe for to slay this fiende,
  Thoughe he be stiffe and stowre."

"Goe fetch him downe the Eldridge sworde,"
  The king he cryde, "with speede:
Nowe heaven assist thee, courteous knighte;
  My daughter is thy meede."

The gyaunt he stepped into the lists,
   And sayd : " Awaye, awaye ;
I sweare, as I am the hend soldan,
   Thou lettest me here all daye."

Then forthe the stranger knight he came,
   In his blacke armoure dight :
The ladye sighed a gentle sighe,
   "That this were my true knighte ! "

And nowe the gyaunt and knighte are mett
   Within the lists soe broad ;
And now with swordes soe sharpe of steele,
   They gan to lay on load.

The soldan strucke the knighte a stroke,
   That made him reele asyde ;
Then woe-begone was that fayre ladye,
   And thrice she deeply sighde.

The soldan strucke a second stroke,
   And made the bloude to flowe :
All pale and wan was that ladye fayre,
   And thrice she wept for woe.

The soldan strucke a third fell stroke,
   Which brought the knighte on his knee :
Sad sorrow pierced that ladye's heart,
   And she shriekt loud shriekings three.

The knighte he leapt upon his feete,
   All recklesse of the pain :
Quoth hee, " But heaven be now my speede,
   Or else I shall be slaine."

He grasped his sworde with mayne and
   And spying a secrette part,   [mighte,
He drave it into the soldan's syde,
   And pierced him to the heart.

Sir Cauline

Then all the people gave a shoute,
   Whan they sawe the soldan falle:
The ladye wept, and thankèd Christ,
   That had reskewed her from thrall.

And nowe the kinge with all his barons
   Rose uppe from offe his seate,
And downe he stepped into the listes,
   That curteous knighte to greete.

But he for payne and lack of bloude
   Was fallen into a swounde,
And there all walteringe in his gore
   Lay lifelesse on the grounde.

"Come downe, come downe, my daughter deare,
   Thou art a leeche of skille;
Farre lever had I lose halfe my landes,
   Than this good knighte sholde spille."

Downe then steppeth that fayre ladye,
   To helpe him if she maye;
But when she did his beavere raise,
"It is my life, my lord," she sayes,
   And shriekte and swound awaye.

Sir Cauline juste lifte up his eyes
   When he hearde his ladye crye,
"O ladye, I am thine owne true love;
   For thee I wisht to dye."

Then giving her one partinge looke,
   He closed his eyes in death,
Ere Christabelle, that ladye milde,
   Begane to drawe her breath.

But when she found her comelye knighte
   Indeed was dead and gone,
She layde her pale cold cheeke to his,
   And thus she made her moane:

"O staye, my deare and onlye lord,
   For mee thy faithfulle fere;
'T is meet that I shold followe thee,
   Who hast bought my love soe deare."

Then fayntinge in a deadlye swoune,
   And with a deepe-fette sighe,
That burst her gentle hearte in twayne,
   Fayre Christabelle did dye.

RUTH.*

When Ruth was left half desolate,
Her Father took another Mate;
And Ruth, not seven years old,
A slighted Child, at her own will
Went wandering over dale and hill,
In thoughtless freedom bold.

And she had made a Pipe of straw,
And from that oaten Pipe could draw
All sounds of winds and floods;
Had built a Bower upon the green,
As if she from her birth had been
An Infant of the woods.

* See Appendix.

Beneath her Father's roof alone
She seem'd to live; her thoughts her own,
Herself her own delight;
Pleased with herself, nor sad, nor gay;
And, passing thus the livelong day,
She grew to woman's height.

There came a Youth from Georgia's shore—
A military Casque he wore,
With splendid feathers drest;
He brought them from the Cherokees:
The feathers nodded in the breeze,
And made a gallant crest.

From Indian blood you deem him sprung:
Ah no! he spake the English tongue,
And bore a Soldier's name;
And, when America was free
From battle and from jeopardy,
He cross the ocean came.

With hues of genius on his cheek,
In finest tones the Youth could speak:
—While he was yet a Boy,
The moon, the glory of the sun,
And streams that murmur as they run,
Had been his dearest joy.

He was a lovely Youth! I guess
The panther in the wilderness
Was not so fair as he;
And, when he chose to sport and play,
No dolphin ever was so gay
Upon the tropic sea.

Among the Indians he had fought;
And with him many tales he brought
Of pleasure and of fear;
Such tales as told to any Maid
By such a Youth, in the green shade,
Were perilous to hear.

Ruth

He told of Girls—a happy rout!
Who quit their fold with dance and shout,
Their pleasant Indian Town,
To gather strawberries all day long;
Returning with a choral song
When daylight is gone down.

He spake of plants divine and strange
That every hour their blossoms change,
Ten thousand lovely hues!
With budding, fading, faded flowers
They stand the wonder of the bowers
From morn to evening dews.

He told of the Magnolia, spread
High as a cloud, high over head!
The Cypress and her spire;
—Of flowers that with one scarlet gleam
Cover a hundred leagues, and seem
To set the hills on fire.

The Youth of green savannahs spake,
And many an endless, endless lake,
With all its fairy crowds
Of islands, that together lie
As quietly as spots of sky
Among the evening clouds.

And then he said: "How sweet it were
A fisher or a hunter there,
A gardener in the shade
Still wandering with an easy mind,
To build a household fire, and find
A home in every glade!

"What days, and what sweet years! Ah me!
Our life were life indeed, with thee
So pass'd in quiet bliss;
And all the while," said he, "to know
That we were in a world of woe,
On such an earth as this!"

And then he sometimes interwove
Fond thoughts about a Father's love:
"For there," said he, "are spun
Around the heart such tender ties,
That our own children to our eyes
Are dearer than the sun.

"Sweet Ruth! and could you go with me,
My helpmate in the woods to be,
Our shed at night to rear;
Or run, my own adopted Bride,
A sylvan Huntress at my side,
And drive the flying deer!

"Beloved Ruth!"—No more he said.
The wakeful Ruth at midnight shed
A solitary tear:
She thought again—and did agree
With him to sail across the sea,
And drive the flying deer.

"And now, as fitting is and right,
We in the Church our faith will plight,
A Husband and a Wife."
Even so they did; and I may say
That to sweet Ruth that happy day
Was more than human life.

Through dream and vision did she sink,
Delighted all the while to think,
That on those lonesome floods,
And green savannahs, she should share
His board with lawful joy, and bear
His name in the wild woods.

But, as you have before been told,
This Stripling, sportive, gay, and bold,
And with his dancing crest
So beautiful, through savage lands
Had roam'd about. with vagrant bands
Of Indians in the West.

The wind, the tempest roaring high
The tumult of a tropic sky,
Might well be dangerous food
For him, a Youth to whom was given
So much of earth—so much of Heaven,
And such impetuous blood.

Whatever in those Climes he found
Irregular in sight or sound
Did to his mind impart
A kindred impulse, seem'd allied
To his own powers, and justified
The workings of his heart.

Nor less, to feed voluptuous thought,
The beauteous forms of nature wrought
Fair trees and lovely flowers;
The breezes their own languor lent;
The stars had feelings, which they sent
Into those gorgeous bowers.

Yet, in his worst pursuits, I ween
That sometimes there did intervene
Pure hopes of high intent;
For passions link'd to forms so fair
And stately, needs must have their share
Of noble sentiment.

But ill he lived, much evil saw,
With men to whom no better law
Nor better life was known;
Deliberately, and undeceived,
Those wild men's vices he received,
And gave them back his own.

His genius and his moral frame
Were thus impair'd, and he became
The slave of low desires:
A Man who without self-control
Would seek what the degraded soul
Unworthily admires.

And yet he with no feign'd delight
Had woo'd the Maiden, day and night
Had loved her, night and morn:
What could he less than love a Maid
Whose heart with so much nature play'd?
So kind and so forlorn!

Sometimes, most earnestly, he said,
"O Ruth! I have been worse than dead;
False thoughts, thoughts bold and vain,
Encompass'd me on every side
When first, in confidence and pride,
I cross'd the Atlantic Main.

"It was a fresh and glorious world,
A banner bright that was unfurl'd
Before me suddenly:
I look'd upon those hills and plains,
And seem'd as if let loose from chains,
To live at liberty.

"But wherefore speak of this? For now,
Sweet Ruth! with thee, I know not how,
I feel my spirit burn—
Even as the east when day comes forth,
And to the west, and south, and north,
The morning doth return."

Full soon that purer mind was gone;
No hope, no wish remain'd, not one,—
They stirr'd him now no more;
New objects did new pleasure give,
And once again he wish'd to live
As lawless as before.

Meanwhile, as thus with him it fared,
They for the voyage were prepared,
And went to the sea-shore;
But when they thither came, the Youth
Deserted his poor Bride, and Ruth
Could never find him more.

Ruth

"God help thee, Ruth!"—Such pains she had,
That she in half a year was mad,
And in a prison housed;
And there she sang tumultuous songs,
By recollection of her wrongs
To fearful passion roused.

Yet sometimes milder hours she knew,
Nor wanted sun, nor rain, nor dew,
Nor pastimes of the May,
—They all were with her in her cell;
And a wild brook with cheerful knell
Did o'er the pebbles play.

When Ruth three seasons thus had lain
There came a respite to her pain;—
She from her prison fled;
But of the Vagrant none took thought;
And where it liked her best she sought
Her shelter and her bread.

Among the fields she breathed again
The master-current of her brain
Ran permanent and free;
And, coming to the banks of Tone,
There did she rest, and dwell alone
Under the greenwood tree.

The engines of her pain, the tools
That shaped her sorrow, rocks and pools,
And airs that gently stir
The vernal leaves, she loved them still,
Nor ever tax'd them with the ill
Which had been done to her.

A Barn her *winter* bed supplies;
But, till the warmth of summer skies
And summer days is gone
(And all do in this tale agree),
She sleeps beneath the greenwood tree,
And other home hath none.

An innocent life, yet far astray!
And Ruth will, long before her day,
Be broken down and old:
Sore aches she needs must have! but less
Of mind than body's wretchedness,
From damp, and rain, and cold,

If she is prest by want of food,
She from her dwelling in the wood
Repairs to a road-side;
And there she begs at one steep place,
Where up and down with easy pace
The horsemen-travellers ride.

That oaten Pipe of hers is mute,
Or thrown away; but with a flute
Her loneliness she cheers:
This flute, made of a hemlock stalk,
At evening in his homeward walk
The Quantock Woodman hears.

I, too, have pass'd her on the hills
Setting her little water-mills
By spouts and fountains wild—
Such small machinery as she turn'd
Ere she had wept, ere she had mourn'd,
A young and happy Child!

Farewell! and when thy days are told,
Ill-fated Ruth! in hallow'd mould
Thy corpse shall buried be;
For thee a funeral bell shall ring,
And all the congregation sing
A Christian psalm for thee.

ROBIN HOOD AND GUY OF GISBORNE.*

When shaws beene sheene, and shradds full fayre
  And leaves both large and longe,
Itt is merrye walking in the fayre forrèst
  To heare the small birdes songe.

The woodweele sang, and wold not cease,
  Sitting upon the spraye,
Soe lowde, he awakened Robin Hood,
  In the greenwood where he lay.

"Now by my faye," said jolly Robin,
  "A sweaven I had this night;
I dreamt me of two wighty yemen,
  That fast with me can fight.

" Methought they did me beate and binde,
  And took my bow mee froe;
If I be Robin alive in this lande,
  Ile be wroken on them towe."

* See Appendix.

"Sweavens are swift, master," quoth John,
  "As the wind that blowes ore a hill;
For if itt be never so loude this night,
  To morrow itt may be still."

"Buske yee, bowne yee, my merry men all,
  And John shall goe with mee,
For Ile goe seeke yond wight yeomen,
  In greenwood where the bee."

Then the cast on their gownes of grene,
  And tooke theyr bowes each one;
And they away to the greene forrèst
  A shooting forth are gone.

Until they came to the merry greenwood,
  Where they had gladdest bee,
There were the ware of a wight yeomàn,
  His body leaned to a tree.

A sword and a dagger he wore by his side,
  Of manye a man the bane;
And he was clad in his capull hyde
  Topp and tayll and mayne.

"Stand you still, master," quoth Little John,
  "Under this tree so grene;
And I will go to yond wight yeoman
  To know what he doth meane."

"Ah! John, by me thou settest noe store,
  And that I farley finde:
How offt send I my men beffore,
  And tarry my selfe behinde?

"It is no cunning a knave to ken,
  And a man but heare him speake;
And itt were not for bursting of my bowe,
  John, I thy head would breake."

As often wordes they breeden bale,
  So they parted Robin and John;

And John is gone to Barnesdale :
  The gates he knoweth eche one.

But when he came to Barnesdale,
  Great heaviness there hee hadd,
For he found tow of his owne fellowès
  Were slaine both in a slade.

And Scarlette he was flyinge a-foote
  Fast over stocke and stone,
For the sheriffe with seven score men
  Fast after him is gone.

"One shoote now I will shoote," quoth John,
  "With Christ his might and mayne ;
Ile make yond fellow that flyes soe fast,
  To stopp he shall be fayne."

Then John bent up his long bende-bow,
  And fetteled him to shoote :
The bow was made of a tender boughe,
  And fell downe to his foote.

"Woe worth, woe worth thee, wicked wood,
  That ere thou grew on a tree ;
For now this day thou art my bale,
  My boote when thou shold bee."

His shoote it was but loosely shott,
  Yet flewe not the arrowe in vaine ;
For itt mett one of the sheriffes men,
  Good William a Trent was slaine.

It had bene better of William a Trent
  To have bene abed with sorrowe,
Than to be that day in the green wood slade
  To meet with Little John's arrowe.

But as it is said, when men be mett,
  Fyve can doe more than three,
The sheriffe hath taken Little John,
  And bound him fast to a tree.

"Thou shalt be drawen by dale and downe,
  And hanged hye on a hill."
"But thou mayst fayle of thy purpose,"
  "If itt be Christ his will." [quoth John,

Let us leave talking of Little John,
  And thinke of Robin Hood,
How he is gone to the wight yeomàn,
  Where under the leaves he stood.

"Good morrowe, good fellowe," said Robin
    so fayre,
  "Good morrowe, good fellowe," quoth he :
"Methinkes by this bowe thou beares in thy
  A good archere thou sholdst bee." [hande

"I am wilfull of my waye," quo the yeman,
  "And of my morning tyde."   [Robin ;
"Ile lead thee through the wood," sayd
  "Good fellow, Ile be thy guide."

"I seeke an outlàwe," the straunger sayd,
  "Men call him Robin Hood ;
Rather Ile meet with that proud outlàwe
  Than fortye pound soe good."

"Now come with me thou wighty yeman,
  And Robin thou soone shalt see :
But first let us some pastime find
  Under the greenwood tree.

"First let us some masterye make
  Among the woods so even,
Wee may chance to meet with Robin Hood
  Here att some unsett steven."

They cutt them downe two summer shroggs,
  That grew both under a breere,
And sett them threescore rood in twaine
  To shoot the prickes y-fere.

"Leade on, good fellowe," quoth Robin
"Leade on, I doe bidd thee."   [Hood,
"Nay by my faith, good fellowe," he sayd,
"My leader thou shalt bee."

The first time Robin shot at the pricke,
He mist but an inch it froe:
The yeoman he was an archer good,
But he cold never shoote soe.

The second shoote had the wightye yeoman,
He shote within the garlànde:
But Robin he shot far better than he,
For he clave the good pricke wande.

"A blessing upon thy heart," he sayd;
"Good fellowe, thy shooting is goode;
For an thy hart be as good as thy hand,
Thou wert better than Robin Hoode."

"Now tell me thy name, good fellowe,"
"Under the leaves of lyne."   [sayd he,
"Nay by my faith," quoth bolde Robìn,
"Till thou have told me thine."

"I dwell by dale and downe," quoth he,
"And Robin to take Ime sworn;
And when I am called by my right name
I am Guye of good Gisbòrne."

"My dwelling is in this wood," sayes Robin,
"By thee I set right nought:
I am Robin Hoode of Barnèsdale,
Whom thou so long hast sought."

He that had neither beene kithe nor kin,
Might have seen a full fayre sight,
To see how together these yeomen went
With blades both browne and bright.

To see how these yeomen together they
Two howres of a summers day: [fought

Yett neither Robin Hood nor Sir Guy
  Them fettled to flye away.

Robin was reachles on a roote,
  And stumbled at that tyde;
And Guy was quicke and nimble with-all,
  And hitt him ore the left side.

"Ah, deare lady," sayd Robin Hood, "'thou
  That art both mother and may,'
I think it was never mans destinye
  To dye before his day."

Robin thought on our ladye deere,
  And soone leapt up againe,
And strait he came with a backward stroke,
  And he Sir Guy hath slayne.

He took Sir Guy's head by the hayre,
  And sticked itt on his bowes end:
"Thou hast been a traytor all thy liffe,
  Which thing must have an ende."

Robin pulled forth an Irish kniffe,
  And nicked Sir Guy in the face,
That he was never of woman born.
  Cold tell whose head it was.

Saies "Lye there, lye there, now Sir Guye,
  And with me be not wrothe;   [hand,
If thou have had the worse strokes at my
  Thou shalt have the better clothe."

Robin did off his gowne of greene,
  And on Sir Guy did it throwe;
And he put on that capull hyde,
  That cladd him topp to toe.

"The bowe, the arrowes, and litle horne,
  Now with me I will beare;
For I will away to Barnèsdale,
  To see how my men doe fare."

Robin Hood and Guy of Gisborne   263

Robin Hood sett Guy's horne to his mouth,
   And a loud blast in it did blow,
That beheard the sheriffe of Nottingham,
   As he leaned under a lowe.

"Hearken, hearken," sayd the sheriffe,
   "I heare nowe tydings good,
For yonder I heare Sir Guye's horne blowe,
   And he hath slaine Robin Hoode.

"Yonder I heare Sir Guye's horne blowe,
   Itt blowes soe well in tyde,
And yonder comes that wightye yeoman,
   Cladd in his capull hyde.

"Come hyther, come hyther, thou good Sir [Guye,
   Aske what thou wilt of mee."
"O, I will none of thy gold," sayd Robin,
   "Nor I will none of thy fee:

"But now I've slaine the master," he sayes,
   "Let me goe strike the knave;
This is all the rewarde I aske;
   Nor noe other will I have."

"Thou art a madman," said the sheriffe,
   "Thou sholdest have had a knight's fee:
But seeing thy asking hath beene soe bad,
   Well granted it shale be."

When Litle John heard his master speake,
   Well knewe he it was his steven:
"Now shall I be looset," quoth Litle John,
   "With Christ his might in heaven."

Fast Robin he hyed him to Litle John,
   He thought to loose him belive;
The sheriffe and all his companye
   Fast after him did drive.

"Stand abacke, stand abacke," sayd Robin;
   "Why draw you mee soe neere?

Itt was never the use in our countryè,
  One's shrift another shold heere."

But Robin pulled forth an Irish kniffe,
  And loosed John hand and foote,
And gave him Sir Guy's bow into his hand
  And bade it be his boote.

Then John he tooke Guy's bow in his hand,
  His boltes and arrowes eche one: [bow
When the sheriffe saw Litle John bend his
  He fettled him to be gone.

Towards his house in Nottingham towne
  He fled full fast away;
And soe did all his companye:
  Not one behind wold stay.

But he cold neither runne soe fast,
  Nor away soe fast cold ryde,
But Litle John with an arrowe so broad
  He shott him into the syde.

Robin Hood's Death and Burial

ROBIN HOOD'S DEATH AND BURIAL.*

When Robin Hood and Little John,
  Went o'er yon bank of broom,
Said Robin Hood to Little John,
  " We have shot for many a pound ;

"But I am not able to shoot one shot more,
  My arrows will not flee ;
But I have a cousin lives down below,
  Please God she will bleed me."

* See Appendix.

Now Robin is to fair Kirkley gone,
  As fast as he can win;
But before he came there, as we do hear,
  He was taken very ill.

And when that he came to fair Kirkley-hall,
  He knock'd all at the ring,
But none was so ready as his cousin herself
  For to let bold Robin in.

"Will you please to sit down, cousin Robin," she said,
  "And drink some beer with me?"
"No, I will neither eat nor drink,
  Till I am blooded by thee."

"Well, I have a room, cousin Robin," she said,
  "Which you did never see,
And if you please to walk therein,
  You blooded by me shall be."

She took him by the lilly-white hand,
  And led him to a private room,
And there she blooded bold Robin Hood,
  Whilst one drop of blood would run.

She blooded him in the vein of the arm,
  And locked him up in the room;
There did he bleed all the live-long day,
  Untill the next day at noon.

He then bethought him of a casement door,
  Thinking for to be gone,
He was so weak he could not leap,
  Nor he could not get down,

He then bethought him of his bugle-horn,
    Which hung low down to his knee,
He set his horn unto his mouth,
    And blew out weak blasts three.

Then Little John, when hearing him,
    As he sat under the tree,
" I fear my master is near dead,
    He blows so wearily."

Then Little John to fair Kirkley is gone,
    As fast as he can dree;
But when he came to Kirkley-hall,
    He broke locks two or three:

Untill he came bold Robin to,
    Then he fell on his knee;
" A boon, a boon," cries Little John,
    " Master, I beg of thee."

" What is that boon," quoth Robin Hood,
    " Little John, thou begs of me?"
" It is to burn fair Kirkley hall,
    And all their nunnery."

" Now nay, now nay," quoth Robin Hood,
    " That boon I 'll not grant thee;
I never ' hurt ' woman in all my life,
    Nor man in woman's company.

" I never hurt fair maid in all my time,
    Nor at my end shall it be;
But give me my bent bow in my hand,
    And a broad arrow I 'll let flee;
And where this arrow is taken up,
    There shall my grave digg'd be.

" Lay me a green sod under my head,
    And another at my feet;
And lay my bent bow by my side,

Which was my music sweet;
And make my grave of gravel and green,
Which is most right and meet.

"Let me have length and breadth enough,
With a green sod under my head;
That they may say when I am dead,
Here lies bold Robin Hood."

These words they readily promis'd him,
Which did bold Robin please;
And there they buried bold Robin Hood,
Near to the fair Kirklèys.¹

SIR JAMES THE ROSE.*

Of all the Scottish northern chiefs,
    Of high and warlike name,
The bravest was Sir James the Rose,
    A knight of meikle fame.

His growth was as the tufted fir,
    That crowns the mountain's brow;
And, waving o'er his shoulders broad,
    His locks of yellow flow.

* See Appendix.

The chieftain of the brave clan Ross,
   A firm undaunted band;
Five hundred warriors drew the sword,
   Beneath his high command.

In bloody fight thrice had he stood,
   Against the English keen,
Ere two and twenty opening springs
   This blooming youth had seen.

The fair Matilda dear he loved,
   A maid of beauty rare;
Ev'n Margaret on the Scottish throne
   Was never half so fair.

Lang had he wooed, lang she refused,
   With seeming scorn and pride;
Yet aft her eyes confessed the love
   Her fearful words denied.

At last she blessed his well-tried faith,
   Allowed his tender claim:
She vowed to him her virgin heart,
   And owned an equal flame.

Her father, Buchan's cruel lord,
   Their passion disapproved;
And bade her wed Sir John the Graeme,
   And leave the youth she loved.

At nicht they met, as they were wont,
   Deep in a shady wood,
Where, on a bank beside the burn,
   A blooming saugh-tree stood.

Concealed among the underwood,
   The crafty Donald lay,
The brother of Sir John the Graeme,
   To hear what they would say.

Sir James the Rose

When thus the maid began: "My sire
  Your passion disapproves,
And bids me wed Sir John the Graeme;
  So here must end our loves.

"My father's will must be obeyed;
  Nocht boots me to withstand;
Some fairer maid, in beauty's bloom,
  Must bless thee with her hand.

"Matilda soon shall be forgot,
  And from thy mind effaced:
But may that happiness be thine,
  Which I can never taste."

"What do I hear? Is this thy vow?"
  Sir James the Rose replied:
"And will Matilda wed the Graeme,
  Though sworn to be my bride?

"His sword shall sooner pierce my heart
  Than reave me of thy charms!"
Then clasped her to his beating breast,
  Fast locked into his arms.

"I spake to try thy love," she said:
  "I'll ne'er wed man but thee:
My grave shall be my bridal bed,
  Ere Graeme my husband be.

"Take then, dear youth, this faithful kiss,
  In witness of my troth;
And every plague become my lot,
  That day I break my oath!"

They parted thus: the sun was set:
  Up hasty Donald flies;   [youth!"
And "Turn thee, turn thee, beardless
  He loud insulting cries.

Soon turned about the fearless chief,
    And soon his sword he drew;
For Donald's blade, before his breast,
    Had pierced his tartans through.

"This for my brother's slighted love;
    His wrongs sit on my arm."
Three paces back the youth retired,
    And saved himself frae harm.

Returning swift, his hand he reared
    Frae Donald's head above,
And through the brain and crashing bones
    His sharp-edged weapon drove.

He staggering reeled, then tumbled down,
    A lump of breathless clay:
"So fall my foes!" quoth valiant Rose,
    And stately strode away.

Through the green-wood he quickly hied,
    Unto Lord Buchan's hall;
And at Matilda's window stood,
    And thus began to call:

"Art thou asleep, Matilda dear?
    Awake, my love, awake!
Thy luckless lover on thee calls,
    A long farewell to take.

"For I have slain fierce Donald Graeme;
    His blood is on my sword:
And distant are my faithful men,
    Nor can assist their lord.

"To Skye I'll now direct my way,
    Where my two brothers bide,
And raise the valiant of the Isles
    To combat on my side.'

Sir James the Rose

"O do not so," the maid replies;
  "With me till morning stay;
For dark and dreary is the night,
  And dangerous the way.

"All night I'll watch you in the park;
  My faithful page I'll send,
To run and raise the Ross's clan,
  Their master to defend."

Beneath a bush he laid him down,
  And wrapped him in his plaid;
While, trembling for her lover's fate,
  At distance stood the maid.

Swift ran the page o'er hill and dale,
  Till, in a lowly glen,
He met the furious Sir John Graeme,
  With twenty of his men.

"Where go'st thou, little page?" he said;
  "So late who did thee send?"
"I go to raise the Ross's clan,
  Their master to defend:

"For he hath slain Sir Donald Graeme;
  His blood is on his sword:
And far, far distant are his men,
  That should assist their lord."

"And has he slain my brother dear?"
  The furious Graeme replies:
"Dishonour blast my name, but he
  By me, ere morning dies!

"Tell me where is Sir James the Rose;
  I will thee well reward."
"He sleeps within Lord Buchan's park;
  Matilda is his guard."

They spurred their steeds in furious mood,
    And scoured along the lee;
They reached Lord Buchan's lofty towers
    By dawning of the day.

Matilda stood without the gate;
    To whom the Graeme did say,
"Saw ye Sir James the Rose last night?
    Or did he pass this way?"

"Last day, at noon," Matilda said,
    "Sir James the Rose passed by:
He furious pricked his sweaty steed,
    And onward fast did hye.

"By this he is at Edinburgh,
    If horse and man hold good."
"Your page, then, lied, who said he was
    Now sleeping in the wood."

She wrung her hands, and tore her hair:
    "Brave Rose, thou art betrayed;
And ruined by those means," she cried,
    "From whence I hoped thine aid!"

By this the valiant knight awoke;
    The virgin's shrieks he heard;
And up he rose, and drew his sword,
    When the fierce band appeared.

"Your sword last night my brother slew;
    His blood yet dims its shine:
And, ere the setting of the sun,
    Your blood shall reek on mine."

"You word it well," the chief replied:
    "But deeds approve the man:
Set by your band, and, hand to hand,
    We'll try what valour can.

Sir James the Rose

"Oft boasting hides a coward's heart;
  My weighty sword you fear,
Which shone in front of Flodden-field,
  When you kept in the rear."

With dauntless step he forward strode,
  And dared him to the fight:
Then Graeme gave back and feared his arm;
  For well he knew its might.

Four of his men, the bravest four,
  Sunk down beneath his sword:
But still he scorned the poor revenge,
  And sought their haughty lord.

Behind him basely came the Graeme,
  And pierced him in the side:
Out spouting came the purple tide,
  And all his tartans dyed.

But yet his sword quat not the grip,
  Nor dropt he to the ground,
Till through his enemy's heart his steel
  Had forced a mortal wound.

Graeme, like a tree with wind o'erthrown,
  Fell breathless on the clay;
And down beside him sank the Rose,
  And faint and dying lay.

The sad Matilda saw him fall:
  "Oh, spare his life!" she cried;
"Lord Buchan's daughter begs his life;
  Let her not be denied!"

Her well-known voice the hero heard;
  He raised his death-closed eyes,
And fixed them on the weeping maid,
  And weakly thus replies:

"In vain Matilda begs the life
  By death's arrest denied:
My race is run—adieu, my love "—
  Then closed his eyes and died.

The sword, yet warm, from his left side
  With frantic hand she drew:
"I come, Sir James the Rose," she cried;
  "I come to follow you!"

She leaned the hilt against the ground,
  And bared her snowy breast;
Then fell upon her lover's face,
  And sunk to endless rest.

THE CLERK'S TWA SONS
O' OWSENFORD.*

O I will sing to you a sang,
  Will grieve your heart full sair;
How the Clerk's twa sons o' Owsenford
  Have to learn some unco lear.

They hadna been in fair Parish
  A twelvemonth and a day,
Till the Clerk's twa sons fell deep in love
  Wi' the Mayor's dauchters twae.

* See Appendix.

The Clerk's Twa Sons

And aye as the twa clerks sat and wrote,
    The ladies sewed and sang;
There was mair mirth in that chamber,
    Than in a' fair Ferrol's land.

But word 's gane to the michty Mayor,
    As he sailed on the sea,
That the Clerk's twa sons made licht lemans
    O' his fair dauchters twae.

"If they hae wranged my twa dauchters,
    Janet and Marjorie,
The morn, ere I taste meat or drink,
    Hie hangit they shall be."

And word 's gane to the Clerk himself,
    As he was drinking wine,
That his twa sons at fair Parish
    Were bound in prison strang.

Then up and spak the Clerk's ladye,
    And she spak tenderlie:
"O tak wi' ye a purse o' gowd,
    Or even tak ye three;
And if ye canna get William,
    Bring Henry hame to me."

O sweetly sang the nightingale,
    As she sat on the wand;
But sair, sair mourned Owsenford,
    As he gaed in the strand.

When he came to their prison strang,
    He rade it round about,
And at a little shot-window,
    His sons were looking out.

"O lie ye there, my sons," he said,
    "For owsen or for kye?
Or what is it that ye lie for,
    Sae sair bound as ye lie?"

The Clerk's Twa Sons

"We lie not here for owsen, father;
  Nor yet do we for kye;
But it 's for a little o' dear-boucht love,
  Sae sair bound as we lie.

"Oh, borrow us, borrow us, father," they
  "For the luve we bear to thee!"   [said,
"O never fear, my pretty sons,
  Weel borrowed ye sall be."

Then he 's gane to the michty Mayor,
  And he spak courteouslie:
"Will ye grant my twa sons' lives,
  Either for gold or fee?
Or will ye be sae gude a man,
  As grant them baith to me?"

"I 'll no grant ye your twa sons' lives,
  Neither for gold nor fee;
Nor will I be sae gude a man,
  As gie them baith to thee;
But before the morn at twal o'clock,
  Ye 'll see them hangit hie!"

Ben it came the Mayor's dauchters,
  Wi' kirtle coat, alone;
Their eyes did sparkle like the gold,
  As they tripped on the stone.

"Will ye gie us our loves, father,
  For gold, or yet for fee?
Or will ye take our own sweet lives
  And let our true loves be?"

He 's taen a whip into his hand,
  And lashed them wondrous sair:
"Gae to your bowers, ye vile limmers;
  Ye 'se never see them mair."

The Clerk's Twa Sons

Then out it speaks auld Owsenford,
    A sorry man was he:
"Gang to your bouirs, ye lilye flouirs;
    For a' this maunna be."

Then out it speaks him Hynde Henry:
    "Come here, Janet, to me;
Will ye gie me my faith and troth,
    And love, as I gae thee?"

"Ye sall hae your faith and troth,
    Wi' God's blessing and mine."
And twenty times she kissed his mouth,
    Her father looking on.

Then out it speaks him gay William:
    "Come here, sweet Marjorie;
Will ye gie me my faith and troth,
    And love, as I gae thee?"

"Yes, ye sall hae your faith and troth,
    Wi' God's blessing and mine."
And twenty times she kissed his mouth,
    Her father looking on.

"O ye 'll take aff your twa black hats,
    Lay them down on a stone,
That nane may ken that ye are clerks,
    Till ye are putten doun."

The bonnie clerks they died that morn;
    Their loves died lang ere noon;
And the waefu' Clerk o' Owsenford
    To his lady has gane hame.

His lady sat on her castle wa',
    Beholding dale and doun;
And there she saw her ain gude lord
    Come walking to the toun.

The Clerk's Twa Sons

"Ye 're welcome hame, my ain gude lord,
    Ye 're welcome hame to me;
But where-away are my twa sons?
    Ye suld hae brought them wi' ye."

"O they are putten to a deeper lear,
    And to a higher scule:
Your ain twa sons will no be hame
    Till the hallow days o' Yule."

"Oh sorrow, sorrow, come mak my bed;
    And, dule, come lay me doun;
For I will neither eat nor drink,
    Nor set a fit on groun'!"

The hallow days o' Yule were come,
    And the nights were lang and mirk,
When in and cam her ain twa sons,
    And their hats made o' the birk.

It neither grew in syke nor ditch,
    Nor yet in ony sheuch;
But at the gates o' Paradise
    That birk grew fair eneuch.

"Blow up the fire, now, maidens mine,
    Bring water from the well;
For a' my house shall feast this night,
    Since my twa sons are well.

"O eat and drink, my merry-men a',
    The better shall ye fare;
For my two sons they are come hame
    To me for evermair."

And she has gane and made their bed,
    She 's made it saft and fine;
And she 's happit them wi' her gay mantil,
    Because they were her ain.

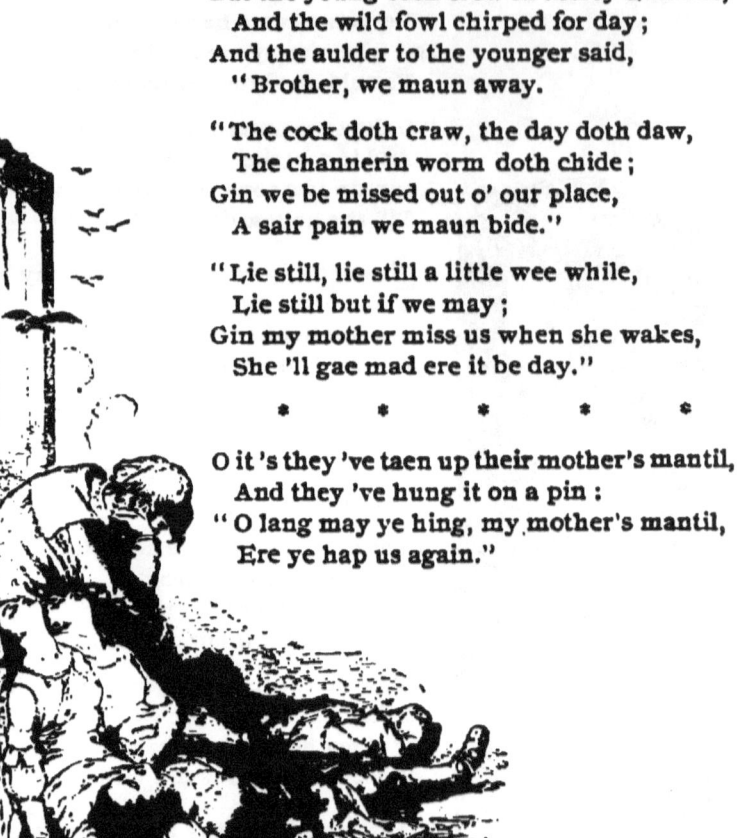

But the young cock crew in merry Linkum,
  And the wild fowl chirped for day;
And the aulder to the younger said,
  "Brother, we maun away.

"The cock doth craw, the day doth daw,
  The channerin worm doth chide;
Gin we be missed out o' our place,
  A sair pain we maun bide."

"Lie still, lie still a little wee while,
  Lie still but if we may;
Gin my mother miss us when she wakes,
  She 'll gae mad ere it be day."

   *   *   *   *   *

O it's they've taen up their mother's mantil,
  And they've hung it on a pin:
"O lang may ye hing, my mother's mantil,
  Ere ye hap us again."

SIR ANDREW BARTON.*

When Flora with her fragrant
   flowers
  Bedeckt the earth so trim and
    gaye,
And Neptune with his daintye
   showers,
  Came to present the monthe
    of Maye:
King Henrye rode to take the
   ayre,
  Over the river of Thames past
    hee;
When eighty merchants of Lon-
   don came,
  And downe they knelt upon
    their knee.

* See Appendix.

"O yee are welcome, rich merchànts;
  Good saylors, welcome unto mee." [good,
They swore by the rood, they were saylors
  But rich merchànts they cold not bee:
"To France nor Flanders dare we pass:
  Nor Bourdeaux voyage dare we fare;
And all for a rover that lyes on the seas,
  Who robbs us of our merchant ware."

King Henrye frownd, and turned him rounde,
  And swore by the Lord, that was mickle of might,
"I thought he had not beene in the world,
  Durst have wrought England such unright."
The merchants sighed, and said, "Alas!"
  And thus they did their answer frame,
"He is a proud Scott, that robbs on the seas,
  And Sir Andrew Barton is his name."

The king lookt over his left shouldèr,
  And an angrye look then looked hee:
"Have I never a lorde in all my realme,
  Will feitch yond traytor unto mee?"
"Yea, that dare I"; Lord Howard sayes;
  "Yea, that dare I with heart and hand;
If it please your grace to give me leave,
  Myselfe wil be the only man."

"Thou art but yong"; the kyng replyed:
  "Yond Scott hath numbred manye a yeare."
"Trust me, my liege, Ile make him quail,
  Or before my prince I will never appeare."
"Then bowemen and gunners thou shalt have
  And chuse them over my realme so free;
Besides good mariners, and shipp-boyes,
  To guide the great shipp on the sea."

The first man, that Lord Howard chose,
   Was the ablest gunner in all the realm,
Thoughe he was threescore yeeres and ten;
   Good Peter Simon was his name.
"Peter," sais hee, "I must to the sea,
   To bring home a traytor live or dead:
Before all others I have chosen thee;
   Of a hundred gunners to be the head."

"If you, my lord, have chosen mee
   Of a hundred gunners to be the head,
Then hang me up on your maine-mast tree,
   If I misse my marke one shilling bread."
My lord then chose a boweman rare,
   Whose active hands had gained fame;
In Yorkshire was this gentleman borne,
   And William Horseley was his name.

"Horseley," sayd he, "I must with speede
   Go seeke a traytor on the sea;
And now of a hundred bowemen brave,
   To be the head I have chosen thee."
"If you," quoth hee, "have chosen mee
   Of a hundred bowemen to be the head;
On your main-màst Ile hanged bee,
   If I miss twelvescore one penny bread."

With pikes and gunnes, and bowemen bold,
   This noble Howard is gone to the sea;
With a valyant heart and a pleasant cheare,
   Out at Thames mouth sayled he.
And days he scant had sayled three,
   Upon the "voyage," he tooke in hand,
But there he mett with a noble shipp,
   And stoutely made itt stay and stand.

"Thou must tell me," Lord Howard said,
   "Now who thou art, and what's thy name;

And shewe me where thy dwelling is:
  And whither bound, and whence thou came."
"My name is Henry Hunt," quoth hee,
  With a heavye heart, and a carefull mind;
"I and my shipp doe both belong
  To the Newcastle, that stands upon Tyne."

"Hast thou not heard, nowe, Henry Hunt,
  As thou hast sayled by daye and by night,
Of a Scottish rover on the seas;
  Men call him Sir Andrew Barton, knight?"
Then ever he sighed, and sayd, "Alas!
  With a grieved mind, and well away!
But over-well I knowe that wight,
  I was his prisoner yesterday.

"As I was sayling upon the sea,
  A Burdeaux voyage for to fare;
To his hachborde he clasped me,
  And robd me of all my merchant ware;
And mickle debts, God wot, I owe,
  And every man will have his owne;
And I am nowe to London bounde,
  Of our gracious king to beg a boone."

"That shall not need," Lord Howard sais;
  "Lett me but once that robber see,
For every penny tane thee froe
  It shall be doubled shillings three."
"Nowe God forefend," the merchant said,
  "That you shold seek soe far amisse!
God keepe you out of that traitor's hands!
  Full litle ye wott what a man hee is.

"Hee is brasse within, and steele without,
  With beames on his topcastle stronge;
And eighteen pieces of ordinance
  He carries on each side along:

And he hath a pinnace deerlye dight,
  St. Andrew's crosse that is his guide;
His pinnace beareth ninescore men,
  And fifteen canons on each side.

"Were ye twentye shippes, and he but one,
  I sweare by kirke, and bower, and hall;
He wold overcome them everye one,
  If once his beames they doe downe fall."
"This is cold comfort," sais my lord,
  "To wellcome a stranger thus to the sea:
Yet Ile bring him and his shipp to shore,
  Or to Scottland hee shall carrye mee."

"Then a noble gunner you must have,
  And he must aim well with his ee,
And sinke his pinnace into the sea,
  Or else hee never orecome will bee:
And if you chance his shipp to borde,
  This counsel I must give withall,
Let no man to his topcastle goe
  To strive to let his beams downe fall.

"And seven pieces of ordinance,
  I pray your honour lend to mee,
On each side of my shipp along,
  And I will lead you on the sea.
A glasse Ile sett, that may be seene,
  Whether you sayle by day or night:
And to-morrowe, I sweare, by nine of the
    clocke,
  You shall meet with Sir Andrew Barton,
    knight."

The merchant sett my lorde a glasse
  Soe well apparent in his sight,
And on the morrowe, by nine of the clocke,
  He shewed him Sir Andrew Barton, knight.

His hacheborde it was "gilt" with gold,
   Soe deerlye dight it dazzled the ee:
"Nowe by my faith," Lord Howard sais,
   "This is a gallant sight to see.

"Take in your ancyents, standards eke,
   So close that no man may them see;
And put me forth a white willowe wand,
   As merchants used to sayle the sea."
But they stirred neither top, nor mast;
   Stoutly they past Sir Andrew by.
"What English churles are yonder," he sayd,
   "That can soe litle curtesye?"

"Nowe by the roode, three yeares and more
   I have beene admirall over the sea;
And never an English nor Portingall
   Without my leave can passe this way."
Then called he forth his stout pinnace;
   "Fetch backe yond pedlars nowe to mee:
I sweare by the masse, yon English churls
   Shall all hang att my maine-mast tree."

With that the pinnace itt shott off,
   Full well Lord Howard might it ken;
For itt stroke down my lord's fore mast,
   And killed fourteen of his men.
"Come hither, Simon," sayes my lord.
   "Looke that thy word be true, thou said;
For at my maine-mast thou shalt hang,
   If thou misse thy marke one shilling bread."

Simon was old, but his heart itt was bold.
   His ordinance he laid right lowe;
He put in chaine full nine yardes long,
   With other great shott lesse and moe;
And he lette goe his great gunnes shott:
   Soe well he settled it with his ee,

Sir Andrew Barton

The first sight that Sir Andrew sawe,
 He see his pinnace sunke in the sea.
And when he saw his pinnace sunke,
 Lord, how his heart with rage did swell!
"Nowe cutt my ropes, itt is time to be gon;
 Ile fetch yond pedlars backe mysell."
When my Lord sawe Sir Andrew loose,
 Within his heart hee was full faine:
"Nowe spread your ancyents, strike up drummes,
 Sound all your trumpetts out amaine."

"Fight on, my men," Sir Andrew sais,
 "Weale howsoever this geere will sway;
Itt is my lord admirall of Englànd,
 Is come to seek mee on the sea."
Simon had a sonne, who shott right well,
 That did Sir Andrew mickle scare;
In att his decke he gave a shott,
 Killed threescore of his men of warre.

Then Henry Hunt with rigour hott
 Came bravely on the other side,
Soone he drove down his fore-mast tree,
 And killed fourscore men beside.
"Nowe, out alas!" Sir Andrew cryed,
 "What may a man now thinke, or say?
Yonder merchant theefe, that pierceth mee,
 He was my prisoner yesterday.

"Come hither to me, thou Gordon good,
 That aye wast readye att my call;
I will give thee three hundred markes,
 If thou wilt let my beames downe fall."
Lord Howard hee then calld in haste,
 "Horseley, see thou be true in stead;
For thou shalt at the maine-mast hang,
 If thou misse twelvescore one penny breed."

Then Gordon swarved the maine-mast tree,
  He swarved it with might and maine;
But Horseley with a bearing arrowe,
  Stroke the Gordon through the braine;
And he fell unto the haches again,
  And sore his deadlye wounde did bleede:
Then word went through Sir Andrew's men,
  How that the Gordon hee was dead.

"Come hither to mee, James Hambilton,
  Thou art my only sister's sonne,
If thou wilt let my beames downe fall,
  Six hundred nobles thou hast wonne."
With that he swarved the maine-mast tree,
  He swarved it with nimble art;
But Horseley with a broad arrowe
  Pierced the Hambilton thorough the heart:

And downe he fell upon the deck,
  That with his blood did streame amaine:
Then every Scott cryed, "Well-away!
  Alas, a comelye youth is slaine!"
All woe begone was Sir Andrew then,
  With griefe and rage his heart did swell:
"Go fetch me forth my armour of proofe,
  For I will to the topcastle mysell.

"Goe fetch me forth my armour of proofe;
  That gilded is with gold soe cleare:
God be with my brother John of Barton!
  Against the Portingalls hee it ware;
And when he had on this armour of proofe,
  He was a gallant sight to see:
Ah! nere didst thou meet with living wight,
  My deere brother, could cope with thee."

Sir Andrew Barton

"Come hither, Horseley," sayes my lord,
  "And looke your shaft that itt goe right,
Shoot a good shoote in time of need,
  And for it thou shalt be made a knight."
"Ile shoot my best," quoth Horseley then,
  "Your honour shall see, with might and
    maine:
But if I were hanged at your maine-mast,
  I have now left but arrowes twaine."

Sir Andrew he did swarve the tree,
  With right good will he swarved then:
Upon his breast did Horseley hitt,
  But the arrow bounded back agen.
Then Horseley spyed a privye place
  With a perfect eye in a secrette part;
Under the spole of his right arme
  He smote Sir Andrew to the heart.

"Fight on, my men," Sir Andrew sayes,
  "A little Ime hurt, but yett not slaine;
Ile but lye downe and bleede a while,
  And then Ile rise and fight againe.
Fight on, my men," Sir Andrew sayes,
  "And never flinche before the foe;
And stand fast by St. Andrew's crosse
  Untill you heare my whistle blowe."

They never heard his whistle blow,
  Which made their hearts waxe sore adread.
Then Horseley said, "Aboard, my lord,
  For well I wott Sir Andrew 's dead."
They boarded then his noble shipp,
  They boarded it with might and maine;
Eighteen score Scotts alive they found,
  The rest were either maim'd or slaine.

Lord Howard tooke a sword in hand,
   And off he smote Sir Andrew's head,
"I must have left England many a daye,
   If thou wert alive as thou art dead."
He caused his body to be cast
   Over the hatchbord into the sea,
And about his middle three hundred crownes:
   "Wherever thou land this will bury thee."

Thus from the warres Lord Howard came,
   And backe he sayled ore the maine,
With mickle joy and triumphing
   Into Thames mouth he came againe.
Lord Howard then a letter wrote,
   And sealed it with seale and ring;
"Such a noble prize have I brought to your grace
   As never did subject to a king:

"Sir Andrew's shipp I bring with mee;
   A braver shipp was never none:
Nowe hath your grace two shipps of warr,
   Before in England was but one."
King Henryes grace with royall cheere
   Welcomed the noble Howard home,
"And where," said he, "is the rover stout,
   That I myselfe may give the doome?"

"The rover, he is safe, my leige,
   Full many a fadom in the sea;
If he were alive as he is dead,
   I must have left England many a day:
And your grace may thank four men i' the ship
   For the victory wee have wonne,
These are William Horseley, Henry Hunt,
   And Peter Simon, and his sonne."

To Henry Hunt, the king then sayd,
  "In lieu of what was from thee tane,
A noble a day now thou shalt have,
  Sir Andrew's jewels and his chayne.
And Horseley thou shalt be a knight,
  And lands and livings shalt have store;
Howard shall be Erle Surrye hight,
  As Howards erst have beene before.

"Nowe, Peter Simon, thou art old,
  I will maintaine thee and thy sonne:
And the men shall have five hundred markes
  For the good service they have done."
Then in came the queene with ladyes fair
  To see Sir Andrew Barton, knight;
They weend that hee were brought on shore,
  And thought to have seen a gallant sight.

But when they see his deadlye face,
  And eyes soe hollow in his head,
"I wold give," quoth the king, "a thousand markes,
  This man were alive as hee is dead:
Yett for the manfull part hee playd,
  Which fought soe well with heart and hand,
His men shall have twelvepence a day,
  Till they come to my brother kings high land."

FRENNET HALL.*

When Frennet's Castle ivied walls
 Through yellow leaves were seen;
When birds forsook the sapless boughs,
 And bees the faded green;

* See Appendix.

Then Lady Frennet, vengefu' dame,
  Did wander frae the ha',
To the wide forest's dewie gloom,
  Among the leaves that fa'.

Her page, the swiftest of her train,
  Had clumb a lofty tree,
Whase branches to the angry blast
  Were soughing mournfullie.

He turn'd his een towards the path
  That near the castle lay,
Where good Lord John and Rothiemay
  Were riding down the brae.

Swift darts the eagle through the sky,
  When prey beneath is seen:
As quickly he forgot his hold,
  And perch'd upon the green.

"O hie thee, hie thee, lady gay,
  Frae this dark wood awa'!
Some visitors of gallant mein
  Are hasting to the ha'."

Then round she row'd her silken plaid,
  Her feet she did na spare,
Until she left the forest's skirts
  A long bow-shot and mair.

"O where, O where, my good Lord John,
  O tell me where ye ride?

Within my castle-wall this nicht
  I hope ye mean to bide.

" Kind nobles, will ye but alicht,
  In yonder bower to stay,
Soft ease shall teach you to forget
  The hardness of the way."

" Forbear entreaty, gentle dame,
  How can we here remain?
Full well you know your husband deir
  Was by our father slain:

" The thoughts of which with fell revenge,
  Within your bosom swell:
Enraged you 've sworn that blood for blood
  Should this black passion quell."

" O fear not, fear not, good Lord John,
  That I will you betray,
Or sue requital for a debt
  Which Nature cannot pay.

" Bear witness a' ye powers on high!
  Ye lichts that 'gin to shine!
This nicht shall prove the sacred cord
  That knits your faith and mine."

The lady slie, with honey'd words,
  Enticed the youths to stay;
But morning sun ne'er shone upon
  Lord John and Rothiemay.

KING ESTMERE.*

Hearken to me, gentlemen,
   Come and you shall heare;
Ile tell you of two of the boldest brethren
   That ever borne y-were.

The tone of them was Adler younge,
   The tother was King Estmere;
They were as bolde men in their deeds,
   As any were farr and neare.

* See Appendix.

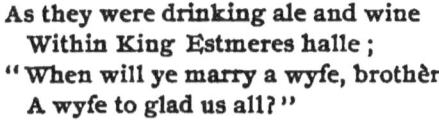

As they were drinking ale and wine
  Within King Estmeres halle;
"When will ye marry a wyfe, brothèr,
  A wyfe to glad us all?"

Then bespake him King Estmere,
  And answered him hastilee:
"I know not that ladye in any land
  That 's able to marrye with mee."

"King Adland hath a daughter, brother,
  Men call her bright and sheene;
If I were king here in your stead,
  That ladye shold be my queene."

Saies, "Reade me, reade me, deare brother,
  Throughout merry Englànd,
Where we might find a messenger,
  Betwixt us towe to sende."

Saies, "You shal ryde yourselfe, brothèr,
  Ile beare you companye;
Many throughe fals messengers are deceived,
  And I feare lest soe shold wee."

Thus the renisht them to ryde
  Of twoe good renisht steeds,
And when they came to King Adlands halle,
  Of redd gold shone their weeds.

And when they came to King Adlands hall,
  Before the goodlye gate,
There they found good King Adlànd
  Rearing himselfe thereatt.

"Now Christ thee save, good King Adlànd;
  Now Christ you save and see,"
Sayd, "You be welcome, King Estmere,
  Right hartilye to mee."

"You have a daughter," said Adler younge,
　"Men call her bright and sheene,
My brother wold marrye her to his wiffe,
　Of Englande to be queene."

"Yesterday was att my deere daughter
　Syr Bremor the Kyng of Spayne;
And then she nicked him of naye,
　And I doubt sheele do you the same."

"The King of Spayne is a foule paynim,
　And 'leeveth on Mahound;
And pitye it were that fayre ladyè
　Shold marrye a heathen hound.

"But grant to me," sayes King Estmere,
　"For my love I you praye;
That I may see your daughter deere,
　Before I goe hence awaye."

"Although itt is seven yeers and more
　Since my daughter was in halle,
She shall come once downe for your sake,
　To glad my guestès alle."

Downe then came that mayden fayre,
　With ladyes laced in pall,
And halfe a hundred of bold knightes,
　To bring her from bowre to hall;
And as many gentle squiers,
　To tend upon them all.

The talents of golde were on her head sette,
　Hanged low downe to her knee;
And everye ring on her small fingèr
　Shone of the chrystall free.

Saies, "God you save, my deere madàm";
　Saies, "God you save and see."
Said, "You be welcome, King Estmere,
　Right welcome unto mee.

King Estmere

"And if you love me as you saye,
  Soe well and hartilèe,
All that ever you are comen about
  Soone sped now itt shal be."

Then bespake her father deare:
  "My daughter, I saye naye;
Remember well the King of Spayne,
  What he sayd yesterdaye.

"He would pull downe my halles and
  And reave me of my lyfe,   [castles,
I cannot blame him if he doe,
  If I reave him of his wyfe."

"Your castles and your towres, father,
  Are stronglye built aboute;
And therefore of the King of Spayne
  Wee neede not stande in doubt.

"Plight me your troth, nowe, King Estmère,
  By heaven and your righte hand,
That you will marrye me to your wyfe,
  And make me queene of your land."

Then King Estmere he plight his troth
  By heaven and his righte hand,
That he wolde marrye her to his wyfe,
  And make her queene of his land.

And he tooke leave of that ladye fayre,
  To goe to his owne countree,
To fetche him dukes and lordes and knightes,
  That married they might bee.

They had not ridden scant a myle,
  A myle forthe of the towne,
But in did come the King of Spayne,
  With kempès many a one.

But in did come the King of Spayne,
　With manye a bold baròne,
Tone day to marrye King Adlands daughter,
　Tother daye to carrye her home.

Shee sent one after King Estmère
　In all the spede might bee,
That he must either turne againe and fighte,
　Or goe home and loose his ladyè.

One whyle then the page he went,
　Another while he ranne;
Till he had oretaken King Estmere,
　I wis, he never blanne.

"Tydings, tydings, King Estmere!"
"What tydinges nowe, my boye?"
"O tydinges I can tell to you,
　That will you sore annoye.

"You had not ridden scant a mile,
　A mile out of the towne,
But in did come the King of Spayne
　With kempès many a one:

"But in did come the King of Spayne,
　With manye a bolde baròne,
Tone daye to marrye King Adlands daughter,
　Tother daye to carry her home.

"My ladye fayre she greetes you well,
　And ever-more well by mee:
You must either turne againe and fighte,
　Or goe home and loose your ladyè."

Saies, "Reade me, reade me, deere brothèr,
　My reade shall rise at thee,
Whether it is better to turne and fighte,
　Or go home and loose my ladye."

"Now hearken to me," sayes Adler younge,
  "And your reade must rise at me,
I quicklye will devise a waye
  To sette thy ladye free.

"My mother was a westerne woman,
  And learned in gramaryè,
And when I learned at the schole,
  Something shee taught itt mee.

"There growes an hearbe within this field,
  And iff it were but knowne,
His color, which is whyte and redd,
  It will make blacke and browne:

"His color, which is browne and blacke,
  Itt will make redd and whyte;
That sworde is not in all Englande,
  Upon his coate will byte.

"And you shal be a harper, brother,
  Out of the north countrye;
And Ile be your boy, soe faine of fighte,
  And beare your harpe by your knee.

"And you shal be the best harpèr,
  That ever tooke harpe in hand;
And I wil be the best singèr
  That ever sung in this lande.

"Itt shal be written in our forheads
  All and in gramaryè,
That we towe are the boldest men
  That are in all Christentyè."

And thus they renisht them to ryde,
  On tow good renish steedes;
And whan they came to King Adlands hall,
  Of redd gold shone their weedes.

And whan they came to King Adlands hall,
　Untill the fayre hall yate,
There they found a proud portèr
　Rearing himselfe thereatt.

Saies, "Christ thee save, thou proud portèr";
　Saies, "Christ thee save and see."
'Now you be welcome," sayd the portèr,
　"Of what land soever ye bee."

"Wee beene harpers," sayd Adler younge,
　"Come out of the northe countrye;
Wee beene come hither untill this place,
　This proud weddinge for to see."

Sayd, "And your color were white and redd,
　As it is blacke and browne,
I wold saye King Estmere and his brother,
　Were comen untill this towne."

Then they pulled out a ryng of gold,
　Layd itt on the porters arme:
"And ever we will thee, proud portèr,
　Thow wilt saye us no harme."

Sore he looked on King Estmère,
　And sore he handled the ryng,
Then opened to them the fayre hall yates,
　He lett for no kind of thyng.

King Estmere he stabled his steede
　Soe fayre att the hall bord;
The froth, that came from his brydle bitte,
　Light on King Bremors beard.

Saies, "Stable thy steed, thou proud harpèr,"
　Saies, "Stable him in the stalle:
It doth not beseeme a proud harpèr
　To stable him in a kings halle."

King Estmere 305

"My ladde he is so lither," he said,
 "He will doe nought that's meete;
And is there any man in this hall
 Were able him to beate?"

"Thou speakst proud words," sayes the King
 "Thou harper, here to mee: [of Spayne,
There is a man within this halle
 Will beate thy ladde and thee."

"O let that man come downe," he said,
 A sight of him wold I see;
And when hee hath beaten well my ladde,
 Then he shall beate of mee."

Downe then came the kemperye man,
 And looked him in the eare;
For all the gold that was under heaven,
 He durst not neigh him neare.

"And how nowe, kempe," said the King of
 "How nowe, what aileth thee?" [Spayne,
He saies, "It is writt in his forhead
 All and in gramaryè,
That for all the gold that is under heaven,
 I dare not neigh him nye."

Then King Estmere pulld forth his harpe,
 And playd a pretty thinge:
The ladye upstart from the borde,
 And wold have gone from the king.

"Stay thy harpe, thou proud harpèr,
 For Gods love I pray thee,
For and thou playes as thou beginns,
 Thou 'lt till my bryde from mee."

He stroake upon his harpe againe,
 And playd a pretty thinge;
The ladye lough a loud laughter,
 As shee sate by the king.

King Estmere

Saies, "Sell me thy harpe, thou proud harper,
 And thy stringès all,
For as many gold nobles thou shalt have
 As heere bee ringes in the hall."

"What wold ye doe with my harpe," he sayd,
 "If I did sell it yee?"
"To playe my wiffe and me a Fitt,
 When abed together wee be."

"Now sell me," quoth hee, "thy bryde so gay,
 As shee sitts by thy knee,
And as many gold nobles I will give
 As leaves been on a tree."

"And what wold ye doe with my bryde soe
 Iff I did sell her thee?"   [gay,
"More seemelye it is for her fayre bodye
 To lye by mee then thee."

Hee playd agayne both loud and shrille,
 And Adler he did sing,
"O ladye, this is thy owne true love;
 Noe harper, but a king.

"O ladye, this is thy owne true love,
 As playnlye thou mayest see;
And Ile rid thee of that foule paynim,
 Who partes thy love and thee."

The ladye looked, the ladye blushte,
 And blushte and lookt agayne,
While Adler he hath drawne his brande,
 And hath the Sowdan slayne.

Up then rose the kemperye men,
 And loud they gan to crye:
"Ah! traytors, yee have slayne our king,
 And therefore yee shall dye."

King Estmere

King Estmere threwe the harpe asyde,
    And swith he drew his brand;
And Estmere he, and Adler younge,
    Right stiffe in stour can stand.

And aye their swords soe sore can byte,
    Through help of gramaryè,   [men,
That soone they have slayne the kempery
    Or forst them forth to flee.

King Estmere tooke that fayre ladyè,
    And marryed her to his wiffe,
And brought her home to merry Englànd,
    With her to leade his life.

THE CRUEL SISTER.*

There were two sisters sat in a bour;
  Binnorie, O Binnorie;
There came a knight to be their wooer;
  By the bonny mill-dams of Binnorie.

* See Appendix.

The Cruel Sister

He courted the eldest with glove and ring,
But he lo'ed the youngest abune a' thing;

He courted the eldest with broach and knife,
But he lo'ed the youngest abune his life;

The eldest she was vexed sair,
And sore envied her sister fair;

The eldest said to the youngest ane,
"Will ye go and see our father's ships come
    in?"—

She's ta'en her by the lily hand,
And led her down to the river strand;

The youngest stude upon a stane,
The eldest came and push'd her in;

She took her by the middle sma',
And dash'd her bonny back to the jaw;

"O sister, sister, reach your hand,
And ye shall be heir of half my land."—

"O sister, I'll not reach my hand,
And I'll be heir of all your land;

"Shame fa' the hand that I should take,
It's twin'n me, and my world's make."—

"O sister, reach me but your glove,
And sweet William shall be your love."—

"Sink on, nor hope for hand or glove!
And sweet William shall better be my love;

"Your cherry cheeks and your yellow hair,
Garr'd me gang maiden evermair."—

The Cruel Sister

Sometimes she sunk, and sometimes she swam,
Until she cam to the miller's dam;

"Oh father, father, draw your dam!
There 's either a mermaid, or a milk-white swan."—

The miller hasted and drew his dam,
And there he found a drown'd woman;

You could not see her yellow hair,
For gowd and pearls that were so rare;

You could not see her middle sma',
Her gowden girdle was sae bra';

A famous harper passing by,
The sweet pale face he chanced to spy;

And when he look'd that lady on,
He sigh'd and made a heavy moan;

He made a harp of her breast-bone,
Whose sounds would melt a heart of stone;

The strings he fram'd of her yellow hair,
Whose notes made sad the list'ning ear;

He brought it to her father's hall,
And there was the court assembled all;

He laid his harp upon a stone,
And straight it began to play alone;

"Oh yonder sits my father, the king,
And yonder sits my mother the queen;

"And yonder stands my brother Hugh,
And by him my William, sweet and true."—

But the last tune that the harp play'd then,
  Binnorie, O Binnorie;
Was—"Woe to my sister, false Helen!"—
  By the bonny mill-dams of Binnorie.

FAIR HELEN.*

PART FIRST.

O! sweetest sweet, and fairest fair,
Of birth and worth beyond compare.
Thou art the causer of my care,
  Since first I loved thee.

* See Appendix.

Yet God hath given to me a mind,
The which to thee shall prove as kind
As any one that thou shalt find
   Of high or low degree.

The shallowest water makes maist din,
The deadest pool, the deepest linn;
The richest man least truth within,
   Though he preferred be.

Yet, nevertheless, I am content,
And never a whit my love repent,
But think the time was a' weel spent,
   Though I disdained be.

O! Helen sweet, and maist complete,
My captive spirit 's at thy feet!
Thinks thou still fit thus for to treat
   Thy captive cruelly?

O! Helen brave! but this I crave,
Of thy poor slave some pity have,
And do him save that 's near his grave,
   And dies for love of thee.

PART SECOND.

I wish I were where Helen lies,
Night and day on me she cries;
O that I were where Helen lies,
   On fair Kirconnell Lee!

Curst be the heart that thought the thought,
And curst the hand that fired the shot,
When in my arms burd Helen dropt,
   And died to succour me!

O think na ye my heart was sair,   [mair!
When my love dropt down and spak nae
There did she swoon wi' meikle care,
   On fair Kirconnell Lee.

Fair Helen

As I went down the water side,
None but my foe to be my guide,
None but my foe to be my guide,
   On fair Kirconnell Lee;

I lighted down my sword to draw,
I hacked him in pieces sma',
I hacked him in pieces sma',
   For her sake that died for me.

O Helen fair, beyond compare!
I 'll make a garland of thy hair,
Shall bind my heart for evermair,
   Until the day I die.

O that I were where Helen lies!
Night and day on me she cries;
Out of my bed she bids me rise,
   Says, "Haste and come to me!"—

O Helen fair! O Helen chaste!
If I were with thee, I were blest,
Where thou lies low, and takes thy rest,
   On fair Kirconnell Lee.

I wish my grave were growing green,
A winding-sheet drawn ower my een,
And I in Helen's arms lying,
   On fair Kirconnell Lee.

I wish I were where Helen lies!
Night and day on me she cries;
And I am weary of the skies,
   For her sake that died for me.

THE LUCK OF EDEN-HALL.*

On Eden's wild romantic bowers,
　The summer moonbeams sweetly fall,
And tint with yellow light the towers—
　The stately towers of Eden-Hall.

* See Appendix.

There, lonely in the deepening night,
  A lady at her lattice sits,
And trims her taper's wavering light,
  And tunes her idle lute by fits.

But little can her idle lute,
  Beguyle the weary moments now;
And little seems the lay to suit
  Her wistful eye and anxious brow.

For, as the chord her finger sweeps,
  Oft-times she checks her simple song,
To chide the forward chance that keeps
  Lord Musgrave from her arms so long.

And listens, as the wind sweeps by,
  His steed's familiar step to hear—
Peace, beating heart! 't was but the cry
  And foot-fall of the distant deer.

In, lady, to thy bower; fast weep
  The chill dews on thy cheek so pale;
Thy cherished hero lies asleep—
  Asleep in distant Russendale!

The noon was sultry, long the chase—
  And when the wild stag stood at bay,
BURBEK reflected from its face
  The purple lights of dying day.

Through many a dale must Musgrave hie—
  Up many a hill his courser strain,
Ere he behold, with gladsome eye,
  His verdant bowers and halls again.

But twilight deepens—o'er the wolds
  The yellow moonbeam rising plays,
And now the haunted forest holds
  The wanderer in its bosky maze.

The Luck of Eden-Hall

No ready vassal rides in sight;
  He blows his bugle, but the call
Roused Echo mocks: farewell, to-night,
  The homefelt joys of Eden-Hall!

His steed he to an alder ties,
  His limbs he on the greensward flings;
And, tired and languid, to his eyes
  Woos sorceress slumber's balmy wings.

A prayer—a sigh, in murmurs faint,
  He whispers to the passing air;
The Ave to his patron saint—
  The sigh was to his lady fair.

'T was well that in that Elfin wood
  He breathed the supplicating charm,
Which binds the Guardians of the good
  To shield from all unearthly harm.

Scarce had the night's pale Lady staid
  Her chariot o'er th' accustomed oak,
Than murmurs in the mystic shade
  The slumberer from his trance awoke.

Stiff stood his courser's mane with dread—
  His crouching greyhound whined with fear;
And quaked the wild-fern round his head,
  As though some passing ghost were near.

Yet calmly shone the moonshine pale
  On glade and hillock, flower and tree;
And sweet the gurgling nightingale
  Poured forth her music, wild and free.

Sudden her notes fall hushed, and near
  Flutes breathe, horns warble, bridles ring;
And, in gay cavalcade, appear
  The Fairies round their Fairy King.

The Luck of Eden-Hall

Twelve hundred Elfin knights and more
   Were there, in silk and steel arrayed;
And each a ruby helmet wore,
   And each a diamond lance displayed.

And pursuivants with wands of gold,
   And minstrels scarfed and laurelled fair,
Heralds with blazoned flags unrolled,
   And trumpet-tuning dwarfs were there.

Behind, twelve hundred ladies coy, [Queen;
   On milk-white steeds, brought up their
Their kerchiefs of the crimson soy,
   Their kirtles all of Lincoln-green.

Some wore, in fanciful costume,
   A sapphire or a topaz crown;
And some a hern's or peacock's plume,
   Which their own tercel-gents struck down.

And some wore masks, and some wore hoods,
   Some turbans rich, some ouches rare;
And some sweet woodbine from the woods,
   To bind their undulating hair.

With all gay tints the darksome shade
   Grew florid as they passed along,
And not a sound their bridles made
   But tuned itself to Elfin song.

Their steeds they quit;—the knights ad-
   And in quaint order, one by one, [vance,
Each leads his lady forth to dance,—
   The timbrels sound—the charm 's begun.

Where'er they trip, where'er they tread,
   A daisy or a bluebell springs;
And not a dew-drop shines o'erhead,
   But falls within their charmed rings.

"The dance lead up, the dance lead down,
  The dance lead round our favourite tree;
If now one lady wears a frown,
  A false and froward shrew is she!

"There's not a smile we Fays let fall
  But swells the tide of human bliss;
And if good luck attends our call,
  'T is due on such sweet night as this.

"The dance lead up, the dance lead down,
  The dance lead round our favourite tree;
If now even Oberon wears a frown,
  A false and froward churl is he!"

Thus sing the Fays;—Lord Musgrave hears
  Their shrill sweet song, and eager eyes
The radiant show, despite the fears
  That to his bounding bosom rise.

But soft—the minstrelsy declines;
  The morris ceases—sound the shaums!
And quick, whilst many a taper shines,
  The heralds rank their airy swarms.

Titania waves her crystal wand:
  And underneath the green-wood bower,
Tables, and urns, and goblets stand,
  Metheglin, nectar, fruit, and flower.

"To banquet, ho!" the seneschals
  Bid the brisk tribes, that, thick as bees
At sound of cymbals, to their calls
  Consort beneath the leafy trees.

Titania by her king, each knight
  Beside his ladye love; the page
Behind his 'scutcheon'd lord,—a bright
  Equipment on a brilliant stage!

The monarch sits;—all helms are doffed,
  Plumes, scarfs, and mantles cast aside;
And, to the sound of music soft,
  They ply their cups with mickle pride.

Or sparkling mead, or spangling dew,
  Or livelier hyppocras they sip;
And strawberries red, and mulberries blue,
  Refresh each elf's luxurious lip.

With "nod, and beck, and wreathed smile,"
  They heap their jewelled patines high;
Nor want their mirthful airs the while
  To crown the festive revelry.

A minstrel dwarf, in silk arrayed,
  Lay on a mossy bank, o'er which
The wild thyme wove its fragrant braid,
  The violet spread its perfume rich;

And whilst a page at Oberon's knee
  Presented high the wassail-cup,
This lay the little bard with glee
  From harp of ivory offered up:

"Health to our sovereign!—fill, brave boy,
  Yon glorious goblet to the brim!
There's joy—in every drop there's joy
  That laughs within its charmed rim!

"'T was wrought within a wizard's mould,
  When signs and spells had happiest power;—
Health to our King by wood and wold!
  Health to our Queen in hall and bower!"

They rise—the myriads rise, and shrill
  The wild-wood echoes to their brawl,—
"Health to our King by wold and rill!
  Health to our Queen in bower and hall!"

A sudden thought fires Musgrave's brain,—
So help him all the Powers of Light,—
He rushes to the festal train,
And snatches up that goblet bright!

With three brave bounds the lawn he crossed,
The fourth it seats him on his steed;
"Now, Courser! or thy lord is lost—
Stretch to the stream with lightning speed!"

'T is uproar all around, behind,—
Leaps to his selle each screaming Fay,
"The charmed cup is fairly tined,
Stretch to the strife,—away! away!"

As in a whirlwind forth they swept,
The green turf trembling as they passed;
But forward still good Musgrave kept,—
The shallow stream approaching fast.

A thousand quivers round him rained
Their shafts or ere he reached the shore;
But when the farther bank was gained,
This song the passing whirlwind bore:

"Joy to thy banner, bold Sir Knight!
But if yon goblet break or fall,
Farewell thy vantage in the fight!—
Farewell the luck of Eden-Hall!"

The forest cleared, he winds his horn,—
Rock, wood, and wave return the din;
And soon, as though by Echo borne,
His gallant Squires come pricking in.

'T is dusk of day;—in Eden's towers
A mother o'er her infant bends,
And lists, amid the whispering bowers,
The sound that from the stream ascends.

It comes in murmurs up the stairs,—
  A low, a sweet, a mellow voice,—
And charms away the lady's cares,
  And bids the mother's heart rejoice.

" Sleep sweetly, babe ! " 't was heard to say ;
  " But if the goblet break or fall,
Farewell thy vantage in the fray !—
  Farewell the luck of Eden-Hall ! "

Though years on years have taken flight,
  Good-fortune 's still the Musgrave's thrall ;
Hail to his vantage in the fight !
  All hail the LUCK OF EDEN-HALL !

LADY ANNE BOTHWELL'S LAMENT.*

Balow, my boy; lie still and sleip!
It grieves me sair to see thee weip:
If thou'se be silent, I'se be glad;
Thy maining make my heart full sad.
Balow, my boy, thy mother's joy;
Thy father breids me great annoy.
   Balow, my boy; lie still and sleip!
   It grieves me sair to see thee weip,

* See Appendix.

When he began to court my luve,
And with his sugred words to muve,
His feignings false and flattering cheir
To me that time did not appeir:
But now I see, most cruel he
Cares neither for his babe nor me.
   Balow, my boy; lie still and sleip!
   It grieves me sair to see thee weip.

Lie still, my darling; sleip awhile,
And, when thou wakest, sweetlie smile:
But smile not as thy father did,
To cozen maids: nay, God forbid!
But yet I feir, thou wilt gae neir
Thy father's heart and face to beir.
   Balow, my boy; lie still and sleip!
   It grieves me sair to see thee weip.

Farewell, farewell, thou falsest youth,
That ever kist a woman's mouth!
Let nevir any, after me,
Submit unto thy courtesie;
For, if they do, Oh, cruel thou
Wilt her abuse, and care not how.
   Balow, my boy; lie still and sleip!
   It grieves me sair to see thee weip.

I was too credulous at first,
To yield thee all a maiden durst.
Thou swore for ever true to prove,
Thy faith unchanged, unchanged thy love;
But, quick as thought, the change is wrought,
Thy love's no more, thy promise noucht.
   Balow, my boy; lie still and sleip!
   It grieves me sair to see thee weip.

Balow, my boy; weep not for me,
Whose greatest grief's for wronging thee;
Nor pity her deserved smart,
Who can blame none but her fond heart.

The too soon trusting, latest finds,
With fairest tongues are falsest minds.
    Balow, my boy; lie still and sleip!
    It grieves me sair to heir thee weip.

Oh, do not, do not, prettie mine,
To feinings false thy heart incline.
Be loyal to thy lover true,
And never change her for a new:
If good or fair, of her have care;
For women's banning 's wondrous sair.
    Balow, my boy; lie still and sleip!
    It grieves me sair to see thee weip.

Balow, my boy; thy father 's fled,
When he the thriftless son has play'd.
Of vows and oaths forgetful, he
Prefers the wars to thee and me.
But now, perhaps, thy curse and mine
Make him eat acorns with the swine.
    Balow, my boy; lie still and sleip!
    It grieves me sair to heir thee weip.

Yet I can't chuse, but ever will
Be loving to thy father still:
Where'er he gae, where'er he ride,
My luve with him doth still abide:
In weel or wae, where'er he gae,
My heart can ne'er depart him frae.
    Balow, my boy; lie still and sleip!
    It grieves me sair to heir thee weip.

Then curse him not: perhaps now he,
Stung with remorse, is blessing thee:
Perhaps at death; for who can tell,
Whether the judge of heaven or hell,
By some proud foe has struck the blow,
And laid the dear deceiver low.
    Balow, my boy; lie still and sleip!
    It grieves me sair to heir thee weip.

Lady Anne Bothwell's Lament

I wish I were into the bounds
Where he lies smothered in his wounds—
Repeating, as he pants for air,
My name, whom once he called his fair.
No woman 's yet so fiercely set,
But she 'll forgive, though not forget.
   Balow, my boy; lie still and sleip !
   It grieves me sair to see thee weip.

Balow, my boy! I 'll weip for thee;
Too soon, alas, thou 'lt weip for me:
Thy griefs are growing to a sum—
God grant thee patience when they come;
Born to sustain thy mother's shame,
A hapless fate, an outcast's name !
   Balow, my boy; lie still and sleip !
   It grieves me sair to see thee weip.

AULD ROBIN GRAY.*

When the sheep are in the fauld, when the cows come hame,
When a' the weary warld to quiet rest are gane;
The woes of my heart fa' in showers frae my ee,
Unken'd by my gudeman, who soundly sleeps by me.

Young Jamie loo'd me weel, and sought me for his bride;
But saving ae crown piece, he 'd naething else beside,
To make the crown a pound, my Jamie gaed to sea;
And the crown and the pound, O they were baith for me!

* See Appendix.

Before he had been gane a twelvemonth and a day,
My father brak his arm, our cow was stown away;
My mother she fell sick—my Jamie was at sea—
And Auld Robin Gray, oh! he came a-courting me.

My father cou'dna work—my mother cou'dna spin;
I toil'd day and night, but their bread I cou'dna win;
Auld Rob maintain'd them baith, and, wi' tears in his ee,
Said "Jenny, oh! for their sakes, will you marry me!"

My heart it said na, and I look'd for Jamie back;
But hard blew the winds, and his ship was a wrack:
His ship it was a wrack! Why didna Jamie dee?
Or, wherefore am I spar'd to cry out, Woe is me!

My father argued sair—my mother didna speak,
But she look'd in my face till my heart was like to break;
They gied him my hand, but my heart was in the sea;
And so Auld Robin Gray, he was gudeman to me.

I hadna been his wife, a week but only four,
When mournfu' as I sat on the stane at my door,
I saw my Jamie's ghaist—I cou'dna think it he,
Till he said, "I 'm come hame, my love, to marry thee!"

O sair, sair did we greet, and mickle say of a';
Ae kiss we took, nae mair—I bad him gang awa.
I wish that I were dead, but I 'm no like to dee;
For O, I am but young to cry out, Woe is me!

I gang like a ghaist, and I carena much to spin,
I darena think o' Jamie, for that wad be a sin.
But I will do my best a gude wife aye to be,
For Auld Robin Gray, oh! he is sae kind to me.

THE CONTINUATION.

The wintry days grew lang, my tears they were a spent;
May be it was despair I fancied was content.
They said my cheek was wan; I cou'dna look to see—
For, oh! the wee bit glass, my Jamie gaed it me.

My father he was sad, my mother dull and wae;
But that which grieved me maist, it was Auld Robin Gray;
Though ne'er a word he said, his cheek said mair than a',
It wasted like a brae o'er which the torrents fa'.

He gaed into his bed—nae physic wad he take;
And oft he moan'd and said, "It 's better, for her sake."
At length he look'd upon me, and call'd me his "ain dear,"
And beckon'd round the neighbours, as if his hour drew near.

"I 've wrong'd her sair," he said, "but ken't the truth o'er late;
It 's grief for that alone that hastens now my date;
But a' is for the best, since death will shortly free
A young and faithful heart that was ill match'd w' me.

"I loo'd, and sought to win her for mony a lang day;
I had her parents' favour, but still she said me nay;
I knew na Jamie's luve; and oh! it 's sair to tell—
To force her to be mine, I steal'd her cow mysel!

"O what cared I for Crummie! I thought of nought but thee,
I thought it was the cow stood 'twixt my luve and me.
While she maintain'd ye a', was you not heard to say,
That you would never marry wi' Auld Robin Gray?

"But sickness in the house, and hunger at the door,
My bairn gied me her hand, although her heart was sore.
I saw her heart was sore—why did I take her hand?
That was a sinfu' deed! to blast a bonny land.

"It was na very lang ere a' did come to light;
For Jamie he came back, and Jenny's cheek grew white.
My spouse's cheek grew white, but true she was to me;
Jenny! I saw it a'—and oh, I 'm glad to dee!

"Is Jamie come?" he said; and Jamie by us stood—
"Ye loo each other weel—oh, let me do some good!
I gie you a', young man—my houses, cattle, kine,
And the dear wife hersel, that ne'er should hae been mine."

Auld Robin Gray

We kiss'd his clay-cold hands—a smile came o'er his face;
"He 's pardon'd," Jamie said, "before the throne o' grace.
Oh, Jenny! see that smile—forgi'en I 'm sure is he,
Wha could withstand temptation when hoping to win thee?"

The days at first were dowie; but what was sad and sair,
While tears were in my ee, I kent mysel nae mair;
For, oh! my heart was light as ony bird that flew,
And, wae as a' thing was, it had a kindly hue.

But sweeter shines the sun than e'er he shone before,
For now I 'm Jamie's wife, and what need I say more?
We hae a wee bit bairn—the auld folks by the fire—
And Jamie, oh! he loo's me up to my heart's desire.

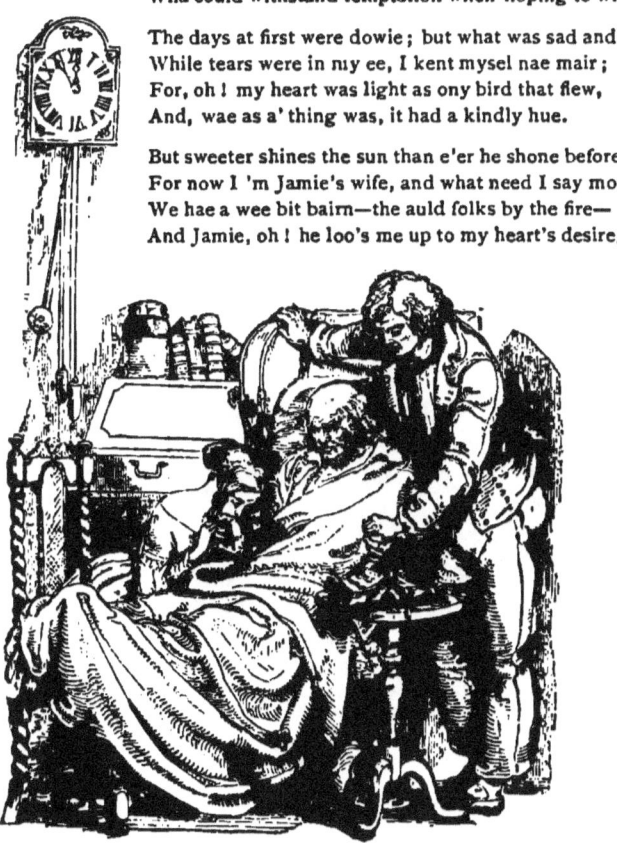

ELFINLAND WUD.*

Erl William has muntit his gude grai stede,
   (Merrie lemis munelicht on the sea.)
And graithit him in ane cumli weid,
   (Swa bonnilie blumis the hawthorn tree.)

* See Appendix.

Elfinland Wud

Erl William rade, Erl William fan—
  (Fast they ryde quha luve trewlie,)
Quhyll the Elfinland wud that gude Erl wan—
  (Blink ower the burn, sweit may, to mee.)

Elfinland wud is dern and dreir,
  (Merrie is the grai goukis sang,)
Bot ilk ane leafis quhyt as silver cleir,
  (Licht makis schoirt the road swa lang.)

It is undirneth ane braid aik tree,
  (Hey and a lo, as the leavis grow grein,)
Thair is kythit ane bricht ladie,
  (Manie flowris blume quhilk ar nocht seen.)

Around hir slepis the quhyte muneschyne,
  (Meik is mayden undir kell.)
Her lips bin lyke the blude reid wyne ;
  (The rois of flowris hes sweitest smell.)

It was al bricht quhare that ladie stude,
  (Far my luve, fure ower the sea.)
Bot dern is the lave of Elfinland wud,
  (The knicht pruvit false that ance luvit me.)

The ladie's handis were quhyte als milk,
  (Ringis my luve wore mair nor ane.)
Her skin was safter nor the silk ;
  (Lilly bricht schinis my luvis halse bane.)

Save you, save you, fayr ladie,
  (Gentil hert schawis gentil deed.)
Standand alane undir this auld tree ;
  (Deir till knicht is nobil steid.)

Burdalane, if ye dwall here,
  (My hert is layed upon this land.)
I wuld like to live your fere ;
  (The shippis cum sailin to the strand.)

Nevir ane word that ladie sayd;
  (Schortest rede hes least to mend.)
Bot on hir harp she evir playd;
  (Thare nevir was mirth that had nocht end.)

Gang ye eist, or fare ye wast,
  (Ilka stern blinkis blythe for thee,)
Or tak ye the road that ye like best,
  (Al trew feeris ryde in cumpanie.)

Erl William loutit doun full lowe;
  (Luvis first seid bin curtesie.)
And swung hir owir his saddil bow,
  (Ryde quha listis, ye 'll link with mee.)

Scho flang her harp on that auld tree,
  (The wynd pruvis aye ane harpir gude.)
And it gave out its music free;
  (Birdis sing blythe in gay grein wud.)

The harp playde on its leeful lane,
  (Lang is my luvis yellow hair.)
Quhill it has charmit stock and stane,
  (Furth by firth, deir lady fare.)

Quhan sho was muntit him behynd,
  (Blyth be hertis quhilkis luve ilk uthir.)
Awa thai flew lyke flaucht of wind;
  (Kin kens kin, and bairnis thair mither.)

Nevir ane word that ladie spak;
  (Mim be maydins men besyde.)
Bot that stout steid did nicher and schaik;
  (Smal thingis humbil hertis of pryde.)

About his breist scho plet her handis;
  (Luvand be maydins quhan thai lyke.)
Bot thay were cauld as yron bandis;
  (The winter bauld bindis sheuch and syke.)

Elfinland Wud

Your handis ar cauld, fayr ladie, sayd hee,
  (The caulder hand the trewer hairt.)
I trembil als the leif on the tree;
  (Licht caussis muve ald friendis to pairt.)

Lap your mantil owir your heid,
  (My luve was clad in the reid scarlett,)
And spredd your kirtil owir my stede;
  (Thair nevir was joie that had nae lett.)

The ladie sho wald nocht dispute;
  (Nocht woman is scho that laikis ane tung.)
But caulder hir fingeris about him cruik.
  (Sum sangis ar writ, bot nevir sung.)

This Elfinland Wud will neir haif end;
  (Hunt quha listis, daylicht for mee.)
I wuld I culd ane strang bow bend,
  (Al undirneth the grein wud tree.)

Thai rade up, and they rade doun,
  (Wearilie wearis wan nicht away.)
Erl William's heart mair cauld is grown;
  (Hey, luve mine, quhan dawis the day?)

Your hand lies cauld on my briest-bane,
  (Smal hand hes my ladie fair,)
My horss he can nocht stand his lane,
  (For cauldness of this midnicht air.)

Erl William turnit his heid about;
  (The braid mune schinis in lift richt cleir.)
Twa Elfin een are glentin owt,
  (My luvis een like twa sternis appere.)

Twa brennand eyen, sua bricht and full
  (Bonnilie blinkis my ladies ee.)
Flang fire flauchtis fra ane peelit skull;
  (Sum sichts ar ugsomlyk to see.)

Elfinland Wud

Twa rawis of quhyt teeth then did say,
(Cauld the boysteous windis sal blaw,)
Oh, lang and weary is our way,
(And donkir yet the dew maun fa'.)

Far owir mure, and far owir fell,
(Hark the sounding huntsmen thraug ;)
Thorow dingle, and thorow dell,
(Luve, come, list the merlis sang)*

* GLOSSARY — Muntit, *mounted*. Gude, *good*. Lemis, *gleams, scintillates*. Graithit, *dressed*. Dern, *hidden, secret, dark*. Swa, *so*. Quha, *who*. Quhyll, *while*. Grai goukis sang, *song of the "cuckoo-gray."* Ilk ane, *each, every one*. Ilka has the same signification. Quhyt, *white*. Schoirt, lang, *short, long*. Braid aik tree, *broad oak tree*. Kythit, *discovered*. Quhilk, nocht, *which, not*. Kell, *a woman's head-dress*. The rois, *the rose*. Stude, *stood*. Fure, *fared*. Bot dern is the lave, *but dark, or hidden, is the remainder*. Als, *as*. Mair nor ane, *more than one*. Schinis, halse bane, *shines, collar bone*. Hert schawis, *heart shows*. Standand alane, *standing alone*. Till, *to*. Burdalane, a term used to denote one who is the only child left in a family ; *bird alone*, or *solitary*. Layed, "lay" means *basis*, or *foundation*, and the signification of "layed," here, is *fixed*, I think, or *set*. Fere, *a companion*. Schortest rede has least to mend, *shortest counsel has least to expiate*. Nocht, *not*. Gang, eist, wast, *go, east, west*. Stern, *star*. Loutit, *stooped*. Seid bin, *offspring is*. Scho, *she*. Its leeful lane, *by itself alone*. Furth by firth, *forth, abroad by frith*. Blyth be hertes quhilkis luve ilk uthir, *blithe be hearts which love each other*. Flaucht, *gust*, and also *flake*. Bairnis, mither, *children, mother*. Mim, *affectedly modest or coy*, prim. Nicher, *neigh*. Quhan thai lyke, *when they choose*. Bauld, sheuch, *bold, a furrow or ditch*. Syke, *a rill, or rivulet, usually dry in summer*. Hairt, *heart*. Ald, pairt, *old, part*. Nae lett, *no obstruction, no hinderance*. Nocht woman is scho that laikis ane tung, *she who lacks a tongue, is not a woman*. Sangis, *songs*. Haif, *have*. Quhan dawis the day, *when breaks the day*. Braid mune, *broad moon*. Lift, *the firmament*. Glentin, *glancing, gleaming*. Brennand, *burning*. Fra ane peelit skull, *from a peeled skull*. Ugsomlyk, *very loathsome, disgusting*. Rawis, *rows*. Boysteous, *boisterous, blustering*. Donkir, *damper, danker*. Maun fa', *must fall*. The merlis sang, *the blackbird's song*. Flude, *flood*. Mudy, *moody*. Blude, *blood*. A seamless shrowd weird schaipis for me] *a seamless shroud fate, or destiny, prepares for me*. To rede aright my spell, *to explain aright my tale*. Eerlie, *awfully, drearily*. Sal, *shall*. Quhill fleand Hevin and raikand Hell, *while avoiding Heaven and ranging Hell*. Ghaist, *ghost*. Luvand, *loving, affectionate*.

Elfinland Wud

Thorow fire, and thorow flude,
  (Mudy mindis rage lyk a sea;)
Thorow slauchtir, thorow blude,
  (A seamless shrowd weird schaipis for me!)

And to rede aricht my spell,
  Eerilie sal nicht wyndis moan,
Quhill fleand Hevin and raikand Hell,
  Ghaist with ghaist maun wandir on.

THE TWA CORBIES

As I was walking all alane,
I heard twa corbies making a mane ;
The tane unto the t'other say,
"Where sall we gang and dine to-day?"—

"In behint yon auld fail dyke,
I wot there lies a new-slain knight ;
And naebody kens that he lies there,
But his hawk, his hound, and lady fair.

* See Appendix.

The Twa Corbies

"His hound is to the hunting gane,
His hawk to fetch the wild-fowl hame,
His lady 's ta'en another mate,
So we may make our dinner sweet.

"Ye 'll sit on his white hause-bane,
And I 'll pick out his bonny blue een;
Wi' ae lock o' his gowden hair,
We 'll theek our nest when it grows bare.

"Mony a one for him makes mane,
But nane sall ken where he is gane;
O'er his white banes, when they are bare,
The wind sall blaw for evermair."

HENGIST AND MEY.*

In ancient days, when Arthur reigned,
  Sir Elmer had no peer;
And no young knight in all the land
  The ladies loved so dear.

His sister, Mey, the fairest maid
  Of all the virgin train,
Won every heart at Arthur's court;
  But all their love was vain.

* See Appendix.

In vain they loved, in vain they vowed;
  Her heart they could not move:
Yet, at the evening hour of prayer,
  Her mind was lost in love.

The abbess saw—the abbess knew,
  And urged her to explain:
"O name the gentle youth to me,
  And his consent I'll gain."

Long urged, long tried, fair Mey replied,
  "His name—how can I say?
An angel from the fields above
  Has 'rapt my heart away.

"But once, alas! and never more,
  His lovely form I 'spied;
One evening, by the sounding shore,
  All by the green-wood side.

"His eyes to mine the love confest,
  That glowed with mildest grace;
His courtly mien and purple vest
  Bespoke his princely race.

"But when he heard my brother's horn,
  Fast to his ships he fled;
Yet, while I sleep, his graceful form
  Still hovers round my bed.

"Sometimes, all clad in armour bright,
  He shakes a warlike lance;
And now, in courtly garments dight,
  He leads the sprightly dance.

"His hair, as black as raven's wing;
  His skin—as Christmas snow;
His cheeks outvie the blush of morn,
  His lips like rose-buds glow.

"His limbs, his arms, his stature shaped
  By nature's finest hand;
His sparkling eyes declare him born
  To love, and to command."

The live-long year, fair Mey bemoaned
  Her hopeless, pining love:
But when the balmy spring returned,
  And summer clothed the grove,

All round by pleasant Humber side,
  The Saxon banners flew,
And to Sir Elmer's castle gates
  The spearmen came in view.

Fair blushed the morn, when Mey looked o'er
  The castle walls so sheen;
And lo! the warlike Saxon youth
  Were sporting on the green.

There Hengist, Offa's eldest son,
  Leaned on his burnished lance,
And all the armed youth around
  Obeyed his manly glance.

His locks, as black as raven's wing,
  Adown his shoulders flowed;
His cheeks outvied the blush of morn,
  His lips like rose-buds glowed.

And soon, the lovely form of Mey
  Has caught his piercing eyes;
He gives the sign, the bands retire,
  While big with love he sighs.

"Oh, thou! for whom I dared the seas,
  And came with peace or war;
Oh! by that cross that veils thy breast,
  Relieve thy lover's care!

"For thee, I 'll quit my father's throne;
 With thee, the wilds explore;
Or with thee share the British crown;
 With thee, the Cross adore."

Beneath the timorous virgin blush,
 With love's soft warmth she glows;
So, blushing through the dews of morn,
 Appears the opening rose.

'T was now the hour of morning prayer,
 When men their sins bewail,
And Elmer heard King Arthur's horn,
 Shrill sounding through the dale.

The pearly tears from Mey's bright eyes,
 Like April dew-drops fell,
When, with a parting, dear embrace,
 Her brother bade farewell.

The cross with sparkling diamonds bright,
 That veiled the snowy breast,
With prayers to Heaven her lily hands
 Have fixed on Elmer's vest.

Now, with five hundred bowmen true,
 He 's marched across the plain;
Till with his gallant yeomandrie,
 He joined King Arthur's train.

Full forty thousand Saxon spears
 Came glittering down the hill,
And with their shouts and clang of arms
 The distant valleys fill.

Old Offa, dressed in Odin's garb,
 Assumed the hoary god;
And Hengist, like the warlike Thor,
 Before the horsemen rode.

Hengist and Mey

With dreadful rage the combat burns,
  The captains shout amain;
And Elmer's tall victorious spear
  Far glances o'er the plain.

To stop its course young Hengist flew,
  Like lightning o'er the field;
And soon his eyes the well-known cross
  On Elmer's vest beheld.

The slighted lover swelled his breast,
  His eyes shot living fire!
And all his martial heat before,
  To this was mild desire.

On his imagined rival's front,
  With whirlwind speed he pressed,
And glancing to the sun, his sword
  Resounds on Elmer's crest.

The foe gave way;—the princely youth
  With heedless rage pursued,
Till trembling in his cloven helm
  Sir Elmer's javelin stood.

He bowed his head—slow dropped his spear;
  The reins slipped through his hand;
And, stained with blood—his stately corse
  Lay breathless on the strand.

"O bear me off (Sir Elmer cried);
  Before my painful sight
The combat swims—yet Hengist's vest
  I claim as victor's right."

Brave Hengist's fall the Saxons saw,
  And all in terror fled;
The bowmen to his castle gates
  The brave Sir Elmer led.

"O, wash my wounds, my sister dear;
  O, pull this Saxon dart,
That, whizzing from young Hengist's arm,
  Has almost pierced my heart.

"Yet in my hall his vest shall hang;
  And Britons yet unborn,
Shall with the trophies of to-day
  Their solemn feasts adorn."

All trembling, Mey beheld the vest;
  "O, Merlin!" loud she cried;
"Thy words are true—my slaughtered love
  Shall have a breathless bride!

"Oh! Elmer, Elmer, boast no more
  That low my Hengist lies!
Oh! Hengist, cruel was thine arm!
  My brother bleeds and dies!"

She spake,—the roses left her cheeks,
  And life's warm spirit fled:
So, nipt by winter's withering blasts,
  The snow-drop bows its head!

Yet parting life one struggle gave,—
  She lifts her languid eyes;
"Return, my Hengist! oh, return,
  My slaughtered love!" she cries.

"Oh—still he lives—he smiles again,
  With all his grace he moves:
I come—I come, where bow nor spear
  Shall more disturb our loves!"

She spake—she died! The Saxon dart
  Was drawn from Elmer's side;
And thrice he called his sister Mey,
  And thrice he groaned,—and died!

Whère in the dale a moss-grown Cross
  O'ershades an aged thorn,
Sir Elmer's and young Hengist's corse
  Were by the spearmen borne.

And there, all clad in robes of white,
  With many a sigh and tear,
The village maids to Hengist's grave
  Did Mey's fair body bear.

And there, at dawn and fall of day,
  All from the neighbouring groves
The turtles wail, in widowed notes,
  And sing their hapless loves.

APPENDIX.

CHEVY CHACE.

There are two versions of this ballad, the more modern of which is here given, as it is more intelligible to the general reader. The earlier one, which was first published by Percy, is more vigorous, if also rugged and uncouth. Nothing authentic can fix the precise date of the poem, which is known to have been popular in the time of Elizabeth. The mention of the battle of Humbledoun (September, 1402) proves that the action took place prior to that date. An Earl of Douglas is known to have been slain by a Percy in the battle of Otterbourne (1388), and it may be that that was the foundation of this ballad, although there are several others which have that battle as their theme.

Douglas had captured the pennon of Percy during an incursion of the Scots into the English marches, and the fight at Otterbourne was the result of an attempt to regain this.

THE CHILDREN IN THE WOOD.

Ritson says that this ballad appears to have been written in 1595, as it was entered in that year on the Stationers' books, but there is some doubt as to the date of its original composition. Dr. Percy credits it to an old play, the scene of which is laid in Padua. It is, however, too English to make an Italian source probable, and the ballad may be regarded as a model of the pure old English style. It was very popular, and was sung to the tune of *Rogero*.

FAIR ROSAMUND.

The fate of Fair Rosamund was a favorite theme with the early minstrels, and historians have not disdained to preserve the memory of her beauty and sad story.

According to Stowe, who follows Higden, the monk of Chester, she was the daughter of Walter, Lord Clifford, and became the favorite of Henry II., and mother of two sons, William Longsword, Earl of Salisbury, and Geoffrey, Bishop of Lincoln. Her royal lover made her a house at Woodstock, so cunningly hidden in a labyrinth that none could come to it. Queen Eleanor, prompted by jealousy, discovered the secret, penetrated to her rival, and so "dealt with her that she lived not long." This was in 1177 A. D. It was believed that she was poisoned, but the fact is not proven. Rosamund was buried at Godstow, " in a house of nunnes besides Oxford."

This version of the ballad appears to have been published in 1612. Percy gives another called "Queen Eleanor's Confession," and there were several others current varying only in details.

THE DEMON LOVER.

This ballad first appeared in the "Minstrelsy of the Scottish Border." Sir Walter Scott received it from Sir William Laidlaw, by whom it was "taken down in recitation."

Sir Walter Scott says the legend here given is "in various shapes current in Scotland," and mentions another song in which a fiend is disconcerted by holy herbs in the bosom of a maiden. Here, unluckily, the lady had no such protection.

The same power of keeping away evil spirits is attributed to the vervain in Ireland.

THE NUT-BROWN MAYD.

The remote antiquity of this beautiful composition is unquestionable. There are, indeed, good reasons for placing it as early as 1400. In the sixteenth century it was so popular that it was parodied, and Prior wrote a poem, "Henry and Emma," taking it as a model.

Appendix

KEMPION.

This ballad is taken from the "Minstrelsy of the Scottish Border," where it is given "chiefly" from Mrs. Brown's MS., "with corrections from a recited fragment." The date of composition is unknown. Sir Walter Scott says it was probably an old metrical romance degraded into a ballad by the lapse of time and the corruption of reciters.

Many tales of fabulous snakes being slain by brave knights are current throughout the British Isles and Denmark, whence they may have been exported by the sea-kings.

THE CHILD OF ELLE.

Percy was the first to publish this ballad, which he probably emended greatly from the MS. in his possession. It is unquestionably Scotch in origin, as many other Scotch poems relate a similar incident.

"Child" is used for knight.

THE TWA BROTHERS.

This ballad is copied from Motherwell's "Minstrelsy, Ancient and Modern." The editor is inclined to trace it to an event which occurred in the family of the Somervilles in 1589 A. D. The master of Somerville and John, his brother, were lying on the grass where their horses were grazing. The master, after sleeping, found that one of his pistols was wet with dew. In rubbing this to dry it, it went off accidentally, and John was killed without having a chance to speak again. In this, or some similar incident, the ballad originated undoubtedly. Other versions are also in existence.

THE BEGGAR'S DAUGHTER OF BEDNALL GREEN.

The ballad, as given here, is Percy's version. Percy places its composition in the reign of Queen Elizabeth, because there is mention of "the Queene's Armes," and also because of the "tune's being quoted in other old pieces written in her time."

History informs us that at the decisive battle of Eversham (August 4, 1265), when Simon de Montfort, the great Earl of Leicester, was slain at the head of his barons, his eldest son Henry fell by his side, and the whole family perished forever, their possessions being bestowed upon Edmund, Earl of Lancaster, second son of the king. There is no date from which to tell whether the story of the blind beggar is pure fiction or founded on fact.

The "angell" mentioned was a gold coin, value about ten shillings. It bore a figure of St. Michael on one side, a ship on the other, and was first coined by Edward IV. in 1466.

ROBIN GOODFELLOW.

This is printed from a black-letter copy in the British Museum. Puck, or Robin Goodfellow, was a "shrewd and knavish sprite," and his tricks and pranks were described by many of the old poets. He has been traced back to the thirteenth century, and may have existed earlier. He is never represented as malicious. Though he leads people into trouble, he gets them out again, and is always generous to those who please him.

The Puck or Chooka of Ireland is a more evil-minded imp, and many stories are related by the peasantry of his merciless cruelties and malicious pranks.

This version of the ballad is attributed to Ben Jonson (1574-1637), probably without sufficient authority, as it is not included in his works. Undoubtedly it was written for some masque in which the character of Robin Goodfellow was assumed by an actor, who describes himself to the audience as being sent by Oberon to

"See the night-sport here."

SIR PATRICK SPENS.

This ballad, in several versions, lays claim to a "high and remote antiquity." It was undoubtedly founded on some actual occurrence, but the earlier annotators were unable to establish the fact.

Mr. Motherwell, from whose collection this is taken, however, con-

Appendix

siders that it records the fate of the band who escorted Margaret, daughter of Alexander III. of Scotland (1249), when she espoused the Fife of Norway, as many of her escort are said to have perished on their return trip. Sir Walter Scott thinks that the expedition was despatched to bring home Margaret's infant daughter, when she became heir to the Scotch throne on the death (or the approaching death) of Alexander III.

The objection of the "skeely" skipper to sail at "this time of the year" is thus accounted for: It was deemed imprudent to navigate in winter. Two hundred years after the date assigned to this poem, an act of Parliament forbade navigation "frae the feast of St. Simon and St. Jude to Candlemas."

GIL MORRICE.

This is taken, in part, from Percy, but it had already been printed —communicated, it is said, to the printers by a lady who took it down from "the mouths of old women and nurses."

The word "Gil" is now considered to be a corruption of "child," which is so frequently used as "knight."

There can be no doubt of the antiquity of the poem, but it has probably undergone many modern improvements. Many of the places referred to can be localized.

The "majer dish" mentioned with the "siller cup" is probably the dish on which the cup stood.

SIR ALDINGAR.

This ballad is taken from Percy. The only information given is that the author seems to have had in his eye the story of Gunhilda, sometimes called Eleanor, married to the Emperor Henry. Sir Walter Scott says the tradition upon which it is founded is "universally current among the Mearns," and he was informed that "until very lately the sword with which Sir Hugh le Blond was believed to have defended the honor of the queen was carefully preserved by his descendants, the Viscounts of Arbuthnot." This Sir

Hugh lived in the thirteenth century, but there is no instance in history in which the good name of a queen of Scotland was committed to the chance of a duel.

SIR LANCELOT DU LAKE.

Printed from a black-letter copy in the British Museum, purer than Percy's version. It is mainly indebted to its celebrity from the fact that Shakespeare mentions it.

The subject is taken from the ancient romance of Morte d'Arthur. Sir Lancelot was one of the most renowned among the twenty-four knights of Arthur's Round Table. This famed table originated with Uther Pendragon, Arthur's father, for whom it was made in token of the roundness of the world. The knights were bound by oath to assist each other and help the distressed. The mirror of all was Arthur. Lancelot's history is the perfection of romance. His father, "King Ban," attacked by his enemy, King Claudas, escaped with queen and child to solicit aid of Arthur, but died of grief on the way. His queen left the infant a moment to attend to her dying husband, and when she returned she found the child in the arms of a nymph, who sprang with him into a lake. She was Vivian, mistress of the enchanter, Merlin, and she brought up the boy in her home beneath the water. When he was eighteen she took him to Arthur's court and obtained knighthood for him. Throughout Lancelot's after-life this lady of the lake continued to be his guardian. In the chapel of Winchester Castle is preserved what is affirmed to be the original round table. It is, however, not considered earlier than the time of Stephen.

KING ARTHUR'S DEATH.

King Arthur and the knights of his round table are familiar to all readers of old romance. The fabulous "History of Geoffrey of Monmouth," published about the middle of the twelfth century, is the undoubted source upon which the minstrels drew so largely. He claims that he translated the story from a very ancient book, but the general opinion on the matter is that it was a pure invention of the "historian." Arthur was the son of Uther Pendragon, King of Britain. The mystery of his life commenced with his birth, his father having been introduced by Merlin, the enchanter, to his mother in the semblance of one whose form it was criminal to assume. Arthur's lineage was kept secret, and he was reared in obscurity by Merlin until his father's death. Then the wizard proposed that the rival competitors to the throne should test their strength by drawing a sword—the far-famed Excalibur—out of a stone. Arthur was, of course, successful, and was crowned in Cardvile, that noble town.

Thenceforth his career was one of conquest, either upon a large scale, surrounded by all his knights, or in single combat. Arthur's death was as mysterious as his birth, and is described in the following ballad. Long after its occurrence his return to life was looked for. It is "believed by the vulgar that he still lives and is to come to restore the Britons to their own." This epitaph is in the "monastic church of Glasinberi":

"Hic jacet Arthurus, rex quondam atque futurus."

THE HEIR OF LINNE.

This is copied from Percy, who emended it from a fragment in his possession. He considers that it was originally Scotch, and observes: "The Heir of Linne seems not to have been a Lord of Parliament, but a laird whose title went along with his land."

LORD SOULIS.

This is the composition of John Leyden (b. 1775). The hero is supposed to be William, Lord Soulis, who was of royal descent and aspired to the Scottish throne with aid of Robert de Bruce (d. 1329). In local tradition, according to Sir Walter Scott, he is represented as a cruel tyrant and sorcerer, using all means, human and infernal, to attain his ends. Tradition relates that the Scottish king, wearied of reiterated complaints, peevishly exclaimed: "Boil him, if you please, but let me hear no more of him." Satisfied with this answer, they hastened to execute the commission. The cauldron which they used for this purpose on the Nine-Stane Rig is said to have been long preserved at Shelf-Hill, a hamlet betwixt Hawick and the Hermitage which was Lord Soulis' castle. The Nine-Stane Rig derives its name from a circle of so-called Druidical stones, five of which are still visible. The king, it is said, sent messengers to prevent the effect of his hasty declaration, but they did not arrive till all was over. The idea of Lord Soulis' familiar, connection with whom was broken by his looking at him, was derived, according to Scott, from "Spirit Orthone and the Lord of Corasse." The formation of ropes of sand was assigned as an interminable task by Michael Scott to a number of spirits for whom he wished to find employment.

LORD THOMAS AND FAIR ANNET.

This is taken from Percy, who copied it from a Scotch MS. He thinks that it is composed from two English ballads, "Lord Thomas and Fair Ellinor," and "Fair Margaret and Sweet William."

FAUSE FOODRAGE.

First published in "Minstrelsy of the Scottish Border," where it was "chiefly given from the MS. of Mrs. Brown of Falkland." There appears to be no historical authority for the leading incident of the poem, the exchange of the children. It is not improbable that some such incident did occur, as the old ballad-makers were seldom inventors. That its age is remote is certain by the reference to King Easter and King Wester, although the former kingdom cannot be positively located. There is internal evidence of its Scottish origin.

GENEVIEVE.

This is the composition of Samuel Taylor Coleridge, and is given as a specimen of his ballad verse.

Appendix

FAIR MARGARET AND SWEET WILLIAM.

Percy took this from a printed copy picked up at a stall. Although the language is modernized, it retains many tokens of antiquity.

THE MERMAID.

"This ballad," writes Sir Walter Scott, "was founded upon a Gaelic traditional ballad called 'Macphail of Colonsay and the Mermaid of Corrivrekin.' The dangerous gulf of Corrivrekin lies between the islands of Jura and Scarba, and the superstition of the islanders has peopled it with all kinds of fabulous monsters, of which the mermaid, who somewhat resembles the siren of the ancients, is the most remarkable." According to the Gaelic story, Macphail of Colonsay was carried off by a mermaid, and passed several years beneath the sea with her. Finally he tired of her society, and prevailed on her to carry him to Colonsay, where he escaped. Such stories are common in the islands, and in Ireland peasants are still to be found who have seen them "combing their yellow hair."

LORD ULLIN'S DAUGHTER.

Thomas Campbell (1777-1843), the author of this ballad, does not mention whether it was pure invention. Probably neither Lord Ullin nor the Chief of Ulva's Isle are altogether fictitious. Loch Gyle or Goil is an arm of Loch Long, a salt-water loch fed by the Frith of Clyde. Being near the counties of the chief Scottish families, it has been the site of many a clan feud.

SIR AGILTHORN.

This is the production of Matthew Gregory Leurs (1773-1818), who was the first to introduce a German element into English fiction. He had some influence on English taste, but most of his compositions have already perished.

JOHNIE OF BRADISLEE.

From "Minstrelsy of the Scottish Border." Scott styles it "an ancient Nithsdale ballad," the hero of which appears to have been an outlaw and deer-stealer. It is said he possessed the old castle of Dumfriesshire, now ruinous. The date of Johnie's history must be very remote, for the scene of his exploits has been cultivated domain "beyond the memory of tradition." There are several versions.

THE DOWIE DENS OF YARROW.

This was first published in the "Minstrelsy of the Scottish Border." Sir Walter Scott collected this form from the several versions in circulation. He says: "Tradition places the event recorded very early, and the ballad was probably composed soon afterwards, though the language has been modernized in the course of oral tradition." He believes that the hero was a knight called Scott, and that the action refers to a duel fought at Deucharswyre, of which Annan's Treat is a part, between John Scott, of Tushielaw, and his brother-in-law Walter Scott, in which the latter was slain. Annan's Treat is a low muir on the banks of the Yarrow. "There are two tall, unhewn masses of stone erected about eighty feet distant from each other, and the least child that can herd a cow will tell you that there lie the two lords who were slain in single combat.

THE BONNIE BAIRNS.

Allan Cunningham "arranged and eked out these old and remarkable verses." It is probable that the original was nothing more than a crude outline. The superstition involved is current in Scotland.

GLENFINLAS.

This is the composition of Sir Walter Scott. The tradition upon which it is founded is briefly as follows: Two Highland hunters were passing the night in a solitary bothy (hunting hut) and making

merry, when they expressed a wish that they had some lassies to
bear them company. Their words were scarcely uttered, when two
beautiful young women entered. One of the hunters was induced
to leave the hut with one of these sirens, but tne other, suspicious,
played a sacred strain upon a jews-harp until day came and the
damsel vanished. He searched for his friend, and found nothing
but his bones. He had been devoured by the fiend. The place was
henceforth called the Glen of the Green Women. Glenfinlas is a
tract of forest land lying in the Highlands of Perthshire, not far
from Callander in Menteith.

THE GAY GOSS-HAWK.

This was first published in the "Minstrelsy of the Scottish Border." Sir Walter Scott says it was taken partly from one in Mrs.
Brown's collection, and partly from a MS. The leading incident,
conveyance of a letter under a goss-hawk's wing, is common
enough. There are several other versions.

COLIN AND LUCY.

This is the composition of Tickell (d. 1740), the friend of Addin,
and seems to have been written in Ireland, though it is not Irish.

KATHARINE JANFARIE.

Sir Walter Scott published this first—combined from several recited copies. The scene of the ballad is said to lie upon the banks
of the "Cadden-water," a small rill which joins the Tweed, betwixt
Inverleithen and Cloverford.

RUDIGER.

A German poem translated by Robert Southey (1774-1843), and
given here only as a specimen of his ballad verse, even though it is
expended on an essentially German theme.

Appendix

THE EVE OF ST. JOHN.

Composition of Sir Walter Scott. The scene of the tragedy, Smaylhome or Smallholme Tower, is on the northern boundary of Roxburghshire. It lies so high that it is seen for "many a myle." The battle of Ancram Moor (1545) was ever famous in the anuals of border warfare.

BARTHRAM'S DIRGE.

Sir Walter Scott says that Mr. Surtees (the historian of Durham County) took this down from the recitation of Anne Douglas, who weeded in his garden. Her memory was defective, and she could only recall snatches of the song which he filled in. Scott adds that if the reciter be correct, the hero of this ditty was shot to death by nine brothers, to avenge the wrongs of their sister, the lady with the "ling long yellow hair." According to her wish, he was laid near their trysting place instead of in holy ground. The name Barthram would argue a Northumberland origin, but the mention of the Nine-Stane Barn and the Nine-Stane Rig seems to refer to the vicinity of the Hermitage (scene of the Ballad of Lord Soulis). The style is decidedly Scottish rather than Northumbrian.

SIR CAULINE.

Percy emended this ballad from a defective MS. in his possession. There is a curious version of the same story preserved by oral tradition in the north of Scotland. Percy begins with "In Ireland far over the sea." But the superstition of the Eldridge Knight is unknown in Ireland, and not one of the incidents or allusions bear the remotest affinity to Irish customs, ancient or modern.

RUTH.

This is given as a specimen of Wordsworth's ballad poetry.

ROBIN HOOD AND GUY OF GISBORNE.

This is taken from Percy who acknowledges that he took some liberties with it. There are a great many ballads and songs about

Appendix

Robin Hood, as he continued a favorite subject for several centuries. It would appear on consulting the several authorities that, about the year 1120, in the reign of Richard II., Robin Hood was the leader of a famous band of thieves who infested the forests of Yorkshire, Cumberland, and Nottingham. He was probably outlawed for slaying royal deer. His mode of selecting his associates was well calculated to create a stout army. "Whersoever he heard of any that were of unusual strength and hardiness he would disguise himself, and rather than fayle, go lyke a beggar to become acquainted with them ; and after he had tryed them with fyghting, never give them over tyl he had used means to drawe (them) to lyve after his fashion." The historion Major pronounces him to have been "of all theeves the most gentle theefe." Ritson has collected two volumes of ballads about his various exploits.

THE DEATH AND BURIAL OF ROBIN HOOD.

The old chronicles are somewhat circumstantial in their accounts of Robin Hood. One says: "Being distempered with cowld and age, he had great payne in his lymmes, his bloud being corrupted; therefor to be eased of his payne by letting bloud he repaired to the priores of Kyrkesly, which some say was his aunt, a woman very skylful in physique and surgery ; who perceyving him to be Robin Hood, and waying how fel an enemy he was to religious persons, toke revenge of him for her owne house and all others by letting him bleed to death."

SIR JAMES THE ROSE.

Of Michael Bruce, the author of this ballad, very little is known. He was born in Kinnassword, Scotland, struggled his life long with poverty, and died of consumption in 1767 The ballad is only worked out, not original. Rose is an ancient and honorable name in Scotland. Johannes de Rose was a witness to the famous charter of Robert II.

THE CLERKE'S TWA SONS O' OWSENFORD.

This ballad is copied from the collection of Robert Chambers by whom it is thus introduced. " This singularly wild old ballad is chiefly taken from the recitation of the editor's grandmother, who learned it in her girlhood from a Miss Gray, resident at Neidpath, Peebleshire. Some additional stanzas and a few variations are borrowed from a less perfect copy and from a fragment called 'The Wife of Usher's Well,' which is evidently the same narrative."

SIR ANDREW BARTON.

Percy says this ballad appears to have been written in Elizabeth's time. The story on which this is founded is briefly this: A certain Scottish captain, Barton by name, greatly worried the English sailors and merchants. The Earl of Surry could not smother his indignation but . . . declared that while he had an estate that could furnish out a ship, or a son capable of commanding one, the narrow seas should not be infested. Barton had the reputation of being one of the ablest sea-captains of his time in addition to being a pirate. The earl's two sons, Sir Thomas and Sir Edward Howard, put to sea in command of two ships. After much rough weather, Sir Thomas came up with the *Lion*, commanded by Barton in person, and Sir Edward came up with the *Union*, Barton's other ship. The engagement that followed was obstinate on both sides but the Howards finally prevailed. Barton was slain fighting and his two Scotch ships were taken into the Thames (Aug. 2, 1511). The story is to be found in most of the English chronicles later than 1511, but the ballad is nearly a century later. The designs illustrating it have been made in strict accordance with ancient authorities.

FRENNET HALL.

This is copied from Herd's "Collection of Ancient and Modern Scottish Songs." It was unaccompanied by note or comment and was probably the work of a modern pen founded on an older ballad called "The Fire of Frendraught."

KING ESTMERE.

Percy emended this from the MS. He says the original would seem to have been written while part of Spain was in the hands of the Moors, whose empire was not fully extinguished before 1491. He adds that the treatment of the minstrels showed the high position they held on their wanderings, that is, they were allowed to mix in the company of kings. All histories of the North are full of the reverence paid to this order of men. As to Estmere's riding into the banquet hall, this was not unusual in the days of chivalry, and even to this day we see a relic of the custom still kept up in the Champion's riding into Westminister Hall during the coronation dinner.

THE CRUEL SISTER.

There are several versions of this ballad, some one of which is to be found in every edition of Scotch ballads. This was composed by Sir Walter Scott from a copy in Mrs. Brown's MS. intermixed with a fragment. There can be little doubt that this ballad may be classed among the compositions founded upon actual occurrences.

FAIR HELEN OF KIRCONNELL.

Sir Walter Scott gives this from the most accurate copy that he could find. The sad catastrophe (date uncertain) upon which this ballad is founded is briefly this: A lady by the name of Helen Irving or Bell (it is a disputed point between two clans), beautiful daughter of the Laird of Kirconnell, in Dumfriesshire, was wooed by two gentlemen. The favored lover was Adam Fleming of Kirkpatrick. The name of the second is lost, though it has been alleged that he was a Bell of Blacket House. The latter was encouraged by the family, and the lovers were obliged to meet secretly in the churchyard of Kirconnell, which is nearly surrounded by the river Kirtle. During one of these interviews the other suitor appeared on the opposite bank of the river and aimed his carbine at the breast of his favored rival. Helen threw herself before her lover, received the bullet and died. A combat ensued in which the murderer was slain. Another account makes Fleming pursue the other to Spain, where he killed him, and then returned to Helen's grave where he died. Their grave is still pointed out in Kirconnell churchyard. "Hic jacet Adamus Fleming."

THE LUCK OF EDEN HALL.

This ballad, the composition of Mr. J. H. Niffen, is founded on a superstition in Cumberland. There is a small village there, Eden Hall, situated on the Eden River. The mansion and estates belong to the Musgraves, who have held property there since the time of Henry VI. and were distinguished in the reign of William the Conqueror, with whom they came over from Normandy.

In the mansion an old drinking-cup, enamelled in colors, is preserved with the greatest care. It is called "The Luck of Eden Hall" and bears the letters I. H. S. on the side, which mark its origin, but tradition affirms it was seized from a company of fairies who were sporting near a spring called St. Cuthbert's well. They made an ineffectual struggle to recover it, and then vanished into thin air, saying:

> "If that glass do break or fall
> Farewell the luck of Eden Hall."

LADY ANNE BOTHWELL'S LAMENT.

This is taken from "Scottish Ballads," edited by Chambers. Percy gives a shorter version and says that he once thought the subject of this pathetic ballad might relate to the Earl of Bothwell, and the desertion of his wife, Lady Jean Gordon, to make room for his marriage with Mary; but he now believes this opinion to be groundless. A young lady by the name of Bothwell, having been, together with her child, deserted by her husband or lover, composed these lines herself.

AULD ROBIN GRAY.

The history of the author and poem is briefly as follows: Lady Ann Lindsay (1750–1825) was the daughter of the Earl of Balcarres and became the wife of Sir Andrew Barton, librarian to George III. The song was written before her marriage. She was very fond of an ancient Scotch melody called "The bridegroom grat when the sun gaed down." The air was sung to her by an aged person, with old, rather free-spoken words. At a time when Lady Ann was feeling rather melancholy after the marriage of a sister, she sought to amuse herself with poetry. "I longed to sing old Sophy's air," as she afterwards wrote to Sir Walter Scott, "to different words and give its plaintive tones some little history of virtuous distress in humble life, such as might suit it." So she created a heroine, sent her Jamie to sea, broke her father's arm, made her mother fall sick, and gave her Auld Robin Gray (a herd at Balcarres), for a lover. She wished to load the poor maiden with a fifth sorrow and called to her little sister to help her. " Steal the cow, sister Ann," which was done and the story finished.

The song became popular immediately. Its authorship was attributed to ever so many people, from David Rizzio down. In process of time a new air was written, by a Mr. Leeves, to the words. It found its way to the stage, where it has been occasionally sung ever since. Finally, in 1823, Lady Ann acknowledged to Sir Walter Scott that she was the author and sent him the two continuations which she had written long after the song itself.

ELFINLAND WUD.

This is the composition of Mr. William Motherwell, written in imitation of the old style.

THE TWA CORBIES.

Of the several versions of this singular fragment the one from "Minstrelsy of the Scottish Border" is here given. It was communicated to the Editor by C. K. Sharpe, "as written down from tradition by a lady."

THE BALLAD OF HENGIST AND MEY.

This is given by William Julian Mickle. It professes to be an imitation of the ancient ballad, the character of which, however, it partakes but little. The author was born, 1734, at Langholme, in Dumfriesshire, and died in 1782 in Oxfordshire. It is conjectured that he was the author of "There's nae luck about the house."

The incident on which this ballad is founded is presumed to have grown out of the wars between the Britons and the Saxons.

GLOSSARY.

Acton, a leather jacket, strongly stuffed, worn under a coat of mail.
Arblast, a cross-bow.
Barmkin, a rampart.
Bartizan, a battlement.
Bewray, to reveal.
Bigged, built.
Bigly, pleasant, delightful.
Birk, *s.* birch; *v.* to give a tart reply.
Bowne, *a.* ready; *v.* to make ready.
Bræ, brow or side of a hill.
Brand, sword.
Bryttled, made brittle.
Busk, to dress, to make ready.
Capull, a horse or mare.
Carle, a man (churl).
Cryance, belief.
Dill, to still, to calm.
Dowie, dull, mournful.
Dule, grief.
Farden, fared, flashed.
Feid, enmity.
Felawe, companion.
Fere, fear, companion.
Fet, fetched.
Fetteled, tied up, put in order.
Fitt, diversion of a song.
Gair, geer, dress.
Galliards, a dance.

Gared, made, caused.
Giffe, if.
Gil, child, knight.
Gin, if.
Gorgett, neck-dress.
Greit, greet, cry.
Grype, griffin.
Gurley, bleak, stormy.
Hachborde, hatch-board.
Hartely, heartily.
Hewberke, a shirt of mail.
Holt, groves, woods, hills.
Hone, delay.
Houzle, to administer the sacrament.
In-fere, in company, together.
Kell, hinder part of a woman's cap.
Kemp, soldier.
Kemperye, soldier.
Kempion, champion.
Kend, known.
Kevils, lots.
Lap, leapt.
Lave, remainder.
Lear, *s.* liar; *a.* rather, liefer.
Lemis, gleams, scintillates.
Lincome, of Lincoln (as Lincoln cloth).
Ling, *s.* a species of grass; *s.* a line; *v.* to move with long steps.

Loot, pret. of *v.* to let.
Losel, a worthless fellow.
Louted, bowed.
Marrow, a companion, one of a pair, an equal.
May, maid.
Mazer dish, saucer under a cup (?)
Merkle, much.
Paynim, pagan.
Pibroch, a Highland air.
Quat, what.
Rede, *s.* remedy; *v.* advise.
Renisht, perhaps a derivative from *renitio*, to shine.
Shent, disgraced.
Sichs, sighs.
Skaith, harm.
Skeely, skilful, intelligent.
Skrieh, peep, dawn.
Spæ-book, a book of necromancy.
Speir, ask, inquire.
Soldan, sultan.
Steven, voice, time.
Stint, stayed, stopped.
Strathspey, a dance.
Stythe, *s.* place, station; *a.* firm, steady.
Sweven, dream.
Tercel-gents, trained falcons.
Tint, lost.
Triest furth, draw forth.
Warwolf, half man and half wolf.
Wæsome, woful.
Weet, know, understand.

www.ingramcontent.com/pod-product-compliance
Lightning Source LLC
Chambersburg PA
CBHW020300240426
43673CB00039B/654